RED TO GREEN

RED TO GREEN

Environmental Activism
in Post-Soviet Russia

LAURA A. HENRY

CORNELL UNIVERSITY PRESS
ITHACA AND LONDON

First published 2010 by Cornell University Press
First printing, Cornell Paperbacks, 2010
Printed in the United States of America

Library of Congress Cataloging-in-Publication Data

Henry, Laura A., 1971–
    Red to green : environmental activism in post-Soviet Russia / Laura A. Henry.
        p. cm.
    Includes bibliographical references and index.
    ISBN 978-0-8014-4840-9 (cloth : alk. paper)
    ISBN 978-0-8014-7641-9 (pbk. : alk. paper)
  1. Environmentalism—Russia (Federation)   2. Green movement—Russia (Federation)   3. Post-communism—Russia (Federation)
4. Social change—Russia (Federation)   5. Non-governmental organizations—Russia (Federation)   I. Title.
    GE199.R8H46   2010
    363.70947—dc22   2009036386

Cornell University Press strives to use environmentally responsible suppliers and materials to the fullest extent possible in the publishing of its books. Such materials include vegetable-based, low-VOC inks and acid-free papers that are recycled, totally chlorine-free, or partly composed of nonwood fibers. For further information, visit our website at www.cornellpress.cornell.edu.

Cloth printing   10 9 8 7 6 5 4 3 2 1
Paperback printing   10 9 8 7 6 5 4 3 2 1

For Vlad, Leo, and Alexei

Map of the Russian Federation

Vladivostok

PRIMORSKII KRAI

NOVOSIBIRSK
OBLAST

Novosibirsk

ST. PETERSBURG

Vladimir

VLADIMIR
OBLAST

BRYANSK
OBLAST

Bryansk

MOSCOW

CONTENTS

PREFACE

Scholars who are drawn to the study of civil society, social movements, and social organizations have been optimistic about the ability of these institutions to generate political and social change. I count myself among their number. In this book, however, I acknowledge this unspoken support for grassroots political actors among scholars and practitioners alike, and question some of the assumptions about civil society, social movements, and organizations that underpin that support. Therefore, I write neither to praise nor to lament the rise of social organizations in Russia—or the policies of foreign donors that hope to support them. Instead, I take seriously the normative claims of political actors involved in civil society development in Russia while engaging in more objective analysis of social organizations and their achievements.

This book is based upon extensive field research in Russia, including more than 125 interviews with environmental activists, government officials, and foreign donors that I conducted in Russia and the United States between 1999 and 2008, with the initial interview period from 1999 to 2001 and a follow-up survey of regional activists in 2005 and 2006. (Interviews with Russian activists were conducted in Russian. All translations of interviews and other Russian language sources are the author's, unless otherwise specified.) These interviews took place in the offices of nongovernmental organizations (NGOs), activists' homes, and NGO resource centers, as well as government and donor offices. Interviews were semistructured, following a standard outline of questions but also allowing each interviewee to address his or her specific concerns and introduce new topics for discussion. Fieldwork included extended research stays in the cities of St. Petersburg, Vladivostok, Khabarovsk, Novosibirsk, Moscow, Bryansk, and Vladimir. In each of these cities, the organizations I studied in depth were selected from a sample of organizations identified in NGO directories, NGO resource-center databases, and through Internet searches. Snowball sampling techniques were then employed to find smaller, lesser-known, or unregistered organizations. Other research strategies included participant observation within environmental organizations, during both day-to-day operations and special events, and at movement-related meetings, seminars, and conferences. Whenever possible, I confirmed information gathered in interviews and at events using third-party responses, the organization's archives, and newspaper and other media resources. The staff at NGO resource centers in St. Petersburg, Vladivostok, Novosibirsk, and Moscow played an invaluable role in the research.

Material from chapters 3 and 4 first appeared in Laura A. Henry, "Shaping Social Activism in Post-Soviet Russia: Leadership, Organizational Diversity, and Innovation," reprinted with permission from *Post-Soviet Affairs* 22, 2 (2006): 99–124, copyright Bellwether Publishing, Ltd., 8640 Guilford Road, Suite 200, Columbia, MD, 21046, all rights reserved. Material from chapter 6 first appeared in Laura A. Henry, "Russian Environmentalists in Civil Society, in *Russian Civil Society: A Critical Assessment,* edited by Alfred B. Evans, Jr., Laura A. Henry, and Lisa McIntosh Sundstrom, 211–28, 2006, and is reprinted with permission from M. E. Sharpe, Inc., Armonk, NY.

Many individuals supported this project, and it is a pleasure to acknowledge them. My interest in Russia and Russian politics began at Wellesley College just as the Berlin Wall fell and was encouraged by scholars including Bill Joseph, Lars Lih, Nina Tumarkin, and Marshall Goldman. Special thanks go to Jane Dawson, who helped me start down this path, serving as an inspiration and mentor. The generous support of the Thomas J. Watson Jr. Foundation allowed me to spend a fascinating year volunteering with new nongovernmental organizations in Russia, Ukraine, and the Baltic states.

Research for this project was supported by the NSEP/Boren Fellowship, the Berkeley Fellowship for Graduate Study, and the Berkeley Program in Soviet and Post-Soviet Studies. This funding enabled many months of fieldwork, including frequent relocations from one Russian region to another. Numerous Russian colleagues and acquaintances offered their insight into Russian politics and social life and assistance with the logistics of daily living. I especially thank Sasha, Natasha, Pavel, and Nikolai Viotosh, the Chebanov family, Maria Tysiachniouk, Alla Bolotova, Natasha Cheremnykh, Rosa Khatskelevich, Natasha Proskurina, Yuri Shirokov, Gennadii Stakhurlov, Aleksei Chizhevskii, and Anastasia, my research assistant in Moscow. I am also indebted to the many Russian environmentalists who shared their time, histories, and good humor during our lengthy interviews.

This project began at the University of California, Berkeley. I relied on many scholars for advice during the research and writing, most notably Steve Fish, George Breslauer, Ned Walker, Kim Voss, Chris Ansell, Victoria Bonnell, Ken Jowitt, and Andrew Janos. My colleagues were an unflagging source of optimism and energy. I particularly am grateful to Jill Hargis, Sara Rushing, Robin Brooks, Maria Rosales, Brian Duff, Ben Goldfrank, Dan Kronenfeld, Ken Foster, and the members of the Triple Rock working group for their willingness to read sections of the manuscript and provide constructive criticism. Alfred Evans and Lisa McIntosh Sundstrom also offered thoughtful comments on several sections. My colleagues at Bowdoin College provided encouragement during the final stages of this project and served as role models through their ability to combine excellent teaching with active research agendas. I thank Lynne Atkinson for her administrative and moral support and her copyediting skills. I also appreciate the excellent advice of Roger Haydon, my editor at Cornell University Press, and two anonymous reviewers for their suggestions for improving the manuscript. Susan Specter, Rachel Post, and Marie Flaherty-Jones shepherded the project to completion.

Finally, I am grateful to my family. My parents, Steve and Diane Henry, instilled in me an appreciation of the natural world and concern for the environment. They offered unquestioning support throughout my years in graduate school. My husband, Vladimir Douhovnikoff, deserves the most credit for the realization of this project. His encouragement saw me through crucial moments at home and in the field, and his endless willingness to debate Russian politics, to battle the bureaucracy, to see the humor in academic life, to drag me out into nature, and to offer emotional support make him an extraordinary and much-appreciated partner. Last but not least, I thank my sons, Leo and Alexei Douhovnikoff, who gave me the last push I needed.

NOTE ON TRANSLITERATION

In this book, I use a modified Library of Congress system for the transliteration of the Russian language. Diacritical marks are largely omitted from the text so as not to distract the reader. In addition, well-known names appear in their most common transliterated form (Yeltsin as opposed to El'tsin), and names of interviewees are transliterated based on the individuals' preferred spelling.

RED TO GREEN

INTRODUCTION

Drive nature out the door, and it returns through the window.

RUSSIAN PROVERB

On June 5, 2005, more than two hundred environmentalists drawn
from fifty-nine regions of the Russian Federation gathered in the town
of Koroleva, just outside Moscow, to form a new political party. This new
party, the Union of Greens, boasted the leadership of several prominent
activists, including Aleksei Yablokov, a former environmental adviser to
President Yeltsin, and Aleksandr Nikitin, a naval officer who had been accused in 1996 of espionage for revealing information about nuclear contamination caused by Russia's Northern Fleet. According to Yablokov, the
Union of Greens was founded "out of despair" in order to combat "the ongoing de-ecologization of the government."[1] Party leaders pledged to join
with other small democratic parties to address the Russian government's
failure to adequately protect the environment and to stem Russia's loom-
ing demographic crisis.

---

1. Aleksei Yablokov, author interview, Moscow, July 15, 2005.

Party building represented a new strategy for Russian environmentalists. After years toiling in nongovernmental organizations, greens chose to form a new, broad-based political coalition explicitly identifying itself as a competitor of the current political regime. When questioned about the difficulties of establishing a party given new legal constraints on party building and the Kremlin's overt hostility to new parties,[2] Yablokov responded that the decision to set up a political wing of the green movement was taken because "nothing else is working."[3] Environmentalists' earlier strategies for generating political change had been stymied by their lack of resources, limited by their difficulty mobilizing the Russian public, and frustrated by a political system that discourages participation and neglects environmental issues. According to Yablokov, a new party could provide an opportunity, however unlikely, to change the rules of the political game.

Amid the fanfare of its founding, however, supporters voiced some misgivings. Sergei Mitrokhin, a leader of the liberal Yabloko Party, offered his party's cooperation but warned, "It is possible that it won't work out for several reasons, mainly because the bureaucrats have a strong distaste for ecological movements and they have lots of opportunities to nip the formation of any kind of organization in the bud" (Bigg 2005). His words proved prophetic. According to Yablokov, at its peak the party attracted sixteen thousand members, an unprecedented number for a green party in Russia but far short of the fifty thousand necessary for registration (Pasko 2008). Less than a year after its founding, a March 2006 Union of Greens party congress decided to constitute a "Green Russia" faction inside the Yabloko Party and to work toward registration as an independent party as a longer-term goal. Meanwhile, Yabloko itself is struggling to survive as a party, having received only 1.6 percent of the vote, and no seats, in the December 2007 parliamentary elections and failing to run a candidate in the 2008 presidential elections.

The efforts made by Russian environmentalists to create a new political party represent just one of the strategies of activism that exist within the green movement. The party's founding illustrates greens' persistent

---

2. A 2001 law designed to promote party consolidation raised the requirements for party registration, and a 2005 law abolished single-member districts in favor of proportional representation and raised the threshold of entry into the State Duma from 5 to 7 percent (Hale 2005).

3. Yablokov interview.

desire for political change within Russia's increasingly centralized political sphere and the difficulty of achieving such a change. For some observers, the party and its fate underscore how significantly Russia has fallen short of its once-anticipated transition to democracy. For others, environmentalists' actions represent the persistence and innovative quality of grassroots activism in Russia and the continued potential for future political transformation. In either case, the struggle of these activists is highly symbolic of Russian citizens' efforts to participate in the political sphere and generate political change.

This book has two objectives: to identify the factors that promote and inhibit different types of citizen mobilization in Russia and to understand the implications of emerging patterns of mobilization for both the development of civil society and the transformation of Russia's politics. Civil society is an expansive, and often ambiguous, term. In 1991, as Soviet Communism collapsed and Russians constructed new democratic institutions, rhetoric about "the rebirth of civil society" encouraged optimistic assessments of the potential for political pluralism in Russia. A reinvigorated public sphere seemed to offer remedy for diverse social and political ills. Almost two decades later, however, it has become commonplace to characterize civil society in Russia as perilously weak owing to the post-Soviet legacy of political cynicism, continuing state ambivalence about the role of society in politics, and a lack of domestic resources to support activism. These extremes of optimism and pessimism distract us from the actual efforts of social activists on the ground in Russia and their complex, inspiring, and often frustrated attempts to increase government accountability and political openness. This book goes beyond simple characterizations of strength or weakness in order to identify the contradictory trends within Russian society that determine whether the public can influence politics. What is it that these social organizations actually do? How do they use the limited economic and political opportunities that are available to them? Does the Soviet legacy continue to shape activism? Have social organizations been able to influence policy in Russia or change how politics is practiced? Is it possible for outside actors to influence patterns of societal change, or, in effect, to increase the "demand" for democracy, if not the supply?

To answer these questions, I investigate the rise of social organizations as political players in Russia, analyzing the causes and consequences of organizational innovation in the post-Soviet period. By situating social organizations within the institutional and normative constraints of the broader post-Soviet environment, I address two questions, the first more theoretical and the second more empirical. First, what mechanisms link the characteristics of Russia's political, economic, and cultural environment to patterns of social activism within civil society, facilitating some kinds of mobilization and not others? Second, what does this process tell us about the effectiveness of Russian social activists at achieving their goals?

Environmental Activism as a Critical Case

In order to investigate the causes and consequences of the emergence of social organizations in Russia, I examine the development of environmental organizations from the mid-1990s to the present. The Russian environmental movement represents a critical case for scholars interested in social activism in post-Soviet Russia because it appeared to be the movement "most likely to succeed" for several reasons. First, environmentalism was the most effective social movement of the late Soviet period. The movement mobilized thousands of citizens, forced state officials to close or cancel construction of numerous nuclear power plants and hydroelectric projects, and offered a broad critique of the Soviet regime. Consequently, it appeared to be well-positioned to influence the direction and practice of post-Soviet politics. In the current period, however, activists scattered across Russia face severe political and economic obstacles to promoting green issues, ranging from tiger protection and nuclear safety to environmental education. The struggle of Russian green activists therefore exemplifies the opportunities for and limits to social activism in Russia.

Second, environmental conditions in Russia remain poor, and public concern about green issues is high. Russian territory encompasses a unique combination of severe degradation and pristine wilderness. A 2002 survey conducted by the presidential administration concluded that approximately 60 percent of the population lives in territory that "does not correspond to standards of ecological safety" (Petrov 2002). The Russian Federation hosts a number of nuclear reactors and a decaying fleet of nuclear submarines. The exploitation of Russia's vast petroleum resources, other mineral deposits, and timber has increased rapidly in the post-Soviet era, as has resulting ecological degradation. At the same time, Russia is the site of many of the world's unique ecosystems, including the taiga forest and the steppe grasslands. Russia possesses more than one-third of the world's wildlife areas and is justly famous for its network of preserved lands. These environmental assets have been under increasing threat, however, as Russia's ability to protect its own natural areas and to implement its environmental policies has deteriorated since the 1990s. The country thus offers great scope for green activism.

Third, Russian environmental organizations benefited from significant transnational support designed to increase their efficacy. In the 1990s, foreign assistance programs that aimed to promote civil society development and democracy in the postcommunist region and international environmental organizations working on global campaigns provided resources for environmental organizations in Russia. Since then, the overall level of funding has declined, but it continues to contribute to the survival of many organizations within the Russian environmental movement. Whether or not this external sponsorship assisted Russian activists in achieving their goals, or promoted progress toward the greater objective of civil society development, are open questions, however, and this book addresses them both.

Finally, environmental movements around the world have been powerful forces of political and social change, advocating indigenous rights and the rights of the poor, combating racism, and demanding a greater public voice in the political process (Pellow 2007; Cole and Foster 2001; Peluso and Watts 2001; Lee and So 1999; Keck 1995; Taylor 1995). If we reject the deterministic view that Russians are somehow doomed to political passivity and authoritarianism by the weight of their history or political culture, then environmental mobilization as a source of political change deserves our attention, even in a regime that is increasingly centralized.

Organizations in Social Activism: The Argument

As with other varieties of social activism in Russia, the growth of the contemporary environmental movement has occurred in a context of economic and political destabilization resulting from the collapse of the Soviet regime in 1991. The end of the Soviet system marked a critical juncture that introduced new actors, rules, and institutions into the arena of social activism, even as elements of the former regime and societal institutions persisted. This book begins by investigating the hypothesis that varying political and economic conditions in Russia's regions should lead to varying types of subnational activism. Unexpectedly, however, what we discover is that while the level of mobilization across regions is strikingly similar, there is intriguing variation in the quality of activism—in the distinct strategies of organizational development that recur within the movement across regions.

While there is no single movement-wide response to Russia's scarce resources and relatively closed political opportunity structure, the evidence suggests that in this constrained environment, social organizations have converged on a limited number of strategies for survival. The narrow array of resulting organizational forms illustrates how activists negotiate a challenging terrain for mobilization—a terrain that appears to contain a small number of organizational niches. These organizational forms serve as a "fossil record" of activists' innovations, frustrations, and compromises.

In the post-Soviet period, Russian activists must negotiate competing beliefs and values that stem from enduring Soviet political traditions on the one hand and new post-Soviet practices on the other. They have to balance the often dissonant preferences of local constituents, the Russian authorities, transnational environmental organizations, and foreign donors operating in Russia in order to construct sustainable organizations. Old and new influences interact in complex ways. Activists' responses to the juxtapositions reflect their earlier experiences with Soviet institutions and practices, experiences that act as a lens through which they interpret their current political and economic environment. Norms, identities, networks, and institutional affiliations developed in the Soviet period condition the way activists view current opportunities for, and obstacles to, mobilization. The Soviet legacy is thus more heterogeneous and contingent than earlier works have implied. While widespread political cynicism and persistent ambivalence about the role of society in governance constrain social activism in the post-Soviet period, activists also have been able to recycle Soviet-era norms, institutions, and networks in order to work toward their goals.

The strategic choices made by organizational leaders are the mechanism that links the diverse characteristics of the post-Soviet field of social activism to the broadly different organizational forms that have emerged within the Russian environmental movement and, correspondingly, to the three distinct varieties of environmental activism—grassroots, professionalized, and government affiliate—embodied in the organizations that

I discuss in this book. Organizational development follows a path dependent process in which early strategies of organization building shape and constrain the range of current activism. The stark juxtaposition of old and new actors, institutions, and norms in the post-Soviet organizational field—even if it proves to be short-lived—has established initial patterns of societal mobilization in post-Soviet Russia. Ultimately these different organizational forms influence the varying degrees of effectiveness that activists achieve as they pursue their goals. That is, while organizational form does not determine outcome, it does set the parameters for the behavior of activists, making some outcomes more likely than others.

When we say that the form adopted by an organization influences its outcome or effectiveness, what do we mean by effectiveness? How to measure the "effectiveness" of social activism has long been a contested question. This book posits that all social organizations attempt to achieve three broad goals: first, to find the resources needed to sustain the organization (internal goals); second, to institute more favorable state policies on a particular issue, in this case environmental protection (substantive goals); and finally, to create a political and social arena more conducive to future activism (transformational goals). Efforts to achieve these goals may reinforce each other, but they also may undermine each other as they compete for activists' energy and resources.

Identifying these diverse objectives of social organizations opens up several lines of inquiry. For example, in the case of the Russian environmental movement, how do efforts to create and sustain organizations shape activists' behavior? Is there an underlying tension among the goals of organizational development, environmental protection, and political transformation, or are these goals mutually supportive? Are green organizations more effective at achieving some of these objectives than others in Russia's current political system? Can transformational political goals, such as democratization, be achieved within the confines of the existing political institutional context?

Advancing the Debate

For scholars interested in contemporary Russian politics, examining the environmental movement underscores not only what has changed in Russia's state-society relations but also what has stayed the same. This point of view is a necessary corrective to our eagerness to study novelty in post-Soviet states and also to the perspective that the Soviet legacy is entirely inimical to autonomous social mobilization. The book moves beyond the characterization of Russian civil society as weak. It argues that what is interesting about post-Soviet Russia's civil society is not the low level of organization and participation but the fact that so many social organizations have been created and persist *in spite of* these infelicitous conditions. While the overall level of activism in Russian society remains low, there is significant variation in the type of activism that is emerging. This variation in the quality of activism has not yet been sufficiently explained. An understanding of why varying strategies of social mobilization emerge is crucial to predicting how activism will develop in Russia's changing political context. These strategies also point to potential sites of political and social change in an increasingly rigid political system, while highlighting trends that make this change more or less likely.

An examination of social activism in Russia also contributes to broader debates about how social movements and other civil society actors may contribute to political change. The book builds upon and challenges the dominant theoretical framework for explaining social activism—the political process model. An organizational approach to the study of social activism and political change offers several insights for social movement theory. First, it emphasizes that grievance identification, resources flows, political access, and issue framing are not independent factors but are often interrelated and mutually reinforcing. Second, it reassesses the significance of grievances, although not in the narrow sense that activism is more likely to arise when grievances are particularly severe—an explanation that has been discredited in past studies of social movements. Instead, grievances that motivate social activism, and the framing of those grievances, may be more or less compelling to the direct beneficiaries or external supporters of a movement, and therefore they hold the promise of easier access to some kinds of resources and eventually may lead to different kinds of activism. Third, an organizational approach such as this book proposes a more nuanced perspective on the role of resources in supporting activism, highlighting the fact that monetary and nonmonetary resources are inextricably bound up in particular cultures of activism. In addition, an organizational approach highlights the importance of "logics of appropriateness" in instigating and sustaining different types of activism. Ultimately, partnership and resource sharing among organizations, domestically and transnationally, depends on shared worldviews as much as shared goals. Finally, the book's organizational approach systematically disaggregates the concept of "effectiveness" to illustrate how the diverse goals of social organizations may reinforce or undermine each other.

This book makes several contributions to the broader literature on comparative politics. It furthers our understanding of the causes and effects of regime change, presenting a bottom-up picture of political change that complements the literature's predominantly elite focus. It unites models from political science and sociology to specify the role of social organizations in political transformation and to build a theory of the conditions that enable societal organizations to contribute to political change. Finally, the book brings together theories from international relations and comparative politics to examine the increasingly transnational nature of social activism and to incorporate transnational actors into a model of domestic political change that is applicable to states around the world.

Research Focus and Terminology

The multiplicity of approaches to studying citizens' organizations has produced a long list of terms and typologies to define the groups that citizens voluntarily create. Self-organizing citizens' groups are variously known as nonprofit organizations, voluntary associations, advocacy groups, interest groups, informals, grassroots organizations, or community-based organizations. The social movement literature refers to similar groups as social movement organizations (SMOs). "Civil society organization" is a common term in the comparative democratization literature, but democracy promoters in the field more often use the term "NGO," translated into Russian as nongovernmental (*negosudarstvennye*) or noncommercial (*nekommercheskie*) organizations.[4] Each term entails its own set of assumptions about why groups form and what role they play in the political

---

4. Salamon and Anheier (1996, 1997) offer thorough discussions of the difficulties in defining the term "NGO." Within the NGO literature, differentiating among the proliferation of terms to describe NGOs and asking whether this terminological tangle indicates any real variation in

process, contributing to the conceptual diversity that presents a barrier to cross-fertilization within the social sciences.

Why focus on organizations rather than protest events or participants? This choice was driven in part by the realities of the post-Soviet political context. Organization building is the preferred method of pursuing environmental goals for Russian environmentalists of all stripes. As mass mobilization declined in the early 1990s, organizations scattered across different regions are what remain as the residue of the perestroika wave of anti-regime protest. These groups could be seen as acting as "abeyance structures," sustaining the goals of the movement and shaping the possibility of renewed mass mobilization (Taylor 1989). For Russian activists, formal organizations also appear to have a legitimacy that networks, campaigns, and individual efforts do not. This is the case even when there is little formal institutionalization behind the organization's title. For state and societal actors accustomed to formal organizations and clear hierarchies from the Soviet period, organizations appear to be more credible than loose networks of individuals. Finally, formal organizations are more likely to meet the requirements of transnational donors who generally direct support toward legally registered groups, further encouraging organization building within the movement.[5]

While this book focuses on organizations, it acknowledges that studies of civil society are too often biased toward the Western experience, searching for institutions and practices that mimic our own history. For that reason, I keep an open mind about exactly what an organization is. The groups I study range from highly institutionalized organizations with a budget, staff, and well-defined projects to those groups that simply consist of a name and a handful of individuals. In other words, if an entity claims to be an environmental organization, it is considered as such even if it boasts few characteristics of a formal organization. The desire to be considered an organization is more important here than the achievement of organizational status, by whatever measure. This approach recognizes that what an organization is or does in post-Soviet Russia may be different

---

organizational type at one point became something of a cottage industry among NGO practitioners (Vakil 1997; Fowler 1997; Edwards and Hulme 1992).

5. As Sampson argues in his examination of foreign aid in Eastern Europe, "Put bluntly, social networks can't get grants, but autonomous associations can" (1996, 141).

from what we have come to expect of Western organizations. The goal is to consider a spectrum of mobilization strategies around a particular issue, capturing mobilizational patterns that are similar to those in the West and patterns that may be particular to the country studied.

Given the wealth of terms, this book simply uses "social organization" to refer to a range of self-organizing, nongovernmental, not-for-profit groups. There are several reasons for remaining agnostic about selecting a term embedded in a particular theoretical model. First, if the purpose of this book is to consider a range of mobilizational strategies and to look for patterns of mobilization that may be unique to Russia's post-Soviet environment, it is important to maintain an open mind and not presuppose what types of organizations are developing. Second, as work on the broad swathe of "contentious politics" makes clear, distinctions among social movement organizations, interest groups or NGOs, and even political parties are often unsustainable in empirical research (Burstein 1998, 8; McAdam, Tarrow, and Tilly 2001). Finally, "social organization" (*obshchestvennaia organizatsiia*) is a direct translation of the term most frequently used for these groups in Russia.

Throughout the book, I refer to environmental organizations as being part of a broader social movement in Russia. There are theoretical and practical reasons for referring to the thousands of green organizations scattered across Russia as an environmental movement (*ekologicheskoe dvizhenie*). First, while movements at the peak of mobilization receive the most attention, the idea of a "movement" and the theoretical tools that are used to understand the emergence of social movements enable us to understand their development and impact even in periods of lower mobilization. Second, "movements," such as the environmental movement and the women's rights movement, persist for decades in terms of their collective consciousness and strategies of cooperative interaction, however minimal their ability to mobilize the public. Actors within the movement recognize each other as working on the same set of problems, and this sense of solidarity and history informs their activism. Finally, in the particular case of the Russian environmental movement, even the most isolated activists frequently cite what they see as a broader movement across the country and recognize federal-level organizations and events that influence their own goals and strategies.

One last terminological point is that the exact word "environmentalism," as distinct from the term "ecology," does not exist in the Russian language as it does in English. Instead, greens in Russia refer to their cause as nature protection (*okhrana prirody*) and their groups as ecological organizations (*ekologicheskie organizatsii*). When not specifically referring to the science of ecosystems but to efforts of state and society actors to resolve the problems of ecological degradation, I have, however, used the terms more familiar to the English-language reader: environmental and environmentalism.

This book reaches conclusions based on several types of comparative analysis. It compares environmental mobilization within five regional capitals in Russia and then considers variation in the form, activism, and effectiveness of specific environmental organizations. The book's theoretical aspect is also implicitly comparative with Western movements as it relies upon social movement theories developed in the context of advanced industrial democracies. However, as Piven and Cloward wisely caution in their seminal work on poor people's movements, "What was won must be judged by what was possible" (1977, xiii). For that reason, this book highlights how Russia's political and economic context differs from that of Western states.

The post-Soviet period has been an exhilarating and exhausting time for Russian environmentalists. New ideas, language, and resources for environmental advocacy flowed across the previously closed border; domestic political opportunities appeared suddenly open but then progressively narrowed again; and the national economy suffered a dramatic recession that left the population focused on issues of basic subsistence before beginning to grow again at the turn of the century. Russian greens suddenly had many choices, but these choices could be divisive. Taking advantage of new opportunities at times seemed to entail abandoning what was valuable in the Soviet tradition and the more recent perestroika-era activism of the late 1980s. Through their strategic choices, environmental leaders, operating within severe political and economic constraints, have chosen where to seek resources, whom to ally themselves with, and what it means to be an "environmentalist" in post-Soviet Russia. Their choices present both advantages and drawbacks to efforts to construct effective environmental governance in Russia.

The development of Russia's contemporary environmental movement offers a number of intriguing puzzles for scholars of social movements.

Although environmental issues mobilized thousands of citizens during the perestroika era of 1986 to 1991 and environmental conditions in Russia remain dire, environmental protest has declined in the post-Soviet period. Despite the lack of mass protest events in the post-Soviet years, the number of Russian environmental organizations increased steadily during the 1990s and early 2000s. Thousands of green groups now exist throughout Russia. In the contemporary period, Russian environmentalists have previously unimagined levels of organizational capacity, access to technology, international partnerships, and funding. The overall number of environmental organizations, their geographic dispersal throughout Russia, and their increasing professionalism all seem to signify the development of a vibrant sector within civil society. And yet greens struggle to advance their agenda. In spite of their limitations, these groups bear the expectations, inside Russia and around the world, that environmental protection and political transformation remain possible in spite of two decades of only haphazard attention to the environment and increasing disregard for civil liberties and the democratic process.

1

CITIZEN ACTIVISM AND
POLITICAL CHANGE

With the collapse of the Soviet Union's Communist Party–dominated regime in 1991, some observers anticipated that Russia's more open post-Soviet political environment would encourage the flowering of social activism.[1] Citizens' groups would spring up naturally in the more benevolent context of new democratic institutions, laws, and practices. In fact, however, the 1990s were difficult years for many fledgling social organizations as political and economic instability hampered their activities. Although social activism has not flourished as optimists hoped, neither is Russian society a wasteland of isolated individuals concerned only with their own survival. Focusing on the weakness of contemporary Russian civil society obscures significant changes that may serve as building blocks of civil society development.

---

1. See, for example, Rau (1991), Starr (1988) and the public comments of various East European dissidents and Western government officials.

A survey of Russia's regions reveals many small nongovernmental, nonprofit organizations doggedly pursuing social and political change in areas such as human rights, women's issues, press freedom, disability rights, and environmentalism. In fact, the number of social organizations spread across the Russian Federation has risen dramatically during the last two decades. Conservative estimates suggested that there were more than sixty thousand legally registered social organizations operating in Russia in 2000, and estimates that encompass smaller unregistered groups were much higher.[2] Of those numbers, environmental groups comprised approximately 6 percent.[3] The Public Chamber estimates that, as of January 2008, there are 655,400 noncommercial organizations in Russia; of social organizations applying to the chamber for funding, 5 to 6 percent are environmental or animal protection organizations (Obshchestvennaia Palata 2008, 42 and 54).[4] While small as a percentage of social organizations, the environmental movement is often recognized for having produced some of the most experienced and professional social organizations in Russia.

In order to explore the nature of social activism in Russia and the effect it is having on politics and society, this book investigates the organizations that survive and the environmental activists who continue to attempt to influence politics. The mere establishment of social organizations alone is not an indicator of civil society development, however. In spite of Russia's growing population of social organizations in the post-Soviet period,

---

2. Estimated by Susan Reichele, USAID-Moscow (author interview, Moscow, April 21, 2000). The "USAID/Russia Strategy Amendment 1999–2005" offered the number sixty-five thousand (USAID 2002). The Charities Aid Foundation's "Russia Annual Review" (1998/99, 6) estimated that as of January 1999 there were two hundred eighty-six thousand NGOs in Russia. In her introductory remarks at the Kremlin-sponsored Civic Forum in 2001, Liudmila Alekseeva, leader of the Moscow Helsinki Group, noted that forum attendees represented more than three hundred fifty thousand nongovernmental organizations (Zolotov 2001).

3. This estimate (from Charities Aid Foundation, *Russia Annual Review*, 1998/99) is likely low. Many surveys of social organizations ask group representatives to select just one issue area, and this may lead to undercounting. In Novosibirsk, environmental groups constituted 4.2 percent of the total surveyed NGO population (Sibirskii Tsentr Podderzhki Obshchestvennykh Initsiativ 1998), while in St. Petersburg, environmental groups composed an estimated 20 percent of the total number of NGOs (TACIS 1995). In Primorskii Krai, in a survey in which groups were allowed to choose several issue areas, 43 percent of NGOs noted some environmental component to their activities (ISAR-Dal'nii Vostok and USAID, 1998).

4. Environmental leader Aleksei Yablokov offered the following estimation in 2008, "In Russia there were more than 50 thousand civic ecological organizations. Of these—around a thousand [are] active ones. Around 500 are left. The overall number has sharply fallen" (Pasko 2008).

we cannot simply assume their role in the political process. This chapter first presents the insights of several schools of thought on the causes and consequences of social mobilization. It then synthesizes this scholarship by developing a novel organizational approach to the study of social activism, offering a more precise means of investigating the process of civil society development. I draw upon social movement theory, organization theory, and scholarship on transnational norms and networks in order to comprehend how nascent civil societies develop and how patterns of development may influence political transformation.

I argue that the legacy of the Communist system is not monolithic, uniform, or inevitably negative for the prospects for social mobilization in post-Soviet Russia. The institutions, networks, and norms that originated in the Soviet era and persist to the present day shape contemporary activism but not always in ways that constrain it. Environmental leaders, depending on the professional norms under which they were socialized and their past experiences interacting with state and societal actors in the Soviet period, have varying access to mobilizational resources. Different experiences also result in different visions of one's identity as an environmentalist and different images of how environmental organizations should behave in relation to the state and citizens. Therefore, patterns of organizational development are not only driven by post-Soviet political and economic opportunities but are also filtered by the perceptions of different actors within Russia's civil society.

How Social Organizations Shape and Are Shaped by Politics

Although there is an abundance of theorizing about civil society broadly and citizen activism more specifically, an integrated theory of how social organizations develop in different political environments and how they promote political change does not exist. Many approaches within the social sciences tackle different questions related to the development and significance of social organizations. Scholarship on civil society and transitions to democracy tends to assume that organizations arise spontaneously from the diverse interests present in any society; these organizations then make an essential contribution to democratic consolidation by representing public interests to the state. Social movement scholars generally focus on the initial appearance of citizen activism, while the interest-group literature is less concerned with the organizations' origination than with the ongoing effect of established organizations on politics and policy. Organization theory, emerging out of the study of private and public sector organizations, investigates the relationship between organizations' structure, environment, and behavior. Another body of scholarship focuses on the increasingly transnational nature of activism.

Civil Society and Democracy

The concept of civil society has enjoyed a long history in political theory. The image of citizen associations as building blocks of a vibrant democracy has been a compelling one, particularly in the United States. Alexis de Tocqueville, the great mythologizer of civil society, was among the first to identify it as an important arena for constructing and sustaining democracy. Since his assertion, "In democratic countries the science of association is the mother of science; the progress of all the rest depends upon the progress it has made" (Tocqueville 1835/1990, 110), a romantic vision of the political power of associations has colored the study of civil society—a concept that Gellner has called a "shining emblem" to fill an "aching void" (1994, 1) and Seligman refers to as the "*cause célèbre*" of Western intellectuals (1992, 200).

Civil society is "that arena of the polity where self-organizing groups, movements, and individuals, relatively autonomous from the state, attempt to articulate values, create associations and solidarities, and advance their interests" (Linz and Stepan 1996, 7). Civil society occupies an unusual position in models of democratic regime change as both a possible instigator and a likely consequence of the democratization process (Bermeo 2003; Diamond 1999; Collier and Mahoney 1999; Hipsher 1998; O'Donnell and Schmitter 1986). In theory, initial movement toward a more open and consultative political system produces a corresponding increase in citizen activism; civil society is thus naturally born or reborn in the collapse of authoritarianism. The interaction between expanding political liberties and increased citizen participation generates a feedback effect, a virtuous cycle of deepening democracy. Citizens' groups in civil society then play an ongoing role in maintaining the new system by "checking, monitoring, and restraining the exercise of power by formally democratic states" (Diamond 1999, 239).

The literature presents two broad dilemmas for scholars engaged in empirical research on whether civil society in fact does assist in routinizing and deepening democratic practices. First and most important, "civil society" presents a relatively static conceptualization that is difficult to incorporate into a dynamic theory of political change. The strength or weakness of civil society is seen as a function of the type of authoritarianism that preceded the transition or the transition process itself (Karl 1990; Karl and Schmitter 1991; Munck and Leff 1999). Civil society's relative strength also may be attributed to a country's political culture, religious tradition, or geographic proximity to the West (Janos 2000; Huntington 1993).[5] Due to this static depiction, civil society as a concept is used most effectively to explain continuity rather than change, enduring weakness or strength rather than the development or decay of voluntary citizen associations. Second, the literatures on democratization and civil society fail to provide useful tools for engaging in empirical research on the interaction of civil society and political change. These literatures answer the normative question of what roles civil society *should* play to facilitate democratization but spend less time addressing under what conditions this role will be played and how, in practice, civil society changes over time.

Social Movements and Organization Theory

To identify the forces that promote continuity or change in a dynamic civil society, we turn to the social movement literature—a literature that attempts to explain the conditions under which citizen activism is likely to arise, why it varies over time, and when it is likely to alter political and social status quo. In social movement theory, the study of organizations generally has been less central than studies of protest events, levels of participation, and mobilizational networks. Organizations are noted for their role in providing resources and an institutional base to social movements and in structuring mass protest (Zald and McCarthy 1987). Organizations also provide professional continuity for activists and serve as a repository for ideas and resources during periods of low mobilization (Taylor 1989). Controversy about the role of organizations in social movements remains,

---

5. To mention just one well-known example, in Robert Putnam's study of northern and southern Italian politics, the weakness of social engagement and organizations hundreds of years ago proves so entrenched that civil society remains weak into the current era (1993, 183).

however. Most scholars agree that expanding the organizational capacity of a movement empowers activists and improves the likelihood that they will achieve their goals (Gamson 1990; Burstein, Einwohner, and Hollander 1995, 285). In contrast, Michels (1962) suggests that as social movement organizations became more professional, they deradicalize, becoming more bureaucratic and less responsive. Over time activists may become more interested in the survival of their organizations than in achieving their original goals (Piven and Cloward 1977).

Social movement scholars offer competing hypotheses to account for the rise and fall of social mobilization and for cross-national variation in the emergence of social movements. Prior to the 1970s, scholars employing the collective behavior model argued that the number of grievances or the intensity of discontent in society influenced the level of mobilization around a particular issue (Gurr 1970; Davies 1962; Smelser 1968). However, grievances alone did not seem a sufficient explanation for social mobilization. Why did social movements arise based on some contentious social issues and not others? Alternatively, theorists working within the resource mobilization school, and borrowing from organization theory, pointed to changing levels of resources available to support collective action as a source of variation in activism (Oberschall 1973; Jenkins and Perrow 1977). According to McCarthy and Zald (1977), an expanding supply of resources in society "will incite political entrepreneurs to found new professional SMOs [social movement organizations], which will compete for these resources and contribute to the organizational development of the movement" (McAdam, McCarthy, and Zald 1996, 159). As a corollary, the organizations that do appear will disproportionately represent those in society who have access to resources (Piven and Cloward 1977).

Scholars drawing on the work of Erving Goffman (1974) attempted to incorporate concerns about culture and identity into models of social mobilization. They argued that social movement "framing" of a contentious issue can change the public's perception, leading to greater activism (Snow et al. 1986; Snow and Benford 1992).[6] Social activists are not the only actors to engage in framing; state officials, the media, and transnational actors

---

6. Framing has both a cultural and instrumental component. Frames are developed out of preexisting societal norms—drawing on particular beliefs and values in a given society—yet activists also manipulate social movement frames strategically, broadening or reinterpreting past beliefs, to increase social activism.

offer supporting or competing frames (McAdam 1982/1999). Activists also articulate new identities, and appropriate and reinterpret existing identities, as an important part of their efforts to mobilize the public (Melucci 1989; Offe 1985; Touraine 1981). Finally, differing political configurations of states may influence the level of mobilization in society (Tarrow 1994). A state's political opportunity structure—encompassing access points to the policymaking process, the availability of elite allies, the stability of elite alliances, and the repressive capacity of the government—may be relatively open or closed to social mobilization (Tarrow 1994, 76–80).

Organization theory draws attention to the *interdependence* of variables similar to those identified by social movement scholars. In so doing, it situates organizations in a complex web of relationships with other actors in their environment (Pfeffer and Salancik 1978). Organization theory scholars reject the notion that organizations are either entirely autonomous or predictably rational actors. Instead, organizations respond to the demands of other actors that control resources in a given environment, often becoming dependent on those actors who possess critical resources (Pfeffer 1982). In addition, an organization's identification of opportunities is subjective, depending on the perceptions of individual actors, who may or may not perceive the situation as favorable. Individuals filter contextual factors and select strategies of organizational development, operating according to institutional logics or "belief systems and associated practices that predominate in an organizational field" (Scott et al. 2000, 170). An organization's leader acts in response to what he or she perceives and believes about the environment, does not necessarily maximize utility.[7] These individuals "may misread interdependence, misinterpret demands, remain committed to past practices, or fail to see the various conflicts in demands" (Pfeffer and Salancik 1978, 89).

Transnational Resources, Norms, and Networks

Political opportunities, resource flows, and framing strategies are no longer purely domestic phenomena. These factors interact with and are influenced

---

7. Leaders' strategic choices may depend on that society's repertoires of contention (Swidler 1986) or the "culturally encoded ways in which people interact in contentious politics" (McAdam, Tarrow, and Tilly 2001, 16).

by institutional, financial, and rhetorical arrangements at the transnational level (Tarrow 2005; Della Porta 2004; Della Porta, Kriesi, and Rucht 1999; McAdam 1998b; Smith, Chatfield, and Pagnucco 1997). As Tarrow points out:

> If it was once sufficient to interpret or predict social movements around the shape of the national state, it is less and less possible to do so today. Because of multiple levels and sectors of movement mobilization, their changing shape in different phases of protest cycles, and their increasingly transnational links, national regularities in state structure must be seen as no more than the initial grid within which movements emerge and operate. (1996, 52)

Particularly for social organizations in relatively closed, postauthoritarian political systems, the transnational arena often has appeared to be a more hospitable context for mobilization than the domestic political environment.

Ascertaining how transnational factors influence movement development and effectiveness poses a greater challenge than simply recognizing the growing significance of cross-border connections. Transnational ties can provide leverage to less powerful actors, allowing movements to exert a "boomerang effect" on resistant domestic governments by activating international condemnation (Keck and Sikkink 1998, 12–13), or a movement may supply information or testimonials to a transnational campaign. Transnational actors rarely offer their resources or partnership for purely altruistic reasons, however. These actors have their own goals that they attempt to achieve through support for certain kinds of social activism in a particular country. Consequently, they often privilege certain kinds of activism over others. In turn, local norms affect activists' response to new transnational information and interactions.[8]

Transnational support is not necessarily an unmitigated advantage for domestic social organizations. Sponsorship by a third party that is not a direct beneficiary of movement success may prove unreliable in the long run or may have a neutralizing effect on activism (Piven and Cloward 1977; McAdam 1998a). Keck argues that the strength of the local movement prior to contact with transnational actors will affect the success of the

---

8. Finnemore suggests that "actors may ask themselves, 'what kind of situation is this?' and 'what am I supposed to do now?' rather than, 'how can I get what I want?'" (1996, 29).

relationship (1995). Brysk suggests that the impact of transnational actors depends in part on the strategy they adopt for interacting with local activists, whether that is to "eschew contact with local social movements, promote nonpartisan 'social capital,' or become movement enablers" (2000, 189).

Civil Society and Social Activism in Russia

Almost as soon as Soviet leader Mikhail Gorbachev initiated his policies of perestroika and glasnost in the Soviet Union in the late 1980s, social scientists began to study the role that social movements, civil society, and transnational actors play in generating political change in Russia. Scholars studying Russia participate in broader debates about the applicability of the concept of civil society to non-Western societies and the range of activities the concept encompasses.[9] For example, Howard advocates a narrow definition of civil society, excluding social movements and networks, arguing that civil society requires "a degree of organization institutionalization that is usually absent in such forms of mobilization" (2003, 39). Gibson disagrees, arguing that the social ties and trust among those within personal networks are what allow for the development of civil society in Russia and suggesting that these networks may evolve into broader and more impersonal formal organizations (2001). The strongest argument against expanding the definition of civil society to include less formal varieties of social interaction is that the concept could become meaningless and lose its explanatory power. In spite of the danger of concept stretching, however, there are sound arguments for eschewing narrow definitions of civil society that are based on advanced industrial democracies, if we want to understand civic life in other parts the world.

Focusing specifically on the Communist legacy, Jowitt presciently identified elements of state-society relations that would prove inimical to the

---

9. Ernest Gellner recognized that the "assumption of an unconstrained and secular individual" as the human norm outside the West can lead to a "naïve universalization" of civil society, but he concluded that the lack of an active civil society in some countries does not preclude the population's desire for it and its possible future development (1994, 13–14). In a volume devoted to examining what civil society means in non-Western settings, Hann suggests "the exploration of civil society requires that careful attention be paid to a range of informal interpersonal practices." For this reason, he advocates including networks and other informal relations within the definition of civil society for the purposes of comparative research (1996, 3).

development of civil society in the region—most notably citizens who "view the political realm as something dangerous, something to avoid" (1992, 287–9). Howard compared civil societies throughout the postcommunist region and found them weak due to citizens' mistrust of organizations based on their experiences in the Communist era, the persistence of Communist-era friendship networks, and disappointment with postcommunist political and economic developments (Howard 2003, 122–45).[10] Developing an "experiential approach" to societal change, Howard argues that an individual's current behavior depends on how they interpret their situation based on past experiences. Rose, Mishler, and Munro's analysis of New Russia Barometer data shows that the Soviet experience significantly influences citizens' evaluations of contemporary politics; for example, most Russians believed that the post-Soviet regime was either less or similarly open to influence by the public as the pre-perestroika Soviet regime (2006, 134).

A number of valuable early works on social activism and state-society relations emerged out of the late Soviet and early post-Soviet period, capturing both the optimism of the era and the constraints that were likely to limit further change (Fish 1995; Dawson 1996; Smith 1996; Sperling 1999; Weigle 2000; McFaul 2001; Hale 2002). Investigations of the development of Russian civil society from the mid-1990s to 2009 chronicle the troubled evolution of postcommunist social organizations (Johnson 2009; Salmenniemi 2008; Hemment 2007; Sundstrom 2006; Henderson 2003; Mendelson and Glenn 2002). These studies, many of them focusing on women's organizations, chronicle the importance of transnational resources in influencing the development of new organizations as well as the challenges of assisting civil society development in the region.

An Organizational Approach to the Study of Social Activism

An organizational approach synthesizes the insights of the literatures reviewed above. In doing so, it makes five contributions to our current understanding of citizen activism and political change. First, it focuses directly on

---

10. The persistence of strong personal networks in Russia and other postcommunist countries is analyzed by Ledeneva (1998), White (1999), Wedel (1992), and Bridger and Pine (1998).

organizational development as a source of dynamism within civil society, demonstrating how organizations persist or fail in a complex field of incentives and constraints. Second, an organizational approach draws attention to the limited number of organizational niches that arise due to historically contingent interactions among grievances, resources, framing, and political opportunities. Third, it highlights the role played by organization leaders, in particular their beliefs and perceptions, in interpreting the broader political context and shaping mobilizational strategies. In doing so, it incorporates the role of individual perception into the study of social organizations. Fourth, it integrates transnational factors more systematically into the study of civil society development. Finally, it examines the goals of social organizations to show how decisions related to an organization's early development influence its ability to achieve sustainability, accomplish issue-based goals, and press for broader political change. In the Russian case, an organizational approach shows that three organizational types—professionalized, grassroots, and government affiliate—have emerged within the country's environmental movement due to the conjunction of the current mobilizational field and the Soviet legacy, linked by the normative commitments, network ties, and institutional affiliations of environmental leaders.

Organizational Niches in a Mobilizational Field

Organizations are a significant element of broad-based social mobilization. They are the "mobilizing structures…through which people come together and engage in collective action" (McAdam, Tarrow, and Tilly 1997, 155). While "different types of organizational structures and participants have consequences for movement goals and activities" (Staggenborg 1988, 585), few studies have examined the factors that give rise to diverse organizational forms within a movement. Such studies could prove invaluable to theory building, however, since the pattern of organizational development within a movement is, in a sense, a fossil record providing evidence of past constraints and opportunities within a broader field of social activism. Organizations, once constructed, shape varieties of activism and influence varying levels of effectiveness within a movement. Therefore, this approach highlights the path dependent process in which social organizations' early development affects their ability to achieve their goals.

In an organizational approach, organizations are the intervening institutions that illustrate how broad contextual factors shape citizens' efforts generate political and change. The evolution of social organizations within a field of mobilization demonstrates that resources, political opportunities, and framing strategies are interdependent in ways not readily apparent in much of the literature on social movements. Strategies of organizational development within a single movement illustrate how contextual factors reinforce or undermine each other and overlap in ways that are more or less likely to lead to sustainable or successful activism. Ultimately, these factors are woven together in such a way that they create a "field" of mobilization—a field that offers only a few niches the organizations can occupy (Ray 1999; Urban 1997).[11] Niches are combinations of political opportunities, resource streams, and cultural resonance that are more likely to sustain social organizations. Over time, the difficulty of surviving outside one of these niches leads to similar strategies of organizational development, resulting in the appearance of distinct organizational types. Clustering naturally occurs as "units subjected to the same environmental conditions or to environmental conditions as mediated through a given key unit acquire a similar form of organization" (Hawley 1968, 334). The result is a limited number of strategies of organizational development within a given social movement. Organizations that occupy a niche tend to develop similar organizational forms, to address similar grievances within the movement, to use similar tactics, and to develop similar relationships with nonmovement actors.

Bringing Legacy Back In

What links contextual factors and the emergence of organizational forms within the movement? Cause and effect are mediated by the perceptions and preferences of organizational leaders. Who recognizes opportunities, seeks resources, and articulates movement framing? Organizational leaders do. Indeed, grievances, political opportunities, resource streams, and framing strategies are interpreted by individual actors who make choices in response to what they perceive and believe about their environment. Far from being driven solely by the need for resources to ensure their own survival, the leaders of social organizations are influenced by "logics of

---

11. In utilizing the concept of a field of social action, I owe a debt to Pierre Bourdieu (1984, 1993) for his depiction of a field as an arena in which agents bearing certain predispositions and power struggle over the allocation of various sorts of capital.

appropriateness" that legitimize some activities while offering less support for others (March and Olsen 1989). Different logics are put into service to answer questions such as: What is the social problem I am concerned about? Who is to blame for this problem? How can the problem be resolved, and who should participate in its resolution? Differences in leaders' relationships and ideologies are particularly stark in postauthoritarian societies, such as the former Soviet Union, in which actors' political allegiances are sharply divided between loyalty to and rejection of the previous regime. Guided by these logics of appropriateness, actors behave according to learned roles or rules that they consider exemplary or desirable. They make choices based on habit or a sense of obligation rather than acting in a purely utilitarian way to gain resources.

Since leaders' preferences are crafted out of their familiarity with existing cultural repertoires of action, their professional socialization and past experiences play a crucial role in determining strategies of organizational development. It is here that we see the role of the Soviet legacy. "Legacy" often has been used as an undertheorized shorthand, or residual category, to capture any and all aspects of postcommunist society unfavorable to the development of democratic politics. This book adopts a more multifaceted understanding of legacy. Although legacy has been seen as something relatively uniform across society, in fact social groups had starkly different experiences under Communist regimes and learned different lessons about politics as a result.

Organization leaders' political judgments are an important way in which the Soviet experience continues to shape post-Soviet state-society interactions. In this view of legacy, behavior in the early post-Soviet period is correlated strongly with activists' professional socialization during the Soviet period. More specifically, activists redeploy their preexisting beliefs, networks, and resources in the post-Soviet context to construct organizations and build relationships. In this sense, the agency of movement leaders is shaped, although not determined, by predispositions related to their Soviet-era experiences, in combination with new incentives and information.[12] Leaders attempt to maximize their impact within what they view as

---

12. Dalton's study of Western European environmentalists also argues that the political identities of social movement organizations will lead them to act differently even if they have similar goals. In other words, a group's identity defines the political opposition it faces (Dalton 1995, 317).

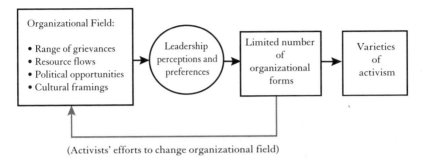

(Activists' efforts to change organizational field)

Figure 1.1. Explaining varieties of activism: mobilizational field,
leadership, and organizational forms

the "appropriate" role for social organizations in the public sphere. Leaders
also are engaged in a constant process of learning and adaptation. Therefore, the influence of the Soviet legacy, which was very powerful in the first
fifteen to twenty years of the post-Soviet experience, will likely fade over
time. However, the new organizations constructed by these activists establish new constraints on mobilization. Thus, predispositions related to experiences in the Soviet era serve to structure "new" patterns of state-society
engagement that will continue to be influential in the years to come.

An individual's allegiance to preexisting norms and access to networks
and institutions influences not only how leaders perceive opportunities and
threats in the political arena but also their ability to take advantage of these
opportunities once recognized. The injection of relatively large amounts of
funding from transnational actors into Russian society creates new opportunities for mobilization, opportunities that some organizations and individuals are better positioned, and more willing, to take advantage of than
others. Therefore, it is not enough that political and economic opportunities exist; the leader must recognize their existence and be able to exploit
them. When possible, leaders will seek resource providers and allies who
possess a worldview or logic of appropriateness similar to their own. When
these logics coincide, organizations are more likely to ensure a stable flow
of resources, allowing them to persist even in a challenging environment
for social activism. Ultimately, organization building may serve either to
create new identities and new forms of political interaction or to reinforce
old identities and interactions.

The Impact of Social Organizations

Even as we recognize the factors that influence the development of social organizations, the effects of those organizations remain challenging
to identify. First, what is meant by "effect"? Which political and social
changes are most likely to be related to social movement activity? Given
that social movements have diverse goals, from changing a particular policy to changing social attitudes, it is not necessarily obvious which outcomes can be attributed to a movement. Second, it is extremely difficult
to assess the intended and unintended consequences of movement activity. Social movements may achieve their goals in a straightforward fashion, but often their actions inspire a backlash—repressive measures from
the government, the emergence of countermovements, or unpredictable
shifts in public opinion. Finally, any assessment of the "effectiveness" of
social movements is subjective. Even actors inside the movement may disagree on how successful they have been depending on how they define
their goals.

Within the limited study of movement outcomes, changes to policy
have received more attention than broader political, social, or cultural
effects (Giugni, McAdam, and Tilly 1999, xxi).[13] Kitschelt differentiates
among outcomes that are procedural (gaining access to the political system) and substantive (policy concessions from authorities), and those that
are structural (changes in the political context itself, its institutions, or alliances) (1986). Kriesi and his collaborators (1995) add a fourth outcome—
"sensitizing" effects, or changes in the political agenda or public attitudes.

An organizational approach synthesizes and simplifies the categori-
zation of outcomes of social mobilization and also takes into account the
imperative of organizational maintenance and survival. The three broad
goals of social organizations include, first, efforts to ensure the organization's survival (internal goals); second, attempts to change policy and win
government concessions in a particular issue area (substantive goals); and
finally, the struggle to transform the political system itself in a way that
makes it more favorable to mobilization and more receptive to future

---

13. Gamson suggests two possible measures of movement success: a movement organization's
acceptance by political authorities as a representative of societal interests and the achievement of
new advantages for the group's beneficiaries (1975/1990, 28–37).

movement demands (transformational goals). The first and third goals of organizations may not be clearly articulated by activists. Organizational maintenance may simply be one of those tasks that must be attended to in order to get on with more substantive projects. Transformational goals are implied by efforts to expand public participation in the policymaking process but may not be explicitly stated. Substantive goals are those that are most commonly understood as the purpose of social activism. These three goals often reinforce each other, but occasionally they may undermine each other by competing for activists' limited time, energy, and resources.

Perhaps because they generally do not focus on organizations, scholars examining social movement outcomes have paid relatively little attention to the groups' efforts to sustain themselves and expand. In fact, internal goals are as significant as policy goals since the achievement of policy goals often depends upon the survival of the organization. Internal goals are also crucial for understanding effectiveness because an organization's strategy for mobilizing resources and the dependencies it develops will constrain its efforts to achieve broader political change. As for transformational goals, many studies of social movements agree that one possible outcome of social movement activity is the democratization of the political process (Giugni, McAdam, and Tilly 1998; Warren 2001). The democratizing potential of collective action stems from the belief that it challenges the existing power distribution within society.[14] Tilly argues that movements may facilitate four aspects of democracy: broadening citizenship; demanding relatively equal citizenship; pursuing binding consultation of citizens by the state; and protecting citizens from arbitrary state action (1999, 256).

An organization's effectiveness at achieving any of these three goals is mediated by its strategic choices—the issue area that it chooses to address, the movement framing it adopts, the mobilizational tactics it employs, its efforts to attract supporters, and the relationships it develops with other political and social actors. The mediating role of strategies and tactics links organizational development and organizational effectiveness.

---

14. Cohen and Arato suggest that the "success of social movements on the level of civil society should be conceived not in terms of the achievement of certain substantive goals or the perpetuation of the movement, but rather in terms of democratization of values, norms, and institutions that are rooted ultimately in political culture" (1992, 562). Foweraker and Landman agree that democracy is often the result of "prolonged struggle" between movements and the state (1997, 42 and 243).

Recognizing the existence of distinct organizational types within a movement, each with a tendency toward different strategic choices, avoids the pitfall of characterizing an entire social movement as broadly successful or as a failure without reference to its internal dynamics. In addition, by acknowledging that social organizations have a variety of goals, it becomes clear that organizational effectiveness is multifaceted, and that effectiveness in one area does not imply achievement in another.

The Russian Environmental Movement
and the Organizational Approach

The development of the Russian environmental movement illustrates how social organizations emerge in a postauthoritarian and resource-poor environment, in part relying on transnational resources. The Russian environmental movement shifted from almost complete isolation in its early years to significant dependence on transnational sponsorship for its continuing survival in the 1990s. Domestically, most resources available for social activism are still held by the state. As predicted by organization theory, transnational and state actors have come to wield disproportionate influence over green organizations. This influence is all the more significant because of the dearth of resources from citizens to support mobilization.

In this context, activists have been forced to make choices and trade-offs in seeking support and allies. These choices have led to the emergence of three organizational types—referred to here as professionalized, grassroots, and government-affiliate organizations—driven primarily by the varying availability of resources (transnational, societal, state) and the varying ability and desire of activists to take advantage of those resource streams. Environmental leaders use their skills and past experiences to cultivate the support that allows an organization to sustain itself. The need to maintain an ongoing relationship with resource providers influences an organization's relationship with other state and societal actors. Grassroots environmental groups tend to be based on domestic, and usually local, resources, relying on the enthusiasm and unpaid labor of their leaders. Professionalized environmental organizations, in contrast, tend to be grant-based groups modeled after Western NGOs. As their name implies, government affiliates, the third and smallest category, are closely linked to the state administration and rely on government sponsors and funds for organizational survival. Based on their resource dependencies, environmentalists develop different organizational forms, pursue broadly different types of environmentalism, and develop different relationships with state, societal, and transnational actors.

As a result of these incentives, environmental organizations of different types may be very effective at achieving some of their goals but less so in accomplishing others. Ultimately, grassroots organizations emphasize the norms of voluntary labor and collective responsibility in caring for the community but do so in a way that avoids politicized issues. Professionalized groups act more confrontationally, in part based on the history of scientific autonomy and dissidence, yet they do so largely with little contact with the general public. Finally, government affiliates eschew criticism in favor of supporting the government, and yet from their position as insiders they may be able to promote environmental protection within local and regional administrations in a limited way or they may serve to provide the appearance of public participation when it does not in fact exist.

Civil society implies a broad and rich intermediary space between the home, the market, and the state that is populated by organizations; less formal initiatives and associations; movements; and other forms of civic engagement. Undoubtedly, a collection of advocacy organizations such as Russian environmental organizations does not capture the diversity of civil society as a whole. Nevertheless, the evolution of these groups offers insight into the dynamic development of civil society based on the opportunities and obstacles faced by Russian activists.

Various organizational types within a movement illustrate the emergence of specific niches for mobilization. Organizations develop resource dependencies, relationships, and styles of activism based on the broader mobilizational context and the leaders' desire and ability to exploit opportunities. Activists' choices are linked to their differing normative commitments, skills, and access to networks and institutions, a concrete manifestation of the Soviet legacy. These organizational types, and the resource dependencies that they develop, have implications for effectiveness at achieving their three broad goals—sustainability, policy change, and political transformation.

Finally, an understanding of the diverse organizations in Russian civil society and the factors behind their development will assist us in anticipating the further development of state-society relations in Russia. These social organizations provide the basis for future opposition to or support for the regime. They demonstrate processes of social reconstruction with tendencies that reinforce or challenge old identities, norms and institutions. They are the actors that state officials must choose to dominate, co-opt, or compromise with in the future.

2

SPACE FOR ACTIVISM?

Russia's Political and Economic Transformation

Russian social organizations have faced a variety of challenges throughout the post-Soviet era, challenges that have changed over time as the chaotic openness of the Yeltsin years has given way to the state's campaign to recentralize political power and rein in dissent under the Putin and Medvedev administrations. Reviewing the changing political and economic circumstances highlights the fact that classifying the country's political transformation as a failed "transition to democracy" oversimplifies the complex, multidirectional nature of Russia's post-Soviet experience—an experience in which Soviet institutions bend to accommodate new realities, formally democratic structures are infused with patronage and corruption, and economic incentives are shaped by both the market and the state. Ultimately, however, domestic factors combine to create a generally inhospitable environment for social activism. Russian social organizations have difficulty influencing state officials, finding allies among the political elite, and participating in the policymaking and regulatory process. They lack access to information and are harassed by the tax and security police. Given this context, foreign funding has played a significant role in the development of social organizations in Russia, providing a basis for development in spite of domestic constraints.

This chapter reviews the conditions that comprise Russia's mobilizational field. First, it considers environmental quality in Russia. Second, it offers a brief history of environmental activism during the Soviet era, noting the changing political context that led to the emergence of the green movement as a mass phenomenon in the late 1980s. Third, the chapter outlines Russia's political and economic transformation under the Yeltsin and Putin administrations, focusing on the political and economic trends that are most significant for social mobilization. The following section examines those factors that specifically affect environmental activism. Next, public response to the environmental movement is considered. The final section examines the influx of foreign assistance to promote civil society development and democratization in Russia.

The State of Russia's Environment

The territory of the Russian Federation presents an environmental contradiction. Russia hosts some of the world's last pristine wilderness areas and natural treasures such as Lake Baikal, the world's deepest freshwater lake. Russian territory also is home to one-fifth of the world's forest cover, including more than half of boreal forests. Indeed, at the 2002 summit in Johannesburg, Prime Minister Mikhail Kasyanov characterized Russia as an "environmental donor" to the rest of the world.[1]

In spite of this claim to environmental stewardship, however, Russia faces severe environmental degradation in many regions, degradation that is the result of Soviet economic planning. Economic planners in the Soviet era believed that industries should be concentrated in order to gain efficiencies in investment, production, and transportation (Peterson 1993). As a result, a map of Russia now depicts a landscape encompassing relatively untouched natural expanses punctuated by highly degraded areas of concentrated industry. According to OECD data, more than 50 percent of the country's surface water was polluted in the 1990s, and air quality violated

1. The text of Kasyanov's speech is available at http://www.un.org/events/wssd/statements/russiaR.htm.

maximum allowable concentrations in more than two hundred cities (OECD 1999, 57 and 74–75). Prior to 1991, Russia produced 17 percent of the world's carbon dioxide emissions, which contribute to global climate change. In addition, Russia possesses thirty-one nuclear reactors in ten power plants, half of which are considered to be high risk by experts, and a decaying fleet of nuclear submarines. A 2006 report from the Blacksmith Institute stated that three of the world's ten dirtiest cities are in Russia (Blacksmith Institute 2006).

In the 1990s, Russia experienced some improvement in water and air quality and a general reduction in greenhouse gas emissions, largely attributable to the country's industrial collapse. Yet the environmental benefits of industrial decline must be balanced against the growing extraction of natural resources since 1999, the year Russia's economy began to recover, including the rapid development of the oil and gas sector. Russia has the world's largest natural gas reserves and the second-largest oil reserves; since the turn of the century it has become the world's largest exporter of natural gas. Russia exports considerable quantities of timber and minerals such as uranium, copper, and nickel. Russia also faces significant challenges with illegal logging in the Far East.

The effects of environmental degradation on human health are difficult to prove, but many scientists argue that in Russia they are severe. The most strongly worded prediction of an environmentally related health catastrophe in Russia was made in Feshbach and Friendly's *Ecocide in the USSR,* published in 1992, which recounted a litany of health problems in the Soviet Union's highly industrialized cities. According to the 2003 UN Human Development Report, health problems resulting from environmental pollution in Russia cost the state 6.3 percent of GDP on average (UN 2003, 112). Environmental factors may aggravate Russia's demographic crisis, which includes a drop in the life expectancy of Russian men from sixty-five years to just above fifty-eight between 1989 and 1994, and a decline in birth rates in the same time period (Field 2000).

Russia's Soviet-Era Environmental Movement

The evolution of Russia's environmental movement in the Soviet period highlights the role of the political system in creating, and limiting, space for environmental activism. In the Soviet period, the Communist

Party–dominated state attempted to control the public sphere and public debate through its monopoly of political and economic resources.[2] State institutions penetrated society, taking over autonomous public associations and developing state-sponsored organizations to promote the party's ideology. Soviet citizens, dependent upon the state for basic needs such as employment, housing, health care, and education, were not allowed to create an associational sphere independent of the hegemonic party-state. During the Soviet era, social mobilization was characterized by participation in state-sponsored mass mobilization organizations such as the Komsomol (the Communist-Party youth organization), local soviets, trade unions, and the party itself (Friedgut 1979).

In this context, scientists advocating the protection of Russia's natural environment were exceptional. Soviet biologists, geologists, and other scientists were able to preserve a few semiautonomous public organizations, justifying their existence based on the need for apolitical scientific expertise in policymaking. Douglas Weiner, in his history of the Soviet environmental movement, points out the unusual role played by "scientific public opinion" (*nauchnaia obshchestvennost'*) in governance. The phrase signified conformity with Soviet norms of public participation, yet at the same time it allowed scientists to use their expertise as a basis for critical opposition to state policies, particularly in the realm of environmental protection (1999, 30).[3]

Scientists advocating nature protection faced significant obstacles. While the Soviet Constitution and other laws were largely favorable to environmental protection (Pryde 1991; Ziegler 1987), preserving the natural environment for its own sake ran counter to the ideology of Marxism-Leninism, which envisioned nature as a resource for industrialization. As Trotsky wrote:

> The present distribution of mountains and rivers, of fields, of meadows, of steppes, of forests and of seashores, cannot be considered final.... Man will occupy himself with re-registering mountains and rivers and will earnestly

---

2. State control of the public arena was a defining feature of the Soviet system (see Bunce 1999, 21–25; Jowitt 1992).

3. Weiner points out that Soviet-era environmental organizations did not intend to represent general public opinion. Instead they justified their activities based on their status as experts.

and repeatedly make improvements in nature. In the end, he will have re-
built the earth, if not in his own image, at least according to his own taste.
(Trotsky 1925, 251)

Soviet strategies of economic development, based on the logic of the
planned economy, evaluated resource use by the achievement of output
quotas rather than efficiency. Therefore the system failed to price raw materials and to assess externalities, leading to massive waste of natural resources.[4] The Soviet regime also frequently disregarded scientific advice in
its pursuit of grandiose development projects, including Khrushchev's vir-
gin lands program to develop agriculture in Central Asia and plans to di-
vert northern rivers to bring water to dry lands in the country's south.

Given the regime's prohibition against autonomous social mobilization and ambivalence about independent scientific inquiry, the history of
the Soviet-era nature-protection movement is characterized by the search
for institutional space in which environmental advocates could be shel-
tered from government scrutiny yet still occupy a prestigious position from
which they could speak on behalf of the environment. Weiner describes
how the center of gravity in the movement successively shifted from the
All-Russian Society for Nature Protection (VOOP) to the Moscow Society
of Naturalists (MOIP) and the Moscow branch of the Geographical Society
and finally to the university-based *Druzhina* student movements. Along
the way, sympathizers in the republic-level administrations and main-
stream Soviet organizations such as the Academy of Sciences and even
the Komsomol provided cover for environmental activities (Weiner 1999,
405–6). From these perches of relative security, environmentalists waged
campaigns to protect unique ecosystems.

Two organizational forms can be discerned within the Soviet nature-
protection movement: semiautonomous organizations such as VOOP and
MOIP, and the *Druzhina,* or student brigades, movement. Activists within
the former organizations attempted to preserve the tradition of scientific
autonomy and apolitical expertise within institutions that were slowly
bureaucratized and taken over by the state during the Khrushchev and
Brezhnev eras. The student brigades for nature protection (*druzhiny po*

---

4. For more information on the Soviet planned economy and its effects on the environment,
see DeBardeleben 1985, Jancar 1987, Weiner 1988, and Pryde 1991.

okhrane prirody) emerged in the 1960s at the initiative of MOIP activists, and included around five thousand students by the 1980s. They diverged from their increasingly tame parent organization due to the vigor with which they pursued independent activities such as environmental inspections, monitoring, and antipoaching campaigns (Weiner 1999, 6). Collectively these activists succeeded in establishing and defending one of the world's most extensive systems of preserved lands, known as the *zapovedniki* (Pryde 1991, 136). Intermittent battles over the *zapovedniki*, seen by many inside the movement as "islands of freedom" within the Soviet system, illustrate scientists' willingness to oppose the state (Weiner 1999).

The April 1986 Chernobyl nuclear accident sounded the alarm to the broader Russian public about what scientists had long insisted—that all was not well in the state's management of the environment. The Chernobyl disaster also became a catalyst for Gorbachev's effort to restructure the Soviet political and economic system. In his memoirs, Gorbachev recounts a speech he gave at a Politburo meeting several months after Chernobyl in which he berated the official behavior that led to the accident, charging that, "Throughout the entire system there has reigned a spirit of servility, fawning, clannishness and persecution of independent thinkers, window dressing, and personal and clan ties between leaders" (Gorbachev 1995, 191). Gorbachev's response to these entrenched systemic problems was to mount an unprecedented reform effort. Policies such as perestroika (economic restructuring) and glasnost (openness) somewhat circumscribed the Communist Party's monopoly in the economic and political sphere. Glasnost, in particular, was intended to allow limited public debate in order to demonstrate support for the reform program, draw attention to problems in the implementation of the reform, and provide a safety valve for public frustration that had grown during the stagnation of the Brezhnev years. The environmental movement especially benefited from this new policy of openness in which Soviet citizens were encouraged to identify social ills and offer suggestions for their remedy. State officials saw environmentalism as a relatively benign outlet for citizen complaint. As in the past, environmentalism "looked so little like serious 'politics'" (Weiner 1999, 429).[5]

---

5. Weiner also notes that during the Soviet period, there was a sense that scientists were *chudaki,* or eccentrics, and not worth repressing (1999, 444).

In the late 1980s Russians were able to take advantage of Gorbachev's decision to allow citizens to establish new public associations (Dawson 1996, 14). For the first time, Soviet citizens could organize "informal" groups to address issues ranging from anti-alcoholism campaigns, religious movements, and the protection of monuments, to investigations of Stalin's terror. Environmentalists seized this opportunity to mobilize around issues of river diversion, pollution and health concerns, and nuclear power, and to demand greater information and government responsiveness. Thousands of Soviet citizens signed petitions and demonstrated against further development of the country's nuclear power industry. Few environmentalists during this period were members of organizations per se; instead, green supporters congregated in meetings and initiative groups to strategize how to gather public support and influence the government. In such a brittle yet reform-minded political system, even small protests had profound effects. At its height, the environmental movement succeeded in closing or derailing the construction of more than fifty nuclear reactors and a number of hydroelectric power stations and gas pipelines (Dawson 1996; Yanitsky 1996; Babcock 1997). Environmental demonstrations revealed the level of dissatisfaction with Soviet environmental policies and ultimately with the Soviet regime itself. Reflecting on that period, Russia's leading environmental sociologist, Oleg Yanitsky, has said, "ecological protest during the years 1987–89 in the USSR was the first legal embodiment of broadly democratic protest and solidarity of citizens as citizens" (Yanitsky 1995).

An environmental critique of the Communist Party and its policies played a historic role in mobilizing public grievances, eroding the legitimacy of the party, and helping to precipitate the collapse of the Soviet regime. Society's newfound enthusiasm for criticizing the state quickly grew beyond the control of the Soviet authorities, encroaching on previously sacred Soviet precepts. During this period, the environmental movement benefited from the lack of alternative venues for societal participation and debate, and, as Dawson argues, became a "surrogate movement" used by activists advocating less politically acceptable causes to access mobilized populations and surreptitiously further their own aims such as ending Communist-Party control and achieving independence for the Soviet republics (1996, 6–7).

The last years of Soviet power (1989 to 1991) marked the peak of environmental activism in Russia and also the beginning of the decline in mass mobilization. Why did the movement, which had flourished in the thin soil of the late Soviet political system, find itself eroding so precipitously in the seemingly more fertile ground of the post-Soviet transition to democracy? In retrospect, the decline in mass mobilization appears almost inevitable. The possibility of easily uniting the public against the state's most egregious policies was lost when this single monolithic opponent disappeared after the disintegration of the USSR in December 1991. Suddenly activists had to make hard choices about which environmental issues to address, determine who was an ally and who an opponent among the profusion of new political and economic actors, and devise new tactics, including, most significantly, whether to adopt a cooperative or confrontational attitude toward the reconfigured state. The collapse of the Soviet Union and emergence of Russia as an independent state also created new professional opportunities for activists; many environmentalists moved on to pursue other careers in political and economic institutions. Finally, severe economic recession also played a role; green sympathizers faced economic uncertainty as state-owned factories closed and public services deteriorated. Previously mobilized citizens retreated from the public sphere in order to address private concerns of basic survival.

As the perestroika-era wave of environmental mobilization subsided, a core of activists remained, building upon their small informal organizations to continue environmental activism. For example, the Socio-Ecological Union, founded in 1988, disseminated information and coordinated activism throughout the Soviet Union, and they began to reach out to the international environmental community. Green activists and organizations had operated effectively throughout the perestroika period with few financial resources, but they struggled to survive as indigenous sources of financing and a political elite sympathetic to environmental concerns failed to emerge (Tsepilova 1999, 82). It was at this critical period in the early 1990s that Western governments and private foundations began to offer foreign assistance to promote democracy in the former Soviet states, a development that would prove significant to the evolution of green activism in Russia.

Russia's Post-Soviet Political and Economic Transformation

Political institutions and actors have tremendous power to facilitate or stifle social activism, and the rise and fall of the economy sets the broad context in which social organizations struggle to survive. Russia's political and economic transformation since 1991, although characterized in its early stages as "democratization" and "marketization," has been a complex, multifaceted, and open-ended process. No single label describes the hybrid of democratic and authoritarian features that coexist in post-Soviet Russia. Russia's political system has been characterized variously as competitive authoritarianism (Levitsky and Way 2002), electoral authoritarianism (Fish 2001), weak state authoritarianism (Hanson 2007), and, to describe the power-sharing arrangement between Putin and Medvedev, tandemocracy. Russian political elites have referred to their regime as a managed democracy (*upravliaemaia demokratiia*) or a sovereign democracy (*suvernnaia demokratiia*). While Russian officials often argue that they have constructed a new, uniquely Russian model of political organization, Western scholars tend to emphasize the Russian government's superficial adherence to the formal procedures of democracy, including legally enshrined political rights and civil liberties and regularly held multiparty elections, combined with the simultaneous subversion of democratic norms in practice. Freedom House, a nonprofit organization that evaluates governance around the world, has chronicled a steady erosion of Russia's democracy, lowering the country's political-rights and civil-liberties ranking from an average of 3.4 in 1997 to 5.5 in 2008 based upon on a scale of 1 (fully democratic) to 7 (not democratic).[6]

Merely characterizing the Russian political system as more or less democratic largely misses the complicated landscape of obstacles and opportunities for citizen activism that is explored in this study. Yet, at the same time, democracy remains a goal of many social activists in Russia. It is most useful in this context to conceive of democratic politics as a process that is constantly reinvented by political participants, continuously challenged and modified, and operating more effectively at some levels and in some arenas than in others. It should be looked at as an ongoing struggle between different parties rather than as an outcome. Rather than setting a particular threshold of democracy or authoritarianism, this view highlights the expansion and contraction of different aspects of citizenship and the changing ability of the public to control the state.

---

6. Freedom House, 2008, "Russia." For Freedom House's comparative democracy scores from 1973 to 2007, see http://www.freedomhouse.org/template.cfm?page=15.

This section addresses those trends that have shaped the opportunities for social activism generally and for environmental activism specifically—factors that, in effect, structure Russia's mobilizational field. It will focus primarily on state institutions and actors. In Russia, where the authorities still dominate the economic and public spheres, the state remains "simultaneously target, sponsor, and antagonist for social movements as well as the organizer of the political system and the arbiter of victory" (Jenkins and Klandermans 1995, 3).

The Yeltsin and Putin Administrations

The early years of the Yeltsin regime were a period of great optimism for environmental activists as President Boris Yeltsin seemed to indicate that environmental protection was finally on the government's agenda. In fact, however, the political and economic instability of Yeltsin's tenure as president (1991 to 1999) hampered environmentalists' efforts to press their demands. The early years of the Yeltsin presidency were characterized by a rhetorical adherence to democratic and environmental objectives, weak state capacity, and benign neglect of the new social sector. Green organizations were not harassed or scrutinized by state officials, yet social organizations found it difficult to influence the government's erratic policymaking. More broadly, the most significant features of Yeltsin's tenure were the growing autonomy of regional governments and Russia's severe economic collapse. The later Yeltsin years, marked by the president's increasingly poor health, witnessed a combination of unpredictability and drift in the political and economic realms.

Yeltsin's unexpected resignation on December 31, 1999, brought to power his relatively unknown prime minister, Vladimir Putin. Putin's background offered contradictory evidence of his political convictions, encompassing both a position as head of the Federal Security Service (*Federalnaia sluzhba bezopastnosti* or FSB, formerly the KGB) and a stint as deputy to St. Petersburg's liberal mayor, Anatolii Sobchak, in the early 1990s. In spite of uncertainty about Putin's intentions, many Russians welcomed his ascendancy to the presidency. Putin's youthful demeanor and forceful speaking style promised new energy at the federal level.

Putin's presidency was characterized by two trends. First, Putin reined in independent political forces that challenged federal authority, including regional governors and the powerful economic actors known as oligarchs. Second, the Putin administration engaged in a concerted effort to generate economic growth. These tasks, in many ways necessary after the chaotic Yeltsin years, have been accompanied, however, by Putin's intolerance of political dissent in any form and official willingness to manipulate the legal system to discourage political competitors. Since May 2008, Russia has been officially led by its new president, Dmitri Medvedev, Putin's hand-picked successor, while Putin himself retains significant authority in his new role as prime minister.

Federal Political Institutions   Under Yeltsin, political relations at both the federal and regional level were characterized by a series of negotiated agreements and informal ties that trumped formal rules and institutions (Breslauer 1999). Formally, Russia has a presidential-parliamentary system of government. After the October 1993 constitutional crisis, however, when the president defeated his opponents in the Supreme Soviet during a violent battle, Yeltsin was able to consolidate a "superpresidential system" (Fish 2000). This system ensures that the two federal legislative bodies, the State Duma and the Federation Council, are extremely weak relative to the executive. The Russian president has the ability to issue legally binding decrees and directives, to call for referenda on any issue, and, under certain conditions, to dissolve the Duma. The president also enjoys disproportionate resources, including financial resources through control of the budget and political resources through the courts and security services, further limiting any restraint on executive power.

These political institutions fail to offer much encouragement to social movements and citizen activism. Due to the overwhelming power of the presidency, the legislature has not been the central site of policymaking or political change in post-Soviet Russia. In addition, while political institutions, such as the Duma, are technically accessible to the public, they have very few institutionalized channels for public participation or input on policymaking. Certain legacies of the Soviet era also linger, including government officials' default tendency to consider state information confidential and to hold their hearings behind closed doors regardless of the issue being discussed.

It also is difficult for social actors to find political allies given the weak development of the party system and the fact that personal ties matter more than political programs in influencing political outcomes. Both Yeltsin and Putin resisted party identification—in Putin's case, until leaving office— preferring to stand above politics and tacitly designate a "party of power" responsible for shepherding executive policy preferences through the parliament, which in return benefited from unequal access to resources and the media during elections. United Russia, the party that currently dominates the political system, received 64 percent of the vote and 315 out of 450 seats in 2007 parliamentary elections. The growing strength of the law-enforcement and security ministries under Putin and the use of tax police and the court system for political ends point to the state's continued repressive capacity.[7] The politicized nature of the federally administered court system, and its weakness, mean Russian activists have had difficulty using it as a resource in their opposition to state policies.

Regional Politics   The Russian Federation currently comprises eighty-three federal subjects, including forty-six oblasts (regions), twenty-one republics, nine krai (territories), four autonomous oblasts, one autonomous okrug, and two federal cities, Moscow and St. Petersburg.[8] In spite of the president's dominance of the federal center, the Yeltsin administration was unable to prevent political power from leaching away to the regions, and the 1990s marked a period of growing political and economic differentiation at the regional level (Golosov 2004; Gel'man, Ryzhenkov, and Brie 2003; Ross 2002; Treisman 1999; Gel'man 1999b; Stoner-Weiss 1997). Yeltsin, in an effort to win the regional leaders' backing for his battle with Gorbachev and the Communist Party during the perestroika period, instructed the regional leaders to "take all the sovereignty you can swallow" and initially allowed them wide latitude in organizing their own affairs (Walker 2003). After the dissolution of the Soviet Union, however, fearing a repeat of Soviet disintegration at the level of the Russian Federation, Yeltsin attempted to reassert the supremacy of the federal center, but

---

7. The Putin administration has fostered increasing influence for the *siloviki* (roughly meaning "people of power"), individuals within the administration who have military, intelligence, or law-enforcement backgrounds. Although this was initially viewed as a possible sign of Putin's determination to combat corruption, the rise of the *siloviki* has gone hand in hand with a return to extralegal methods of coercing compliance from political opponents.

8. During most of the 1990s, the Russian Federation hosted eighty-nine federal subjects, but that number has decreased through several mergers among constituent units.

his efforts largely failed. Although the constitution asserts that each region will be treated equally, in fact some regional leaders negotiated much more autonomy than others did, resulting in a system of "asymmetrical federalism" (Lapidus 1999; Walker 1996).[9] Under these conditions, some regional governors were able to rule as minor despots without significant interference from the federal authorities and to promulgate laws that contradicted federal legislation (Gel'man 1999b), creating varying contexts for social mobilization.

One of Putin's primary objectives was to reestablish vertical authority in the Russian Federation—to ensure the supremacy of federal laws over regional laws and to limit the political independence of the regional governors. Putin accomplished this through measures such as the creation, in 2000, of super-regions, a new layer of bureaucratic oversight to ensure conformity with federal laws; the removal of regional executives from the Federation Council, the upper house of the legislature; and the 2004 decision to abolish elections for regional governors and replace them with presidential appointees. Critics charged that gubernatorial despots have been replaced by an overbearing federal center that is eager to dominate media outlets, reactivate the security services, and intervene in regional economies. In addition, regional governments, though now more subservient, continue to be accused of undemocratic practices such as election fraud, intimidation of the media and political opponents, and the misuse of state resources.

Political power in the regions is still formally dispersed across different offices and jurisdictions, including an executive—the regional governor—and a legislature located in the regional capital. In addition, most capital cities elect a mayor and a city soviet or council. Regional governors tend to wield disproportionate power and influence over the decision-making process, as Russia's superexecutive style of governance at the center is mimicked in many of the regions. The personality, political ties, and preferences of the regional executive—rather than legal restrictions—have governed the regional administrations' relations with social groups. Political parties largely have failed to penetrate regional political competition. In the 1990s,

---

9. Each region lobbied for the best-possible bilateral arrangement of tax payments and subsidies based upon the profitability of the region's economic enterprises, the region's de facto control of natural resources, and the clout of its political leader.

fewer than a quarter of successful candidates for regional legislatures in single-member districts were affiliated with a party (Karatnycky, Motyl, and Schnetzer 2001, 316; see also Smyth 2006).

Economic Crisis and Privatization   The Yeltsin administration was incapable of stemming the decline of Russia's economy in the 1990s. A few examples capture the depth of the crisis. During Yeltsin's first term as president (1992 to 1996), hyperinflation, including price increases of more than 1,000 percent, wiped out personal savings and devalued the currency, while GDP fell by an estimated 40 percent. In that same period, state spending on welfare, health, education, and culture dropped by 37.5 percent (Jakobson, Rudnik, and Shishkin 1997, 115). Even given the difficulty of measuring rapid dramatic changes, these numbers indicate significant social and economic dislocation. The result of these trends was the impoverishment of many Russian citizens, culminating in the August 1998 financial crisis, when, after a brief period of economic recovery, the devaluation of Russia's currency once again undermined Russians' confidence. Russia's post-Soviet privatization program created huge financial and industrial conglomerates, overseen by individuals who became known as the oligarchs. Environmentalists charged that these new conglomerates were at the forefront of the unregulated and increasingly rapid exploitation of Russia's natural resources, particularly timber, minerals, and petroleum, in the post-Soviet period and that they attempted to influence environmental policy in their favor. Corruption became pervasive as well.[10]

President Putin has been widely credited with generating economic growth in Russia. Under Putin, the annual growth rates in Russia's GDP averaged almost 7 percent per year. Real incomes more than doubled. Putin reined in the oligarchs, reportedly suggesting that he would not investigate their ill-gotten wealth if they stayed out of politics. The state has reconsolidated its ownership stake in many large firms, especially in strategic industries such as the oil and gas sector. Putin endorsed natural-resource extraction as a means of economic development; in April 2000,

---

10. In 2001, at the end of Yeltsin's presidency, the Transparency International Corruption Perceptions Index showed Russia tied for seventy-ninth place (with Ecuador and Pakistan) out of ninety-one countries. The Transparency International Corruption Perceptions Index 2001 is available at http://www.transparency.org/cpi/2001/cpi2001.html#cpi.

the new president announced, "Russia's economy in the twenty-first century, at least in the first half, will keep to its raw materials orientation" (*Prirodno-resursnye vedomosti,* quoted in Peterson and Bielke 2001, 66). Russia's economy remains highly dependent on natural resources—oil in particular—for economic growth. According to the World Bank, the oil and gas sectors account for almost 25 percent of Russia's GDP (World Bank 2004, 15). An OECD analysis has suggested that 4 percent of Russia's annual 7 percent economic growth rate from 2001 to 2004 is accounted for by the resource sector (Bradshaw 2006, 726). Russian citizens' standard of living has improved since the 1990s, but it is based on a model that is contrary to the sustainable-development model promoted by environmentalists.

Managing Civil Society Russia's constitution enshrines the rights of citizens and social organizations. Russian citizens have the right to "basic human civil rights and freedoms" (Article 17), freedom of association (Article 30), the right to peaceful assembly (Article 31), the right to appeal to state bodies (Article 33), and the right to the protection of their health (Article 41). In practice, however, activists face many obstacles to their use of these rights. Since the late 1990s, state actors have adopted an increasingly negative stance toward independent social organizations.

Once the most obvious challengers to the recentralization of political power were neutralized, Putin turned his attention to other groups he perceived as political opponents, including those in the media and social organizations. Press freedom has been significantly curtailed by the consolidation of media ownership in state hands and by laws affecting the media (Oates 2007). A number of Russian journalists have been detained, attacked, and murdered, including the 2006 murder of Anna Politkovskaya, a vocal critic of the government's actions in Chechnya. Critics argue that these crimes have not been investigated effectively, leading the organization Reporters Without Borders to rank Russia 144th out of 169 countries in terms of press freedom in 2007 (Reporters sans Frontières 2007). The selective prosecutions of scientists who speak out on issues that are perceived as related to national security have also created a climate threatening to independent research.[11]

---

11. For example, in April 2004 Igor Sutiagin, a researcher at the U.S. and Canada Institute in Moscow, was given a fifteen-year sentence for treason purportedly committed when Sutiagin

State regulations on social organizations' registration, taxation, and activities are often applied in a selective and political way (Iur'ev 1999; Human Rights Watch 2008). For example, activists charge that the government's re-registration requirements for social organizations have been used by some officials to refuse registration to groups critical of political elites. Activists report harassment by local police and security services for supposed infractions. Tax audits and inspections also tend to be initiated based on an organization's political stance as opposed to its accounting procedures.[12] A new NGO law, passed in 2006, heightened concerns about the potential for state manipulation of social organizations (Bigg 2006). The government initiated re-registration and annual accounting by NGOs ostensibly to clear the Ministry of Justice's records of defunct and inactive social organizations. Without legal registration, social organizations cannot own property or maintain a bank account, and they are not able to sign contracts or represent themselves in court cases. Annual reporting is a complicated process that involves accounting for all activities and finances. While the government's initiative was similar to oversight exerted by some other states, it occurred in a political context in which activists felt that that state was trying to control their activities and in some cases threaten their existence.[13] At the same time, President Putin warned against the prevalence of foreign funding to support Russian social organizations. At a Moscow meeting with social activists in July 2006, Putin remarked,

> I personally...have only one concern. I will always speak and fight against foreign governments financing political activity in our country, just as our government should not finance political activity in other countries. This is a sphere of activity for our public and our public organizations. They should function on the money of our people, our public or financial organizations. (RIA Novosti 2006)

As president, Putin made several efforts to formally engage social organizations. Under Putin, the state organized a Civic Forum in 2001 to

---

gathered information on the Russian military and weapons systems for his work for a British consulting firm, information that Sutiagin and his lawyers claim was publicly available.

12. Askhat Kaiumov, leader of the environmental organization Dront, notes that "for many organs of power it [has] become normal to ignore or interpret for themselves inconvenient laws" (Kaiumov 2001).

13. For a dissenting opinion, see Lindemann-Komarova 2008, "The Parallel Universes of NGOs in Russia," April 18, 2008. In Johnson's Russia List 2008–79.

gather activists from across Russia. In 2005, President Putin created the Public Chamber (*Obshchestvennaia Palata*), including prominent citizens and NGO representatives, to comment on government policies and to routinize ties between the state and civil society (Richter 2009; Evans 2008). Chamber representatives occasionally have acted as advocates for social organizations, arguing, for example, that the financial documentation required by the 2006 NGO law is too burdensome and should be reformed (*RFE/RL Newsline* 2008). Although its overall influence is still unclear, the chamber also controls increasing financial resources for social groups. The Russian government spent 1.25 billion rubles for NGOs in 2007 and 1.5 billion rubles in 2008, with expectations that funds channeled through the chamber will increase in the future (Moshkin 2008). Given that it is a relatively new organization, the political influence of the Public Chamber is still uncertain, although many activists fear that it represents a top-down strategy to manage, if not coerce, activists.

Opportunities and Constraints for Environmental Activism

As is the case for social organizations more broadly, Russia's basic environmental laws are quite favorable to environmental protection and appear to ensure the public's right to play a role in environmental policy. The Constitution of the Russian Federation endows each citizen with "the right to a favorable environment, reliable information about its condition and to compensation for the damage caused to his or her health or property by ecological violations" (Article 42) and the right to participate in decision making on environmental issues.[14] In practice, however, environmentalists have been frustrated by their lack of access to policymaking and have struggled to promote environmental protection as the government's attention to green issues has declined throughout the post-Soviet period. The early promises of the Yeltsin administration to include environmentalists in deliberation over policy were realized only for a brief period. Under the Putin administration,

---

14. The constitution divides jurisdiction over the environment within the federation, although these divisions are quite vague in practice. The federal government oversees power generation, the armed forces, and security, while there is joint federal-regional jurisdiction over land use, mineral resources, water and other natural resources, public health, scientific facilities, and environmental protection. Regions are responsible for any features not explicitly named in the constitution.

state officials publicly questioned the motivations of environmentalists. Putin's determination to generate economic growth also further demoted environmental issues in the national political discourse. While greens have continued to advocate for the environment, finding some opportunities to propose new preserved lands and contribute to new legislation, the political system remains largely closed to environmental organizations, allowing them to exploit opportunities for participation only on an ad hoc basis.

The post-Soviet period seemed to promise favorable political conditions for environmental protection. In 1991, the Yeltsin administration created the Ministry of Ecology and adopted a new comprehensive law On Environmental Protection. In the early 1990s, Russia also progressively, if mostly rhetorically, committed itself to the principle of sustainable development (Henry 2009). In a sign of political openness on environmental issues, in 1993 a commission chaired by Aleksei Yablokov revealed for the first time that the Soviets had disposed of 2.5 million curies of radioactive waste at sea since 1965. After this initial period of openness, however, in 1996 the Yeltsin administration demoted the Ministry of Ecology to a lower status, renaming it the State Committee on Ecology (*Goskomekologiia*). Observers suggested that the demotion was related to the lack of "a clear constituency for the committee" and the fact that it was not profitable (Fremin 1997). Throughout the 1990s, environmental protection agencies remained relatively weak compared to other state bodies, tending to have fewer resources and less institutional authority (Glushenkova 1999). Other obstacles to environmental protection included frequent bureaucratic reorganization, an uncertain legal environment, lobbying by industrial groups, widespread corruption, and pressure for economic development (Kotov and Nikitina 2002). Then, in May 2000, President Putin dissolved Goskomekologiia and the State Forest Service entirely and transferred their functions to the Ministry of Natural Resources, the agency in charge of licensing mining, oil exploration, and timber extraction.[15] Government officials justified the move as an effort to streamline state structures and cut costs. Observers argued that the dissolution was related to the desire to remove constraints on economic growth after the August 1998 financial crisis (Peterson and Bielke 2001; ZumBrunnen and Trumbull 2003).

---

15. These agencies were dissolved by Presidential Decree 867. Russia's venerable State Forest Service was 202 years old when it was abolished.

Although the State Committee on Ecology had been deeply unpopular with environmentalists for what they deemed its lax enforcement of environmental protection legislation,[16] Russian activists demanded that the committee be reinstated, claiming that a flawed system of environmental protection was better than none at all. *Goskomekologiia* may have been weak and underfunded, but individual bureaucrats within the committee occasionally acted as allies in protection of the environment (Peterson 2000, 6). Viktor Danilov-Danilyan, former head of *Goskomekologiia,* said the decision was "a signal to thieves that they were now free to destroy and steal Russia's environmental wealth" (Lambroschini 2001). Igor Chestin, head of the Russian office of the World Wide Fund for Nature (WWF), commented that increasing the authority of the Ministry of Natural Resources was "like putting a goat in charge of the cabbage patch" (Cockburn 2000). The reactions of regional bureaucrats to the dissolution of the State Committee varied but tended to be fairly muted. Most expected to keep their jobs in some form under the Ministry of Natural Resources. In the absence of an outcry from the general public, environmentalists' protests were not enough to reverse the government's decision.[17]

Since the dissolution of the independent environmental agency, state oversight in the environmental sector has been weak. In 2001, Askhat Kaiumov of Dront in Nizhny Novogorod, one of Russia's most active environmental organizations, stated: "In reality, what we have now are isolated pockets where people try to do something and where state control is maintained, but the exploitation of natural resources is just left to its own devices in a majority of regions" (Kaiumov 2001).

Many laws that were designed to protect the environment have not functioned as intended or have been weakened over time. For example, environmental fines did not reduce pollution and raise funds for environmental protection as intended; fees were generally lower than the cost of new technology and failed to keep pace with inflation; payments were often made in goods or services rather than cash; and many firms have received

---

16. The committee had been called a "Potemkin village of environmental aspirations" (Peterson and Bielke, 2001, 69).

17. The general public remained largely ignorant of and/or unmoved by the government's decision, however, and environmentalists were not successful at attracting attention to the issue. A poll taken in four Siberian cities in early 2001 found that 63 percent of respondents were unaware that the president had abolished *Goskomekologiia* (Kutepova 2001, 14–15).

special dispensation to avoid payment (Kjeldsen 2000). Environmentalist Valentin Yemelin commented, "The problem is, as usual in Russia, that the intentions are very good but the results are quite negative" (Bransten 2002). The 1995 Russian law On Ecological Expertise required any project involving the exploitation of a federal natural resource to undergo an environmental-impact assessment, referred to as an *ekspertiza,* for review by the state environmental-protection body (Cherp 2000).[18] Environmental organizations occasionally were able to favorably prosecute cases on the basis of this law. However, in 2006 a new building code did away with the requirement for environmental review.

In this context of institutional instability and weakness, activists have had difficulty locating paths to participating in governance on environmental issues, despite constitutional guarantees. Russia's 1997 and 2002 reports on sustainable development to the United Nations Department of Social and Economic Affairs acknowledge that mechanisms for NGOs to participate in governance do not yet exist (State Environmental Protection Committee 1997; United Nations 2002). Although they do not play a routine role in policymaking in Russia, environmentalists have continued to try to influence environmental policies at the national level. For example, in the late 1990s the Center for Russian Environmental Policy authored a series of proposals entitled "Priorities for Russia's National Environmental Policy" that elaborated methods for integrating the principles of sustainable development into the Russian system of governance (Zakharov 1999). Activists have tried to propose alternative environmental policies to the government at the three meetings of the All-Russian Congress on Environmental Protection in 1995, 1999, and 2003 (Maleshin 2003/2004; RIA OREANDA 2004). They also have attempted to provide input on major pieces of environmental legislation that have been passed since 2001, including an Environmental Doctrine (2002), a Water Code (2006), and a Forest Code (2007), charging that while these pieces of legislation contain some valuable measures, there are also many inconsistencies and omissions that make them difficult to put into practice.

Promoting the conservation of land has perhaps been the most successful endeavor of greens operating at the federal level. Zapovedniks, the highest

---

18. The organization Ecojuris successfully brought several legal suits on the basis of this law (Mischenko 1998).

level of nature preserve, increased from seventy-seven to one hundred in the 1990s, encompassing more than thirty-three million hectares, and forty national parks have been created (Ostergren and Jacques 2002). However, financing for the management of these lands has fallen, with budgets in the late 1990s only 20 to 40 percent of their former size during the Soviet era (Ostergren and Jacques 2002, 110). Environmentalists question whether there could be money available for environmental protection if government priorities change in the future. Antonina Kuliasova perhaps speaks for many greens when she said, "What does it mean that they don't have any money? I don't know. They have money for Chechnya. They have money for elections."[19] The UNESCO World Heritage Sites program has listed eight natural sites in Russia since 1995.[20] WWF-Russia's Ecoregion program in the Far East has promoted the expansion of existing nature preserves and the creation of new buffer zones around the preserves and wildlife corridors between them.[21] Indeed, Russia ranks first in the world in terms of number of wildlife sanctuaries and national parks, although environmentalists charge that these areas are not well protected in practice.

The tension between economic growth and environmental protection is an obstacle to green activism worldwide, but in Russia the situation has been exacerbated by the country's deep economic recession in the early 1990s and the opportunity to develop the economy by exploiting lucrative natural resources. The government perceives questions of conservation and environmental protection—including protests against the construction of new pipelines and ports—as particularly threatening to continued economic growth. President Putin has singled out environmentalists as agents of espionage working against economic prosperity; industrial elites echo these arguments. Russian environmentalists, in turn, have struggled to address the privatization of natural-resource extraction, necessitating a shift in attention

---

19. Antonina Kuliasova, author interview, Healthy Family and the Center for Independent Social Research, St. Petersburg, April 13, 1999.

20. Russia's participation in the program was initiated by Greenpeace in 1994 when it suggested five Russian territories for consideration by UNESCO. Initially the organization was reprimanded by the Ministry of Foreign Affairs, which argued that only a state organization could make that sort of proposal, but once the issue had been publicized in the press, *Goskomekologiia* decided to contract with Greenpeace to prepare the documents for UNESCO, while the state agency officially would submit them (Sergei Tsyplenkov, author interview, Greenpeace Russia, Moscow, May 31, 2000).

21. Yulia Fomenko, author interview, WWF, Vladivostok, November 15, 1999.

from one big opponent—the state—to many new adversaries, including industrial and natural-resource conglomerates that often have close ties to state actors and small criminal groups that engage in poaching and illegal timber harvesting (Newell 2004). Greens working to monitor the country's environmental-protection laws at the regional level also face corruption that appears to be endemic in the natural-resource sector. As a result of the lack of government support, some environmental groups have undertaken *obshchestvennyi kontrol'*, or social inspections. David Gordon of Pacific Environment, an American organization that funds environmentalists in Russia's Far East, comments that there has been growth in the number of public environmental inspectors, especially student *druzhiny*, trying to enforce environmental laws.[22] Yet environmental organizations and others charge that poaching and illegal tree cutting often occurs with the complicity of regional administrations.[23] Greenpeace Russia has argued that the government is negligent in oversight of, if not overtly complicit in, regional governments' efforts to generate hard-currency revenue through the export of timber and other raw materials.[24]

The Public Response to Environmental Organizations

The Russian public's awareness of the severity of the country's environmental problems has been quite high throughout the post-Soviet period. For example, a 1993 poll showed that approximately 65 percent of Russians evaluated their local environmental quality as fairly bad or very bad, and 85 percent rated the environment at the national level similarly (Dunlap, Gallup, and Gallup 1993, 12). Surveys from the late 1990s indicate that fewer than a third of Russians were "satisfied with the environment"

---

22. Comments made at the World Affairs Council, San Francisco, January 24, 2002.

23. For example, Tiger Volunteer, a Siberian-based environmental organization, was given official permission to patrol natural reserves in Siberia, supplementing the government's few inspectors. The organization found, however, that many tiger poachers were influential locals, and that local environmental-protection officials often turned a blind eye to poaching. In fact, Tiger Volunteer had its agreement with the government terminated after a "member of the group was physically assaulted when trying to stop a former governor from entering a reserve without a permit" (Kyodo News Service 2004).

24. See, for example, Greenpeace, "Results of the Public Opinion Poll Concerning the Use and Protection of the Forests of Karelia," Moscow, February 2000, pamphlet given to the author by a representative of Greenpeace Russia in 2000.

(Petrova 1999). In 1999, 51 percent of Russian respondents expected environmental problems to affect the health of their children and grandchildren "a great deal" (DeBardeleben and Heuckroth 2001). According to Russia's Public Opinion Foundation, between 2001 and 2007 the number of respondents who believed that environmental quality was declining remained fairly stable at 60 to 65 percent (Fond "Obshchestvennoe Mnenie" 2007). The areas of greatest public concern during that period were harmful effects from industrial activity and water quality.

Awareness of environmental problems has not necessarily led to support for more spending on the environment, however. Survey data show that the willingness of Russians to pay the costs of environmental improvement declined 20 percent, from 58.5 percent in 1993 to 38.1 percent in 2001 (Whitefield 2003, 101). A 2008 poll by the Public Opinion Foundation found that only 29 percent of Russian respondents were willing to pay to improve the environmental situation (Fond "Obshchestvennoe Mnenie" 2008). This decline appears to be relatively consistent across all social categories and may have been a result of citizens' anxiety about the economic situation in the 1990s. But concern for the environment does not necessarily translate into support for nongovernmental environmental organizations. In general, the Russian public remains skeptical about social organizations. In a survey asking respondents about social organizations (*obshschestvennye organizatsii*), more than 80 percent of Russian respondents thought that these groups exist only at a formal level, for their own benefit, and do not work to improve the situation in Russia (Fond "Obshchestvennoe Mnenie" 2001a). Olga Alekseeva, head of the Russian office of Charities Aid Foundation, one of the most active resource centers for NGOs in Moscow, acknowledged that the general public tends to have a very poor impression of NGOs—an impression based in part on media coverage of corruption and illegal smuggling by some "charitable" organizations in the mid-1990s.[25] In fact, most Russians are not aware of social organizations at all, including green organizations. Only 30 percent of respondents surveyed in 2001 were aware that environmental groups existed in their region. Of respondents familiar with environmental organizations, they are almost evenly split as to whether the environmentalists' activities are positive (31 percent) or negative (32 percent) (Fond

---

25. Olga Alekseeva, author interview, Charities Aid Foundation, Moscow, April 12, 2000.

"Obshchestvennoe Mnenie" 2001b). Several years later, in 2005, a similar poll found that even in Moscow, site of the greatest number of high profile and active green NGOs, only 33 percent of respondents were aware of the existence of environmental organizations in the city (Fond "Obshchestvennoe Mnenie" 2005).[26] Similarly, in 2008 the Public Chamber found that only 27 percent of Russians surveyed said that they know or have heard of environmental organizations (Obshchestvennaia Palata 2008, 11).

Transnational Funding for Russian Social Organizations

Funding from foreign governments and private foundations has played a significant role in the development of social organizations in Russia. In the post–Cold War period, U.S. presidential administrations have identified "building sustainable democracies" in the postcommunist region as a priority, and European states have made similar commitments (USAID 1998a, 1). In their efforts to support democratization in Russia, many foreign governments and private donors concluded that social organizations could be an effective vehicle for strengthening civil society, and they have expended considerable energy and resources to cultivate these groups (Sundstrom 2006; Henderson 2003, 3–6; Ottaway and Carothers 2000; Carothers 1999, 211–14).[27] Donors were inspired by idealized visions of civil society as a realm in which citizens act together to advocate for the public welfare and call government officials to account.[28] Although civil society includes diverse social interactions—from soccer clubs to choirs and neighborhood associations—for the practical purpose of disbursing aid to promote the

---

26. An analysis of the environmental movement in Samara similarly describes public skepticism and suspicion in regard to environmental advocacy groups (Crotty 2003).

27. Most of the references to donor programs in this study are drawn from the particular efforts of USAID, although I also interviewed representatives of the EU TACIS program, UK DFID, and private American foundations including MacArthur, C. S. Mott, Ford, the Open Society Institute (Soros), World Learning and the public-private Eurasia Foundation. Environmental organizations studied here also received support from international environmental groups, such as the World Wide Fund for Nature, Rockefeller Brothers, Global Green Grants, ISAR, Pacific Environment, and other programs specifically designed to promote environmental protection in Russia. A number of representatives of these programs were interviewed as well.

28. Although scholars have a renewed appreciation for the complexity of actual civil societies, their potentially undemocratic features, and their strengths and limitations (Chambers and Kopstein 2001; Ehrenberg 1999; and Berman 1997), a resolute optimism about civil society persists in both scholarship and democracy promotion.

development of civil society, most donors have chosen to support a particular organizational form: nongovernmental organizations (NGOs). For donors, increasing numbers of NGOs became a proxy measurement for the growth of civil society.[29]

While the quantity of aid dedicated to democracy assistance and specifically for NGO development in Russia has never lived up to Western governments' inflated rhetoric, the relative impact of this aid on the generally impoverished NGO sector has been significant (Quigley 2000; Carothers 1999). Henderson notes that in 2002 civil society programs received the largest share (37 percent, or more than $187 million) of USAID's worldwide democracy and governance portfolio (Henderson 2003, 5). Focusing more narrowly on Russia, the U.S. government gave $133 million and the EU gave $272 million in democracy assistance to Russia from 1990 to 1998 (Mendelson and Glenn 2000, 63).[30] USAID reports indicate that more than $60 million was committed to Russia for democracy and local governance initiatives from 2002 to 2004 (USAID 2005). The OECD estimates that $50 million was given just to support environmental policymaking in Russia from 2003 to 2005 (OECD 2007, 129). In a country with extremely limited domestic sources of funding, these figures—to say nothing of funds donated by private foundations or other states—represent a significant resource for NGO development.

Most of the early funding for social organizations in Russia was disseminated through Moscow, but during the late 1990s and early 2000s a number of donors made providing more funding for social organizations in the regions a priority. Given Russia's size and poor infrastructure, however, no funding agency can work in every region.[31] Even USAID, the largest donor, chooses strategic regions, as a 2002 report notes:

> It is not sufficient, however, to say that we will work "in the regions." Our resources are limited relative to Russia's vast size and population, and the

---

29. For examples, see USAID 1998a, 1998b, and 2002.

30. The $133 million from the U.S. represented only 2.8 percent of the country's total assistance budget to Russia.

31. A 1998 UK Department for International Development report similarly notes, "We have limited the range of sectors and oblasts in which we are involved largely for management reasons. Russia's vast size makes management of a dispersed programme both costly and time consuming" (DFID. October 1998 "Russia Strategy Report," document given to the author by William Pryor, DFID, Moscow, May 2000).

scope of its problems.... U.S. foreign policy priorities, the willingness of local leaders to champion progressive policies, population size, and opportunities to replicate and deepen success from existing programs taken together suggest a geographic focus. (USAID 2002, 11)

Many donors acknowledge that as foreign assistance budgets have declined and as the pressure to show measurable results has increased, they are more likely to offer funding to a region in which the political leadership is willing to work with activists and therefore the likelihood of successful NGO development and increased public participation is greater. When asked why some regions seem to receive significantly more assistance than others, one U.S. donor in Moscow commented, "I think that the greatest determinant I would point to as to whether regions are receptive or good prospects in terms of technical assistance is government—the attitudes of the local government in viewing NGOs as partners and working as partners and as capable implementers of change."[32] She continued, "The biggest indicator of the progressiveness of the region is the local government. What does that mean? That means, who is the mayor. It's all very personality driven."[33]

The unfavorable political climate and the scarcity of domestic funding for social organizations only increased the appeal of funding from external sources. The range of Russian organizations that have received foreign assistance includes women's-rights organizations, media watchdogs, and human-rights monitoring organizations, among others. This funding also became influential in the development and proliferation of Russian environmental organizations throughout the 1990s (Powell 2002). Based on surveys of green activists, Russian sociologists have argued that contacts between Russian environmental leaders and Westerners increased by ten times between 1991 and 1998, and that by the late 1990s about 75 percent of the financial resources of Russian environmental organizations came from the West (Kouzmina and Yanitsky 1999, 180). The fieldwork on which this study is based suggests that approximately 60 percent of Russian environmental organizations have received foreign funding on at least one occasion, and many rely on it as their primary source of support. In

32. Bernadine Joselyn, author interview, Eurasia Foundation, Moscow, March 24, 2000.
33. Joselyn interview.

addition to addressing issue-oriented problems in Russia, donors expect that social organizations will stimulate demand for democracy from below—that organized groups in society will help to generate a constituency for open politics by demanding access to policymaking and government accountability.

In evaluating the impact of democracy assistance, donors use measures such as the number of organizations in existence, the level of technology and infrastructure of organizations, the number of staff members trained, and whether aid money was spent as planned (Smillie and Hemlich 1999, 27–28; USAID 1998b). These measurements do not, however, necessarily capture organizations' effectiveness in achieving their issue-based goals or promoting public participation and government responsiveness. Whether "more NGOs meant more democracy" (Sampson 1996, 121) remains an open question.

Changing state-society relations in Russia thus far have not produced greater transparency, representativeness, responsiveness, or accountability. Despite regular elections during Yeltsin's administration, institutional instability, personalism, corruption, and a general disregard for the rule of law characterized the political system. Yeltsin was a successful revolutionary, helping to overthrow the Soviet state, but he was incapable of building a stable and democratic system of political and economic governance. The state made little effort to incorporate a bewildered and impoverished citizenry into the political process. Putin's legacy has been fiercely debated. He oversaw a return to political stability and economic growth; however, Putin further consolidated superpresidentialism, undermining prospects for greater pluralism. President Putin's "dictatorship of laws" constrained authoritarian practices in the regions, yet his efforts to limit other sources of opposition, particularly in the media, have circumscribed Russia's political debate and inhibited the growth of civil society. Given Putin's consistently high popularity ratings (generally around 70 percent) and his ability to choose his successor, the politically dependent President Dmitrii Medvedev, Russians are unlikely to witness a radical departure from the government's current policies that offer few opportunities for political dissent and opposition.

This examination of Russia's environmental movement and political and economic transformation raises several issues for social organizations.

First, Russia's mobilizational field has not been particularly favorable for social activism. Russia's formally democratic institutions and laws are superseded in practice by personalism, corruption, and manipulation. The few political openings of the early post-Soviet years narrowed further under the Putin administration. Second, the contemporary Russian green movement—shaped by its tumultuous birth during the Soviet era and organizational development during the perestroika years—is now coming of age in the era of transnationalism. Foreign funding, given to promote democracy in Russia, has far outweighed domestic resources for social organization. In this context, what opportunities for mobilization have activists been able to identify? Have these organizations indeed been able to change government policies or contribute to the transformation of Russian politics? The next chapters address the diverse strategies that Russia's environmental organizations have adopted to survive and pursue their goals.

3

Environmental Organizations
in Russia's Regions

This chapter examines the relationship between regional governance and environmental mobilization in post-Soviet Russia. Specifically, it considers how varying levels of political and economic liberalization may affect the level and quality of social movement mobilization by investigating the development of Russian environmental organizations in five regional capitals—St. Petersburg, Vladivostok, Novosibirsk, Vladimir, and Bryansk.[1] While hypotheses of social mobilization would lead us to expect growing variation in mobilization as a result of increasingly diverse political and economic conditions at the regional level, this chapter challenges the conventional wisdom by demonstrating that levels of mobilization across regions are strikingly similar.

---

1. This study examines social mobilization in five subjects of the Russian Federation: the federal city of St. Petersburg; the capital cities of three oblasts including Bryansk, Novosibirsk, and Vladimir; and Vladivostok, the capital city of Primorskii Krai. For terminological simplicity, the terms "region" and "regional" are used throughout.

The *level* of mobilization as an aggregate measure, however, conceals growing diversity in the *nature* or *quality* of environmental activism at the organization level. Russia's regions are home to environmental organizations that exhibit three distinct strategies of organizational development and three models of environmental activism. The clustering of Russian environmental organizations into these three forms points to the existence of a limited number of political and resource niches within Russia's mobilizational field. These three types of environmental organizations are referred to as *grassroots organizations, professionalized organizations,* and *government-affiliate organizations.* It is the relative number of the three organizational types that varies from region to region.

Considering the way grassroots, professionalized, and government-affiliate organizations are distributed unevenly across different regions raises the question of why these organizational types are more likely to appear in some places than in others, and provides clues to the factors that facilitate or inhibit each pattern of organizational development. While grassroots environmental organizations can be found in every Russian region, professionalized organizations tend to emerge where foreign assistance is readily available. Foreign assistance tends to flow either to regions with a relatively open political regime or to regions with well-publicized environmental grievances that attract the attention of the transnational environmental community. Professionalized and grassroots environmental organizations may persist in regions with a more closed political system, but, counterintuitively, government-affiliate organizations appear to require a degree of political openness to survive.

The first section of this chapter briefly sketches the political and economic features of the capital cities of the five Russian regions surveyed here during a crucial period for social-organization development, the late 1990s. It then highlights why, based on hypotheses found in social movement theory, one might expect corresponding variation in the level of social mobilization around environmental issues. Next, evidence is presented demonstrating that there is a broad similarity in levels of environmental mobilization in each region, a finding that runs counter to our initial social-mobilization hypotheses and appears to confirm the negative aspects of the Soviet legacy and of the post-Soviet political and economic transition. The second section of the chapter identifies another important type of variation within the movement—variation in the nature or quality of environmental mobilization. Based on data gathered in interviews with

Russian environmental activists, the chapter reveals three tendencies of organizational development within the environmental movement that are related to the political and economic variables that compose Russia's mobilizational field. The chapter then proceeds to describe the structure of this field and to discuss the independent variables that influence the development of social organizations. I conclude by offering some thoughts about the implications of these patterns of organizational development for the future of the Russian environmental movement.

Regional Diversity in Russia

Why would we expect to see variation in the level of social mobilization across the regions of the Russian Federation? This prospect arises from diverse political and economic conditions at the regional level. Following the Communist Party–dominated economic and political system of the Soviet period, the Russian Federation's constituent regions obtained significant autonomy under the Yeltsin administration. In the 1990s, regional governments implemented political and economic reform programs that differed markedly from those of the federal center. Regional differences, political and economic, persisted even as President Putin attempted to reimpose federal authority. For example, a 2003 United Nations report on variation in the Human Development Index in Russia's regions ranked Moscow at a level of development similar to Slovenia, and the Republic of Tyva as relatively close to Gabon (Zubarevich 2003). According to Western theories of social mobilization, regional experiments in reform—not to mention the uneven distribution of foreign assistance—should generate varying levels of social mobilization within the country's nascent civil society. However, evidence of mobilization in Russia's regions, measured by the number of environmental organizations per capita in a given region and the size and membership of those organizations, shows that there is a lack of substantial regional variation, directly countering expectations raised in the social movement literature and leading to further questions.

Political and Economic Differentiation: Five Regions Compared

The economic and political characteristics of the regional capital cities St. Petersburg, Vladivostok, Novosibirsk, Vladimir, and Bryansk provide evidence of differentiation across Russian regions.[2] This review is not intended to be an exhaustive analysis of regional differentiation or to determine a rigorous ranking system for the regions on an array of political and economic indicators. Instead, these summaries demonstrate that there is a level of regional diversity within Russia sufficient to raise the expectation that variation in social mobilization would follow. Regional cases were selected based on independent variables, notably the degree of political openness and levels of economic development, drawn out of existing hypotheses about social mobilization.

The two regional capitals studied that bear the most overt political differences are St. Petersburg and Vladivostok. They are geographically distant from one another—St. Petersburg sits on the Gulf of Finland and is located within the Baltic region, which includes Finland and the Baltic states, while Primorskii Krai and its capital, Vladivostok, look across the Pacific Ocean toward Alaska and share a border with China and North Korea. Their political differences mirror the geographic. In the late 1990s, Vladimir Gel'man, a scholar of regional politics in Russia, contrasted St. Petersburg's relative political pluralism with the "warlordism" of Vladivostok (1999a). The other three regional capitals reviewed here—Novosibirsk, Vladimir, and Bryansk—are arrayed somewhere in between these two political extremes. Economically, all five regions have struggled during the past fifteen years, but St. Petersburg has far surpassed the others in terms of economic recovery and growth, while Bryansk and Vladimir have lagged behind economically. Socioeconomic measurements mirror the ranking of economic indicators, but show an even greater disparity among the regions.

St. Petersburg   St. Petersburg, one of two federal cities in the Russian Federation and historically Russia's "window on the West," is widely thought to be one of the most politically open regions in Russia. During his electoral campaigns, former governor Vladimir Yakovlev (1996 to 2003) preferred to present himself as a technocrat; when pressed, however, he first

---

2. Information for these sketches is based on my interviews with local political officials, a review of the regional press, and secondary sources such as the *RFE/RL Russian Federation Report* and the Institute for East-West Studies' *Russian Regional Report* and *Russian Regional Investor.* Regional indicators from the Russian State Statistical Agency also illustrate the diversity achieved by the late 1990s and are presented in Appendix B.

claimed a relationship with the liberal democratic Yabloko Party and later with the centrist Fatherland-All Russia Party. His successor as governor, Valentina Matvienko, has been a firm supporter of the United Russia Party and President Putin, but she also emphasizes her pragmatic approach to governance. The Communist Party was weaker in St. Petersburg than in any other major Russian city in the early post-Soviet period, winning no more than 20 percent of the vote in the 1990s. The St. Petersburg political scene also possesses an unusual feature for post-Soviet Russia: a relatively active legislature that has proved itself willing to challenge the governor's policies; however, the legislature has been fragmented among different political blocs and was often deadlocked in the 1990s (Hahn 2004). Another feature of St. Petersburg's government that generates political diversity and competition is the city's active local self-government at the neighborhood, or raion, level (Kirkow 1997).

The city has enjoyed significant domestic and foreign investment during the past fifteen years, and it consistently ranked first or second among Russian regions in terms of its investment climate. Unlike many other regions plagued by budget deficits in early post-Soviet years, the city managed to pay public-sector workers regularly. These political and economic assets for social mobilization are counterbalanced by the region's struggle with corruption, crime, and xenophobia, earning St. Petersburg the moniker "crime capital of Russia" (Tkachenko 2003, 212). Vice Governor Mikhail Manevich was murdered in August 1997, St. Petersburg Legislative Assembly member Viktor Novoselov in October 1999, and State Duma member and liberal reformer Galina Starovoitova was assassinated in the city in November 1998. In general, however, relative political openness and economic growth lead one to expect greater social movement activity in St. Petersburg than in other regions of Russia.

Concerned neighboring states in the Baltic region have offered financial support to St. Petersburg social organizations in order to promote the resolution of transboundary environmental issues. Sweden, Finland, and Norway have provided significant funding to monitor the nearby Leningrad Atomic Energy Station, build water treatment facilities, and study toxic-waste problems in the area (Darst 2001). The Society for German-Russian Exchange established an NGO resource center in the city that fostered social organizations. Environmental organizations also have benefited from regional partnerships, including the Coalition Clean Baltic.

Vladivostok   Primorskii Krai and its capital, Vladivostok, are located at the southern tip of Russia's eastern coast, bordering China and the Sea of Japan. Sitting at the edge of Russia's legendary taiga forests, the region's economy depends primarily on shipping and natural-resource extraction, as well as Russia's Pacific Naval Fleet. In the 1990s, the pathologies of post-Soviet governance were taken to the extreme by the unpredictable and authoritarian governor Yevgenii Nazdratenko (1993 to 2001). The federal government unsuccessfully attempted to remove Nazdratenko from his post in 1997, charging mismanagement and citing his responsibility for the region's economic disarray. During his tenure, Nazdratenko was accused of numerous misdeeds from intimidation of local media to ties to organized crime and the murder of political rivals (Chernyakova 1999).[3] Governance in Vladivostok was marked by Nazdratenko's feuds with on-again, off-again mayor Viktor Cherepkov (Alexseev 2003, 171–2; Hahn 2002, 102–3). In 2001, the Putin administration orchestrated the removal of Nazdratenko from office by appointing him head of the federal fisheries body.[4] Sergei Darkin then became governor. Vladivostok continued to experience problems with crime, including an assault charge against the city's mayor (Weidel 2004).

Primorskii Krai also attracted negative attention for its prolonged energy crisis, failure to pay public-sector employees, and corruption related to illegal timber harvesting. The regional media is quite dependent on the political authorities since the only printing press, Dalpress, is state owned and run by the regional administration.[5] Despite these problems, however, Vladivostok, as gateway to many of Russia's vast forests, has managed to attract foreign investment and the attention of the international environmental community alike. International green organizations were also drawn to the region by the plight of endangered species such as the

3. See also "Primorskii Krai Gubernatorial Campaign Over before It Starts," *Russian Regional Report* 4, no. 34 (September 17, 1999); "Governor Throws Critical Newspaper out of Offices," *Russian Regional Report* 4, no. 34 (September 17, 1999); "Primorskii Kria Relations between Nazdratenko, Putin Not Ideal," *Russian Regional Report* 5, no. 1 (January 7, 2000).

4. Ironically, in 2003 President Putin appointed Nazdratenko to the post of deputy secretary on Russia's Security Council in charge of environmental security and protection of biological resources (Gazeta.ru, May 5, 2003, as cited in Johnson's Russia List 7167).

5. A local newspaper editor commented, "Since every newspaper has debts to Dalpress for newsprint or services, it is enough to get just one call from the governor's office and they would stop printing it" (as quoted in Chernyakova 1999).

Siberian tiger and the Amur leopard (Newell 2004). Infamously, in 1998 Nazdratenko gave Belarusian President Aleksandr Lukashenka the skin of an endangered Siberian tiger as a gift. A WWF–Far East (a branch of WWF-Russia) report estimated that foreign funding for environmental organizations and projects in the Far East increased by approximately 2.5 times from 1994 to 1998, and that Primorskii Krai received 38 percent of that funding.[6] Ultimately, Primorskii Krai has a challenging political and economic environment for mobilization, but its environmental grievances have attracted a high level of transnational interest.

Novosibirsk   Novosibirsk, the largest city in Siberia, and the nearby university town of Akademgorodok are widely recognized as together forming Russia's premier center for scientific research. The region has been governed by largely pragmatic figures including Valery Mukha, governor from 1991 to 1993 and again from 1996 to 1999; and Viktor Tolokonskii, mayor from 1993 to 1999 and governor since 1999. Throughout the first decade of post-Soviet politics, the regional political scene was characterized by tension between these two individuals and competition for political influence between the city of Novosibirsk and the region of Novosibirsk Oblast. Commentators also point out that "Novosibirsk is an exception to the rule that the governor has solid control over the regional legislature and can generally be assured of winning the passage of his legislation" (*Russian Regional Report* 2001). As a result, political power in the region has been comparatively decentralized.

While the region's industrial, agricultural, and defense sectors have suffered, the city of Novosibirsk has attracted significant foreign investment (Stenning 1999). The city is known for its relatively high number of small and medium-sized firms, almost twice the national average in 2000. Internet resources in Novosibirsk are second only to what is available in Moscow and St. Petersburg, likely due to the high number of research institutes and students in the area (Maslennikova 2000a). In addition, Novosibirsk became a regional center for foreign-assistance distribution, boasting three

---

6. WWF, "Analiz finansovoi bazy prirodookhrannykh initsiativ, sushchestvuiushchikh v ekoregione," 1999 (draft given to the author by Yulia Fomenko, WWF-Vladivostok, November 1999). Funding is reported to have increased from $856,636 to $2,285,020, and the number of donors in the region grew from thirty-one to 144.

foreign-sponsored NGO resource centers designed to serve the local NGO community. In summary, Novosibirsk has a relatively competitive political environment, moderate economic performance, and environmental griev- ances that have not attracted a great deal of international publicity.

Vladimir   Vladimir Oblast and the capital city of Vladimir are located 170 kilometers east of Moscow in Russia's Golden Ring of historic cities. Vladi- mir represents the conservative middle path between reform and the status quo opted for by many Russian regions. The region is governed by Nikolai Vinogradov, who was elected by large margins—but with very low voter turnout—in 1996 and 2001 and reappointed by President Putin in 2005. At first Vinogradov declared himself a Communist yet also a proponent of market economics. As a result, the region attempted only limited eco- nomic and political reforms. Now a supporter of United Russia, Vinogra- dov is seen as a pragmatic leader who usually can rely on the support of the regional legislature and the region's relatively homogenous political elite. The collapse of the tourist industry has damaged Vladimir's econ- omy, and the city and region have attracted only moderate amounts of for- eign investment. Without significant natural resources, scientific institutes, or high-profile environmental problems, the region has not drawn much attention from foreign assistance programs.

Bryansk   The predominantly agricultural region of Bryansk Oblast is sit- uated on the border of Ukraine and Belarus. Throughout the 1990s and early 2000s, the region was considered part of the "red belt" of Communist- dominated territory in Russia. The regional government adopted mini- mal economic reforms and experienced poor economic performance. From 1996 until 2004 the dominant political figure in Bryansk Oblast was Governor Yuri Lodkin. Initially an unreformed Communist both in the political and economic spheres, Lodkin possessed sufficient ideological flexibility to retain his position for two terms. Bryansk is now governed by the bland Nikolai Denin, who is affiliated with the pro-Kremlin party United Russia. Denin's loyalty to the current regime is such that some commentators considered him a possible successor to Putin (*Kommer- sant* 2007). Meanwhile, the majority of other political officials in Bryansk have been affiliated with either the Communist Party or United Russia and have demonstrated little interest in changing the political or economic status quo. The Bryansk city charter specifies that the mayor should be

TABLE 3.1. Summary of Political, Economic, and Environmental Characteristics by Region

	Political openness	Economic performance	Quality of life indicators	Foreign assistance	Environmental grievances
Vladivostok	Closed	Medium	Low	Medium	Endangered tiger, leopard; Taiga habitat
Novosibirsk	Partially open	Medium	Medium	Medium	Typical local degradation
Vladimir	Partially closed	Low	Low	Low	Typical local degradation
Bryansk	Closed	Low	Low	Low	Radioactive contamination in Chernobyl zone
St. Petersburg	Open	High	High	High	Baltic Sea pollution; Leningrad atomic-energy station

Note: Rankings are assigned relative to the spectrum of political and economic conditions in Russia's 83 (formerly 89) regions. For detailed information on these rankings, see Appendix B.

indirectly elected by a committee of city-council members and respected citizens, leading to a generally weak mayoral office (Gorelov 1999b). The governor also traditionally exerts control over the regional media; in 1999, the oblast administration controlled all but two of the fifteen newspapers in the region (Gorelov 1999b).

In 1986, Bryansk Oblast was contaminated by radioactive emissions from the Chernobyl nuclear power accident. Lodkin frequently referred to the Chernobyl accident in order to request subsidies from the federal government; indeed, prior to August 1998, these subsidies made up 70 percent of the oblast budget (Levinsky 1998). Some charitable funding from foreign sources has been directed at health issues stemming from the accident (ITAR-TASS 2002). Yet as the regional political regime has demonstrated little potential for either political reform or constructive interaction with civil society, relatively little foreign assistance has been directed toward Bryansk.

Comparing Environmental Activism in the Regions

These political and economic characteristics illustrate substantial variation within the five regions—although, of course, the variation is relative within the context of post-Soviet Russia. Hypotheses related to variation

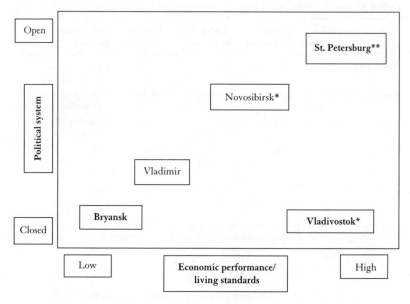

Figure 3.1. Relative political and economic conditions of regions
(bold indicates presence of domestic or international environmental grievance;
** = high foreign assistance, * = medium, no asterisk = low)

in environmental grievances, the availability of material resources, political opportunities for activism, and successful framing of movement goals would lead us to expect varying levels of mobilization in each region, as described below.

Hypothesis 1. Different kinds of environmental grievance may influence environmental activism by mobilizing different constituencies.

Although grievance is a variable that is no longer widely used in social movement literature, in the Russian case grievance can be conceptualized in two ways: 1) the level of dissatisfaction with environmental conditions among the local population; and 2) the level of concern about certain Russian environmental problems within the transnational community. Each aggrieved population would bring its own energy and experiences with activism to bear on the issue of concern. Domestically, while all Russian citizens suffer from living under conditions of environmental degradation that are the legacy of the Soviet period, the citizens of Bryansk have a more obvious grievance due to the lingering effects of radiation from the Chernobyl nuclear accident. In terms of transnational environmental grievances, the plight of charismatic large-mammal species in the area surrounding Vladivostok and the transboundary pollution issues of the Baltic Sea region near St. Petersburg are among the most obvious problems attracting international attention. Therefore, depending on the perceived severity of these grievances among Russian citizens or the transnational environmental community, we could see greater levels of activism in those regions.

Hypothesis 2. Mobilization varies in relation to the amount of resources available.

Resources directed toward supporting environmentalism may flow from: 1) domestic institutions—public and private—and Russian citizens within Russia; or 2) transnational funding from foreign assistance programs and transnational environmental actors. Given the economic collapse in the early post-Soviet period, the overall level of domestic resources in Russia has been low. Of course, some regional economies have recovered more quickly than others. In this study, St. Petersburg is something of an outlier, having a significantly higher GDP and higher standard of living than the other four regions. In addition, St. Petersburg has received the largest share of foreign assistance for civil-society development, and Vladivostok and St. Petersburg have attracted the greatest level of funds from the transnational environmental movement.

Hypothesis 3. A competitive political environment creates a more favorable condition for social mobilization.

Factors such as the degree of concentration of political power, the presence of political allies, and the number of access points to policymaking shape mobilization in Russia. Informal political practices, such as the necessity of finding political allies and connections (*sviazi*) to influence policymaking, are often equally significant in achieving movement goals. By this measure, once again St. Petersburg appears to occupy the most favorable position for social mobilization given its relatively open political environment and dispersed political power; political conditions in Bryansk and Vladivostok suggest lower levels of mobilization due to their more closed political systems, with the concentration of power in the hands of the regional governor.

Hypothesis 4. A larger middle-class population creates a more favorable environment for mobilization.

Environmental issues fall squarely within the quality-of-life concerns that are often thought to be the impetus for new social movements. In the Russian case, however, the industrial-based economy and impoverishment of many citizens during the post-Soviet era mean that the country can hardly be characterized as "postmaterialist." Nevertheless, regional variations in the size of the middle class may affect how many individuals have the leisure time to address their environmental concerns. In addition, some regions may host environmental organizations that have been better able to strategically frame environmental issues for average citizens by linking them to other issues of concern and therefore mobilize the population more effectively.

Level of Mobilization

The level of social mobilization captures the changing volume of participants, organizations, and actions that compose social mobilization around a particular issue area over time.[7] In order to compare the level of activism in regional environmental movements in contemporary Russia, this section considers both the number of environmental organizations in each region and the size of these organizations.[8]

---

7. Another possible indicator for assessing a region's overall level of mobilization is the number of environmental actions, such as public protests and demonstrations, and the number of participants in these actions. Since the peak of environmental mobilization in Russia from 1989 to 1991, however, there have been relatively few mass environmental actions in the county as a whole.

8. Both measures of mobilization—the number of organizations and size of organizational membership—are somewhat more problematic in the Russian context than they might be for similar Western movements. While the accuracy of the data self-reported by environmentalists was verified whenever possible by cross-referencing different sources (i.e., confirming information available on databases with information gathered in interviews), certain features of Russia's nascent NGO sector make data collection difficult. For example, in the directory of NGOs published in Vladivostok, NGO representatives were allowed to classify their organization under several issue-area categories. Consequently, some of what are classified as environmental groups may in fact focus primarily on issues of human rights, youth issues, or cultural promotion, and pursue environmental goals only as a secondary concern; therefore, the number of environmental organizations in Vladivostok may be overstated. In addition, as is widely recognized in Russia, many organizations are formally registered as social organizations with the Ministry of Justice are in fact inactive or are defunct. Conversely, some leaders of environmental organizations choose not

TABLE 3.2. Level of Environmental Mobilization by Regional Capital

Regional capital	Population of regional capital[a]	Estimated number of environmental organizations	Organizations per 100,000 residents	Membership	
				Active	Overall
Vladivostok	610,300	43	7	Avg: 7 Med: 5	Avg: 56 Med: 19
Novosibirsk	1,402,100	28	2	Avg: 9 Med: 5	Avg: 48 Med: 14
Vladimir	336,100	11	3	Avg: 9 Med: 7	Avg: 31 Med: 35
Bryansk	457,000	12	3	Avg: 5 Med: 3	Avg: 47 Med: 10
St. Petersburg	4,695,400	160	3	Avg: 13 Med: 10	Avg: 271 Med: 79

Note: The data presented on the number of organizations and members in this table are drawn from several sources, including author interviews, directories of environmental organizations published by NGO resource centers or environmental-information agencies, and the databases of Russian NGO resource centers. NGO directories include: Ekotok and the Sacred Earth Network, *Handbook of Environmental and Nature Protection Organizations, Users of Electronic Mail,* Moscow: Dialog/MGU, 1998; Transboundary Environmental Information Agency, *Negosudarstvennye ekologicheskie organizatsii Sankt-Peterbuga,* St. Petersburg: Notabene, 1998; *Obshchestvennye ob"edineniia Sibirskogo regiona: Novosibirskaia Oblast',* Sibirskii Tsentr Podderzhki Obshchestvennykh Initsiativ, 1998; *Obshchestvennye Ob"edineniia Dal'nego Vostoka: informatsionyi spravochnik,* ISAR-Dal'nii Vostok and USAID, 1998. Other resources consulted include the ISAR-Moscow and ISAR-RFE NGO resource-center databases, supplemented by author interviews of organizations not in directories and databases.

[a] Goskomstat Rossii, *Regiony Rossii: staticheskii sbornik,* Moscow, 1999.

In spite of our hypotheses, data from five Russian regional capitals (presented in Table 3.2) unexpectedly demonstrate remarkably similar levels of mobilization around environmental issues as measured by environmental organizations per capita and average NGO membership. Focusing narrowly on organizations per capita, the slight variation in the number of organizations per region clearly runs counter to expectations arising from

to register at all. For these reasons, the numbers of organizations listed in table 3.2 remain approximations and not an exact count of environmental NGOs. Membership in Russian social organizations also presents a somewhat thorny issue. Most Russian environmental groups are not membership based, at least in the formal, dues-paying sense. Membership estimates are based on the number of individuals who regularly attend meetings and volunteer. These data limitations create serious challenges for social scientists but are mitigated to a degree by subnational comparison. Since the flaws inherent in these two measures of level of mobilization are held relatively constant across the Russian Federation, the data still provide a reliable comparison of relative levels of mobilization.

the regional descriptions and hypotheses. For example, why does St. Petersburg, with all of its advantages, have roughly a similar number of organizations per capita as Bryansk? Novosibirsk, surprisingly, has the lowest-per-capita number of green organizations in spite of its relatively open political climate and average economic situation. Bryansk, which was predicted to be a laggard in social mobilization by most measures, is instead comparable to other regions in the level of mobilization. Vladivostok, with a closed political system and an average domestic economic environment, has the *highest* number of organizations. Even recognizing that the number of environmental groups in Vladivostok may be overstated due to an unusually broad definition of "environmental" employed by the region's NGO directory, this finding runs counter to both political and resource hypotheses. Instead, it offers support for the assertion that the grievances and resources of the transnational environmental community might outweigh an unpropitious domestic political and economic context.[9]

Membership levels also appear roughly similar across the regions, whether measured by average or median membership. In particular, the number of active members, likely a more accurate assessment of membership strength, is similar in each case.[10] The apparent exception is that environmental organizations in St. Petersburg appear to have slightly higher memberships, especially in terms of their overall membership, when compared with the other regions. What is surprising in this case, however, given St. Petersburg's distinct advantages in political and economic factors, is that these numbers are not even higher and that St. Petersburg does not stand out as a site of greater environmental mobilization.

---

9. Vladivostok appears to have a relatively small population of social organizations in general. Based on information from the State Duma Committee for the Affairs of Social Associations and Religious Organizations charting the number of social and religious organizations by region, Primorskii Krai has the lowest number of social organizations per capita of the five regions studied here (Gosudarstvennaia Duma 2000). Using data from this source, we see that the number of social organizations per 100,000 residents in each region is, approximately, 127 in St. Petersburg; 95 in Bryansk; 94 in Vladimir; 73 in Novosibirsk; and only 55 in Vladivostok. These numbers include only registered organizations.

10. The division of an organization's membership into active members and overall membership is a common practice within the Russian environmental community. Many NGO directories use these terms, and during interviews Russian environmentalists often offered numbers for each category unprompted by me. The active membership indicates the number of individuals working relatively continuously within an organization, while the overall membership represents the number of people who occasionally attend the organization's meetings or events.

Overall, these similar, and relatively low, levels of activism seem to support arguments about the continuing weakness of post-Soviet Russia's civil society. It is widely acknowledged that post-Soviet societies are hampered by the legacy of state-sponsored mass mobilization, the Communist Party's monopoly on organizational resources, and the citizens' lack of trust in public organizations. Against this backdrop of increasing regional differentiation, the Soviet legacy still exerts a significant depressing effect on activism. For example, Howard uses comparative data from the World Values Survey based on the years 1995 to 1997 to show that the average number of memberships in social organizations per person differed significantly across nations surveyed, ranging from 3.59 memberships per person in the United States to 2.12 in West Germany and 0.66 in Russia (Howard 2003, 168). Indeed, Howard shows that membership in social organizations is lower in the postcommunist region than in other postauthoritarian states, with the former averaging 0.82 organizational memberships per person and the latter averaging 1.86 (2003, 168). Russia's Public Chamber offers a similarly low figure for the percentage of social-organization participation, estimating it is between 1 and 4 percent of the population (Obshchestvennaia Palata 2008, 8).

Even acknowledging the depressing effect of the Communist legacy, similar levels of environmental mobilization across Russia's regions in spite of political and economic differentiation demand a more in-depth analysis of each region. In fact, further exploration of the data suggests that this seeming homogeneity masks meaningful variation in the quality, if not quantity, of environmental mobilization at the organization level.

The Quality of Environmental Mobilization

Although variation in the overall level of environmental mobilization in Russia's regions appears to be low, a closer look at the organizational-level data gathered in surveys and interviews reveals that there is another type of variation that shapes environmental activism and influences the effectiveness of the movement as a whole. This section turns to the question of variation in the quality of environmental mobilization by considering the organizational characteristics of environmental groups.

Three Strategies of Organizational Development

Three distinct patterns of organizational development exist within the population of Russian environmental groups in St. Petersburg, Vladivostok, Novosibirsk, Vladimir, and Bryansk. As I mentioned at the start of this chapter, these three organizational types are labeled grassroots organizations, professionalized organizations, and government-affiliate organizations.[11] As inductively derived ideal types, these organizational forms are characterized by patterns of variation in indicators of organizational development, such as staffing, communications, and financial and legal arrangements. Organizations also have substantially different environmental goals, different relationships with other social organizations and state actors, and different ties to local communities.

Table 3.3 summarizes the ideal-type characteristics of each organizational form. Professionalized organizations, on average, possess more than seven of the eleven organizational characteristics listed, while grassroots organizations possess only a few of these features. Thus professionalized organizations appear to be more highly institutionalized. When mission and networks are taken into account, yet another subgroup of organizations emerges: government affiliates. Government affiliates are quite institutionalized but differ from professionalized groups in their mission and close relationship with state agencies. Organizations classified in each category overlap on some characteristics in practice. More important than the presence or absence of any single characteristic, however, is the tendency for these organizational features to be interrelated in predictable patterns. These features cluster in such a way that the presence of one often implies

---

11. These labels have been selected to capture the organizations' developmental trajectory, but due to the use of similar terms in other studies of social mobilization, they may carry unintended connotations. A few caveats are in order. Government affiliates, in spite of the modifier "government," are registered and self-described as nongovernmental organizations and are not formally part of any governing institution; instead the modifier indicates the congruence of their goals with the government's environmental goals and the fact that the government is their primary source of funding. Grassroots groups operate at a local level, but the term "grassroots" should not be taken to imply that these groups have many members. Some do, while most do not. Finally, the term professionalized indicates the emulation of a certain organization form—a "professional" Western-style NGO—and should not be confused with professional associations of doctors, lawyers, or other profession-based groups. Earlier classifications of Russian environmental organizations have primarily been based on issues addressed by the groups—for example, conservation, health, or education (Yanitsky 1996; Tysiachniouk and Bolotova 1999; Fomichev 1997, 33–38).

TABLE 3.3. Three Types of Environmental Organization

	Grassroots organizations	Professionalized organizations	Government affiliates
Mission and Relationships			
Goals	Resolve local environmental issues	Address international environmental issues	Enforce existing environmental laws
Organizational affiliations	A single professionalized group or isolated	International organizations, other professionalized groups	State agencies and officials
Connection to local population	Family, friendship, or neighborhood networks	Intelligentsia networks	Governmental networks
Organization Characteristics			
Registration	Often no	Yes	Yes
Bank Account	No	Yes	Yes
Paid staff	No	Yes	Yes
Organizational structure	Horizontal	Hierarchical or segmented[a]	Hierarchical
Office space	None or donated by local educational or cultural institutions	Rented office or donated by university or research institute	Donated by government administration
Board of directors	No	Yes	No
Computer	No or access through a member	Yes	Yes
Office equipment	No	Yes	Yes
E-mail	No or access through a member	Yes	Yes
Web page	No	Yes	No
Public-relations materials	No	Yes	Yes

[a] Segmented implies a clear division of labor. For example, staff positions are assigned to discrete environmental projects.

the presence of the others. A brief summary of each ideal type illustrates this clustering.

Grassroots environmental organizations are often initiative groups that are quite informal and lack office space, paid staff, and reliable access to technology. Grassroots activists tend to work on issues of practical interest to local communities, such as the cleanliness and safety of local recreational areas, children's environmental awareness and self-esteem, or health issues, although some grassroots organizations also focus on eco-spirituality and constructing new environmental ideologies. Grassroots organizations generally are not tightly networked with other environmental organizations and have few, if any, international ties. As largely apolitical organizations, they tend to have a neutral or distant relationship with state and elected officials. Grassroots organizations, most commonly led by elementary- and secondary-school teachers, rely on local resources to carry out their environmental activities. While some groups have received small grants ($1,500 or less), in general these organizations learn to live without financial resources, surviving either through the enthusiasm and volunteerism of their members or through local in-kind donations.

Professionalized organizations, on the other hand, are relatively institutionalized, modeling themselves after NGOs in other political systems. Professionalized groups often work on transnational environmental issues such as climate change, biodiversity, and sustainable development, and they engage in partnerships with transnational environmental organizations. Professionalized groups also are more likely to have an adversarial or critical relationship with the local and regional government, opposing current environmental policies and regulations. Frequently led by scientists and other academics, they have few ties to the local population. These groups tend to secure resources from outside Russia, most commonly from funding through foreign donors or international environmental organizations.

Government-affiliate organizations, as their name implies, work with the local or regional administrations to enforce existing environmental laws. They have few international ties and are connected to the local population either through the remnants of Soviet-era mass memberships or the collective memberships of research and academic institutes. Environmental groups that fit the government-affiliate profile generally have identified a government sponsor, either an agency or an individual within the local or regional government. This sponsor assists them in securing a resource base for the organization, usually donated office space within government buildings, access to technology in government offices, and frequently some funding from state resources, previously through the regional Ecology Fund, a fund collected through fines from polluting industries.

Distribution of Organizational Types across the Regions

The regional distribution of organizational types (Table 3.4), based on the classification of environmental organizations described above, suggests the factors that shape social mobilization—grievances, resources, identity and framing, and political opportunities—interact with each other, making particular mobilizational niches more available in some regions than in others.

The most striking aspect of the distribution of organization types in the regions is the absence of government-affiliate organizations in Vladivostok and Bryansk, the regions with the most closed political systems. This finding would seem to indicate, counterintuitively, that a closed political system is less conducive to the development of government affiliates than the development of grassroots or professionalized organizations. Domestic political conditions may have less impact on professionalized and grassroots environmental groups due to the former's reliance on external resources for survival on the one hand, and the latter's apolitical nature and its ability to survive on very low levels of resources on the other. In addition, government officials within relatively more open or competitive political environments are more likely to accept that social organizations are players in politics and, if only for public relations purposes, attempt to foster their region's organizations in order to increase their own legitimacy. Politicians in a closed or uncompetitive political system do not share this motivation. Rather than attempting to guide or shape the development of civil society through sponsoring social organizations, politicians and bureaucrats within a closed system may not see any utility in developing ties with activists, including environmentalists. In interviews, environmentalists in Vladivostok and Bryansk expressed the opinion that their regional

TABLE 3.4. Regional Distribution of the Three Organizational Types

	Government affiliates	Grassroots	Professionalized
Vladivostok	0	6 (35%)	11 (65%)
Novosibirsk	2 (14%)	7 (50%)	5 (36%)
Vladimir	3 (33%)	6 (66%)	0
Bryansk	0	7 (58%)	5 (42%)
St. Petersburg	4 (13%)	16 (50%)	12 (38%)

Note: Number of organizations studied in each city are as follows: Vladivostok, 17; Novosibirsk, 14; Vladimir, 9; Bryansk, 12; and St. Petersburg, 32.

governments are less receptive to environmental activism than the authorities in neighboring regions. Thus, a certain degree of political openness may be necessary for the organizational strategy of government affiliation to be successful.

In contrast to the small population of government affiliates—and unexpectedly, given our initial hypotheses—there is a relatively high proportion of professionalized organizations in Vladivostok, and there are more professionalized groups than might have been expected in Bryansk. These findings suggest that high-profile environmental degradation, such as endangered Siberian tigers or nuclear contamination, can be translated into resources for Russian environmental organizations, even in a relatively closed political system, if identified as a grievance by the transnational community.

In Vladivostok, high-profile environmental problems certainly have spurred the flow of foreign aid to the region. Vladivostok has hosted several branch offices of international organizations such as World Wide Fund for Nature (WWF), the Hornocker Institute, Global Survival Network, and ISAR-Far East (affiliated with ISAR in Washington, DC). Representatives of these international environmental groups cultivated and cooperated with other professionalized organizations in Vladivostok. Another strategy particularly suited to a closed political system is to build environmental organizations from within scientific institutes, as several green organizations based in the Institute of Soil Science and the Institute of Marine Biology in Vladivostok have done. These groups tend to fall into the professionalized category owing to their formalized organizations, their access to technology, and their focus on scientific research and transnational environmental issues.

In Bryansk, a few environmental organizations have been able to parlay concern about the health effects of radiation from the Chernobyl accident into support for their environmental projects. Bryansk activists also have proven more willing than environmentalists elsewhere to travel outside their region seeking financial support. In interviews, many Bryansk environmentalists noted the futility of searching for funding and partnerships within their region given the intransigent regional political regime and stated that they have consciously pursued a strategy of frequently traveling to Moscow (a six-hour train ride away) and building relationships with international organizations based there.

The complete lack of professionalized organizations (which generally rely on foreign funding) in Vladimir, a city representing a moderately low score on both political and economic indicators, reaffirms the significance of environmental grievances in mobilizing transnational resources. Vladimir possesses neither high-profile environmental problems nor a particularly high level of foreign aid. As Gennadii Stakhurlov, member of the Green Party of Vladimir, noted, in spite of the region's overall poor environmental quality, "We don't really have severe problems. It is hard to make the case that people's health is affected, for example."[12] While the region lags behind others in terms of professional organizations, it is similar to Bryansk in its number of grassroots groups. Vladimir also has three government-affiliated groups. Unlike Bryansk-based environmentalists, some activists in Vladimir are able to work with regional and municipal authorities to achieve their goals.

Thus, in the cases of Bryansk and Vladivostok—particularly as compared to Vladimir—the evidence indicates that high-profile environmental problems may trump a closed political opportunity structure in the sense that a grievance identified at the transnational level leads to increased resource flows. Arguably, hostile political conditions will still influence the ultimate effectiveness of organizations in closed environments since their ability to shape environmental policy may be impaired. External resources may foster organizational development but in no way guarantee effectiveness at achieving environmental goals.

Finally, the striking similarity between St. Petersburg and Novosibirsk is also interesting. Both cities exhibit a more balanced population of environmental organizations, with all three organizational types represented. What both regions have in common is a fragmented political elite and a greater decentralization of political power. In St. Petersburg, competition between the legislature and the executive results in somewhat dispersed power, while in Novosibirsk wrangling between the mayor of the capital and governor of the region serves the same purpose. A more competitive political environment appears to inspire political officials to take a greater interest in cultivating popular support through social organizations, thereby increasing the availability of elite allies and generating more access to political institutions. The relatively even distribution of organizational types within the environmental movements of Novosibirsk and St. Petersburg thus may signify a pattern of development common to partially

---

12. Gennadii Stakhurlov, author interview, Vladimir Office of the All-Russia Party of Greens, May 23, 2000.

open political systems with a mix of both domestic resources and transnational funding. It is somewhat unexpected that a higher level of foreign aid has not led to more professionalized groups in St. Petersburg. One possible explanation for this, drawn from interview data, is that there has been something of a backlash against aid and what are seen as grant-eating organizations in the city. In fact, several St. Petersburg–based groups stated that they did not enter grant competitions for ideological reasons and that they did not want to be seen as puppets of foreign organizations.

Organizational Niches in a Mobilizational Field

The concept of a mobilizational field offers insight into the prevalence of these organizational niches—why some regions boast a higher proportion of certain organizational types—and may explain the patterns that emerged in Russia's regional environmental movements. The idea of a "field" of political and social contention is a concept that gained currency within the social-scientific literature for its ability to convey the interaction of political, economic, and cultural factors. The image of a mobilizational field is most commonly used to illustrate the distribution of power among different political actors, degrees of cultural homogeneity or diversity, or ideological poles within a given political culture. Organizations develop within this preexisting political, social, and economic environment, subject to its opportunities and constraints. The image of the mobilizational field allows a visual representation of political and economic niches where organizational types have emerged and also illustrates spaces that are not conducive to organization building. Over time, organizations may be able to influence the field itself through their own efforts, perhaps by advocating institutional or attitudinal changes that lead to new opportunities or new resources. Moments of true fluidity are rare, however, although the collapse of Communism was one such moment.

An organization's location within the political field illustrates a coincidence of the resources that group needs to survive and the political environment that allows it to persist. The horizontal axis of the mobilizational field represents the degree of openness or closure of the political system, or in this case, the *relatively* open and closed political systems of contemporary Russia. The vertical axis signifies the availability of resources, ranging from

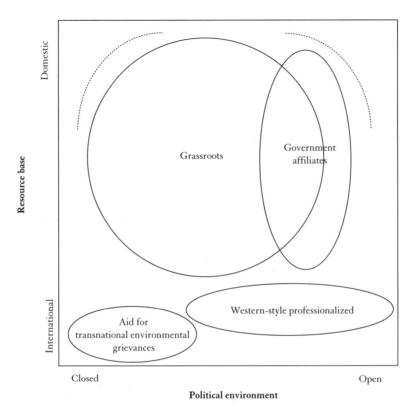

Figure 3.2. Russia's mobilizational field

predominantly external or transnational sources to domestic sources of funding. Political and economic factors are not independent of each other, however. As indicated earlier, transnational resources tend to flow to regions that are open politically or that have environmental problems of concern to the transnational community. Domestic state resources for social organizations also may be more available in those regions that are politically open.

Each Russian region occupies a smaller area of the mobilizational field. For example, St. Petersburg and Novosibirsk would occupy the lower-right quadrant. Relatively open political systems and the availability of international resources create an environment in which all three types of green organizations are able to survive. Vladivostok and Bryansk would be located in the lower left of this field. Closed political systems offer no support for government affiliates, but the presence of high-profile environmental grievances has led to the inflow of foreign support for professionalized groups. Vladimir would occupy the middle of the field as its moderately open political system allows for the emergence of grassroots and government-affiliated groups, but the lack of international funding means that professionalized organizations have not appeared.

As described in the next chapter, environmental activists' preexisting professional identities affect their ability to identify the opportunities presented by these mobilizational niches and to exploit them. Leaders' ties to norms, networks, and institutions shape their vision of environmentalism and identification of their primary constituency, creating resource dependencies over time. Once a resource dependency develops, activists have an incentive to continue to align their selection and framing of issues with the preferences of the primary funder, thereby ensuring a steady basis of support.

The depiction of Russia's mobilizational field also illustrates the organizational niches that are not available to Russian social organizations. For example, the upper-left corner of the figure, which indicates a completely closed political structure and purely domestic resources, is unlikely space for mobilization because of the difficulty of operating in any extremely closed political environment. In addition, because of the initially low level of resources available from Russian citizens and the government's continuing hostility toward social activism, we have not yet seen the development of domestically funded professionalized environmental organizations that are autonomous from both state and foreign donors, although that may change in the future. Thus there is no indigenous-professional-organizations niche on the upper half of the figure. Most significantly, the image of the field suggests that grassroots organizations are the most flexible, demonstrating the ability to occupy almost any political and economic niche owing to their largely apolitical activism and ability to pursue their goals with minimal material support.

In contradiction to initial hypotheses, political and economic variation in Russia's regions has not led to variation in the level of environmental mobilization. Activism across Russia's regions is similarly low. However, intriguing and consequential variation at the organizational level lurks below what at first appears to be a relatively weak and homogenous sector—variation in strategies of organizational development. Variation in the quality, but not quantity, of mobilization raises three points. First, the evidence supports the claim that negative features of the Soviet legacy and the post-Soviet period, including the lack of significant private-sector resources and the concentration of political power, have served to lower social mobilization overall and helps to explain the similarity in the level of environmental mobilization across regions.

Second, as the concept of "field" illustrates, there is no single factor that fully explains variation in strategies of organizational development. Instead, the data presented highlight the interdependence of explanatory factors. Understanding the basic elements of Russia's post-Soviet environmental field increases our analytical and predictive power. By tracking changes that are due to political and economic trends, we are able to see how mobilizational niches expand or contract. For example, when foreign aid declines, professionalized organizations are likely to suffer. If the domestic economy grows and a stable middle class emerges in Russia, or if the economy of a particular region expands, we might see the emergence of better developed, more stable indigenous organizations autonomous from the government. In fact, some grassroots groups appear poised to fill this niche if it becomes available. If the political system becomes increasingly hostile to social activism or the world financial crisis persists, we may see lower levels of mobilization overall.

Finally, the recognition of different strategies of organizational development is crucial to any effort to assess movement effectiveness. These three organizational types signify patterns of development that involve the successful identification of political and economic niches in Russia's current mobilizational field. Organizations grouped together under the heading of grassroots, professionalized, or government affiliates exhibit similar organizational forms due to the fact that their leaders have identified and exploited political and resource niches in similar ways and in doing so reveal similar understandings of what activism should be like in post-Soviet Russia. Given the different strategies of development, different goals, and different relationships with domestic and international actors across organizational types, environmental organizations have varying abilities to achieve organizational sustainability, to influence environmental policy, and to create a more open political system in Russia. The efforts of Russian environmental organizations to achieve these three goals are the subject of the next three chapters.

4

Seeking Sustainability

Dynamics of Organizational Survival

When asked about the biggest challenges they face, Russian environmentalists did not first mention Russia's alarming environmental problems, the country's largely unreceptive political system, or their difficulty mobilizing the public to support green causes. Most frequently they cited the problem of funding—the need to find scarce resources to continue their activities. This chapter examines the most basic goal of the leaders of social organizations: their desire to maintain and expand their organizations and activities. Environmentalists' efforts to sustain their organizations, and more specifically the strategic choices they make about where to seek resources and support, lead to the emergence of what I described in chapter 3 as the three organizational types within the Russian environmental movement. Organizations cluster into different strategies of development due to three interrelated factors: the limited array of funding for social activism available within Russia; the inclination and ability of environmental leaders to take advantage of various sources of funding; and the implicit constraints on mission, rhetoric, and tactics that go along with different sources of support. Organization leaders' ability to identify crucial resources, and manage dependencies that follow, has profound implications for the sustainability of their organizations.

Although organizational maintenance is a basic objective of many social activists, it tends to be overlooked by social scientists in the rush to study more intriguing outcomes in the realm of policymaking and political and social transformation. Yet organizational maintenance is a goal whose achievement renders other aims possible. It not only represents the continuation of an organization as a potential mobilizational vehicle but also provides professional opportunities and personal security for the activists who inhabit these organizations. The strategies a leader uses to achieve organizational sustainability shape how an organization pursues its other goals. As the leaders of social organizations identify means of mobilizing resources that are effective under existing political and economic conditions, they also are developing certain orientations and relationships that will shape their organization's chances of achieving their substantive and transformational goals.

To make this case, this chapter delves into the development of Russian environmental organizations, considering how they emerge and sustain themselves. I first consider common features of Russia's social organizations and suggest that these features can be attributed in part to aspects of the Soviet legacy and the post-Soviet economic crisis. Next, the differences among grassroots, professionalized, and government-affiliate organizations are elaborated in greater detail. Identifying the factors that account for these different developmental patterns highlights the incentives and constraints of activists' resource environment. These incentives and constraints are mediated by leadership preferences that filter the broader political and economic context and make some strategies of mobilizing resources seem more possible and more appropriate than others. Leaders' preferences for addressing certain issues and using certain tactics to reinforce relationships with some actors and not with others grow out of their past experiences and professional socialization. After reviewing the varieties of organizational development in detail, the chapter considers some other strategies that activists use to manage risk and adapt to Russia's mobilizational field.

Similarities across Social Organizations: Reacting to the Soviet Era

While this chapter focuses on important differences in the strategies of organizational development across Russian environmental groups, there are several commonalities among post-Soviet social organizations that developed in the first decade after the collapse of the Soviet regime. These features are interrelated and include the role of strong leaders and the proliferation of small organizations, and the challenge of attracting members.

The Importance of Leadership and the Proliferation of Small Groups

Individual personalities are extremely important in Russia's national political scene, and likewise among the environmental organizations, no factor is more decisive than the preferences of a single dominant leader. When asked in interviews why one organization was more active, more collaborative, or more successful than another, environmentalists replied time and time again that it depended almost entirely on the group's leader. Of course, it is common everywhere for leaders of social organizations to infuse their group with their own vision and energy and to play an important role attracting supporters and funding. In Russia, however, this tendency toward strong leadership—and leaders' related unwillingness to join together into larger organizations—was further exacerbated or enhanced by activists' reaction to the mass organizations of the Soviet period. Sergei Pashchenko, a Novosibirsk environmentalist, noted that many activists were once members of the Soviet-era mass-membership organization the All-Union (now the All-Russian) Society for Nature Protection, known by its Russian acronym VOOP, and rejected that model because the group's goals were "too amorphous because there were too many people."[1] Others declared their reluctance to "subordinate" themselves to any other organization.[2]

1. Sergei Pashchenko, author interview, Siberian Scholars for Global Responsibility, Novosibirsk, December 7, 1999.

2. Olga Zhiganova, author interview, ENSI, Novosibirsk, December 2, 1999.

A preference for strong leadership was common in the early development of the movement. Liudmila Komogortseva of the Bryansk group For Chemical Safety compared this tendency to Russian politics in the 1990s:

> We don't have interchangeable leaders. Have you paid attention to our political parties? Gaidar leaves—there is no party of Gaidar, Lebed leaves—there is no movement of Lebed. You have to consider this. There is one leader and he has to control everything. (Komogortseva, as quoted in Khalii 1998, 13)

Maria Tysiachniouk and Alla Bolotova, Russian sociologists who have studied St. Petersburg's green organizations, argue, "ENGOs [environmental NGOs] in St. Petersburg are almost all known by the name of their leader and none operate without strong leadership" (Tysiachniouk and Bolotova 1999, 207). Olga Tsepilova, a Russian environmental sociologist, concurs, "In their attempts to avoid the rigid organizational framework of the Communist Party type and in opposition to the idea of democratic centralism, most environmental organizations in St. Petersburg rejected any type of vertical organizational structuring," resulting in what she calls a "leader plus group members" model (Tsepilova 1999, 82, n. 1).

Depending on their point of view, environmental activists saw the dominant role of leaders, and the great number of small organizations that resulted, as an advantage or as a problem for the movement as a whole. For Oleg Bodrov of the St. Petersburg group Green World, the fragmentation of the movement into many small groups was a natural outgrowth of political liberalization:

> When the process of democratization began, the desire arose to leave the system—that is, to stop being cogs on which nothing depended—and to become independent. And this manifestation of individualism...is a desire not to be part of a big system because it might crush you....In the Communist system it was all black or white. It was impossible to be anything else. It was always "either you are with us or you are the enemy." For that reason [environmental] organizations are small because they don't want to be part of something big, because something big might crush them.[3]

---

3. Oleg Bodrov, author interview, Green World, Lomonosov, May 5, 1999.

Some green leaders saw their groups' small size as a sign of selectivity and seriousness. Svetlana Nikitina of the St. Petersburg Democratic Party of Greens admitted that her political party had only about twelve members but expressed pride that they did not "race after numbers (*gonimsia za chislennost'iu*)" (*Pchela* 1997, 80). Others lamented that the proliferation of small groups was the result of "too much freedom" and "each person want[ing] to be his own boss (*khozain*)," leading activists to "forget they are working for same cause."[4]

As with many aspects of social activism in Russia, there was more than one factor contributing to this trend toward numerous small organizations. The post-Soviet condition of resource scarcity also contributed to a general preference for small groups within the movement. A Novosibirsk leader commented:

> We have five people in all.... It is not necessary for us all to unite into one organization. It's expensive and incorrect. Then we would face an economic situation where we would have to work like a business simply in order to feed everyone.[5]

Foreign-funded grant competitions also generated incentives for activists to create many small organizations—each then eligible to apply for funding. It often makes sense for activists in a medium-sized Russian organization with two project ideas to splinter into two smaller groups, at least in name, in order to maximize their funding potential. In that way, external funding may inadvertently reinforce the fragmentation prevalent in the post-Soviet era. Ultimately, the fact that there are many leaders who guard their independence carefully contributes to the proliferation of organizations within the movement, and each organization then has to grapple with the question of its own sustainability.

Citizens' Reluctance to Participate

Those environmental organizations that are inclined to grow by recruiting members from the general public face another feature of the Soviet legacy: Russian citizens' reluctance to participate in social organizations.

4. Valentin Lebedev, author interview, Soyuz, St. Petersburg, April 15, 1999.
5. Igor Ogorodnikov, author interview, EkoDom, Novosibirsk, December 3, 1999.

Low participation rates in post-Soviet Russia have been well documented in comparative research. Based on data from the World Values Survey, at the end of the 1990s membership in environmental organizations averaged 5.2 percent across the fifty-six countries surveyed, but the comparable numbers for Russia were 1.7 percent in 1990 and 0.7 percent in 1999 (Dalton 2005). Russian green organizations studied for this project generally had active memberships ranging from five to thirteen individuals.

Economic factors reinforce obstacles to building social organizations on the basis of membership support. Because of economic instability in the 1990s, most Russian citizens, even if they could be induced to become members, could or would not donate sufficient funds for organizations to continue their activities. Of all Russian environmental organizations, Greenpeace Russia makes the strongest claim to mass membership, although they prefer to use the term "supporters (*storoniki*)." The organization was founded in Russia in 1989, originally as an outpost of the international environmental organization Greenpeace, and then in 1992 became an official Russian organization. In their public outreach materials, Greenpeace argues that they are better able to pressure the government because they are the "only social [*obshchestvennaia*] environmental organization that is financed solely on the voluntary contributions of private individuals."[6] Undoubtedly, Greenpeace's status as the branch office of an international organization, giving it name recognition and a record of environmental achievements, places it in a somewhat exceptional position in terms of attracting supporters. In 2000, 4,680 individuals had signed up as supporters of the organization—an impressive number in post-Soviet Russia, but a number dwarfed by the organization's 250,000 members in the U.S. and 2.5 million members worldwide. At that time, some Russian members did not pay dues, and some dues-paying members of the Russian organization were supporters from other countries, such as Germany and Sweden.[7] By 2008, however, Greenpeace Russia claimed 15,000 supporters from Russia itself;[8] similarly, WWF-Russia had received support from 12,000 Russian citizens by 2006 (WWF 2007).

---

6. "Greenpeace v deistvii" (Greenpeace in Action), brochure given to the author by a representative of Greenpeace Russia, Moscow, 2000.

7. Tsyplenkov interview. In 2000, Greenpeace's suggested membership fees were thirty, fifty, and one hundred rubles (one U.S. dollar = approximately thirty rubles).

8. Greenpeace Russia, "O Nas," available at http://www.greenpeace.org/russia/ru/about.

The Sources of Organizational Variation

While the Soviet legacy exerts a depressing influence on social activism, focusing solely on the obstacles to activism in post-Soviet Russia masks the diversity and dynamism of the social organizations that do exist and overlooks what these trends portend for the future. The labels "grassroots," "professionalized," and "government-affiliate" organizations serve as shorthand to compare different strategies of organizational development. Grassroots organizations generally work on local environmental issues, building on networks of family, friends, and neighbors to resolve largely apolitical questions. Professionalized organizations' activities frequently mirror the goals and language of the transnational environmental movement and draw upon science to critique current environmental policies and practices. Government-affiliate organizations, as their name implies, assist the state administration in environmental protection. This chapter is concerned with the emergence of these organizational types and their sustainability. Table 4.1 classifies the Russian environmental organizations in this study by indicating the percentage of organizations possessing certain characteristics.

TABLE 4.1. Organizational Characteristics of Russian Environmental Groups (percent)

	Grassroots	Professionalized	Government affiliates
Legal registration	64	94	100
Paid staff	10	70	78
Organizational hierarchy	55	85	100
Office space	40	76	67
Computer	50	97	89
E-mail	57	100	67
Web page	2	27	0
International contacts	14	91	22
Public-relations material	50	85	66

Note: Data drawn from author interviews. Percentages are based on a cross-regional sample of 84 organizations, including 42 grassroots, 33 professionalized, and 9 government affiliates completed in 1999–2001. Organizational hierarchy is indicated by the use of formal titles or staff positions within the organization through which individuals rotate. Numbers related to office space include both rented and donated premises, a difference that is explored in the case studies below. Numbers related to computers include either ownership of or regular access to a computer. E-mail statistics include organizational e-mail or the regular use of a personal e-mail account for organizational business. International contact indicates organizations that develop ties to *nonfunder* organizations in the course of their work. The public-relations material category indicates whether an organization produces brochures, pamphlets, or other material used to make the public aware of the organization.

Grassroots organizations are less likely than other environmental groups to be registered (more than one-third are unregistered),[9] to have a paid staff (10 percent versus 78 percent for professionalized groups), or to have office space (less than half versus three-quarters for professionalized groups). They are also less likely to own or have access to a computer, to generate public relations material, or to have international contacts or an e-mail account. Professionalized organizations, on the other hand, are more likely to have the characteristics of highly institutionalized organizations. Government affiliates exhibit a mix of characteristics They are closer to professionalized organizations in terms of legal registration, office space, and organizational hierarchy, while they are similar to grassroots groups in their lower levels of e-mail access, Web pages, and international contacts.

As summarized in Table 4.2, variation in organizational form is related to variation in environmental activism, a subject that will be elaborated upon in chapter 5.

TABLE 4.2. Activist Orientation by Organizational Type

	Grassroots	Professionalized	Government affiliates
Green issues addressed	Local issues	Transnational issues	Government-sanctioned issues
Relations with society	Friendship and family networks	Intelligentsia networks	Bureaucratic networks
Relations with state	Avoidance	Opposition	Cooperation

Resources and Leadership

What is the explanation for these patterns of organizational development? In an environment of resource scarcity, environmental groups seek to develop predictable ties to funding sources. Based on leaders' professional

---

9. This sample of environmental organizations is similar to other studies in terms of the percentage of registered social organizations in the early 2000s. A survey conducted by the Siberian Civic Initiatives Support Center found that, of 2,100 NGOs in their survey of Siberia, 76 percent (1,613 groups) were officially registered (Mishina 2000). Information from the ISAR-RFE database in 1999 showed that 80 percent of social organizations were registered.

TABLE 4.3. Sources of Support for Social Organizations (percent)

	Grassroots	Professionalized	Government Affiliate
Foreign funding	40	97	0
Government funding	38	30	89
Volunteers	71	48	56
Other local resources[a]	81	67	100

Note: Percentages of organizations include any group that received funding from that source, even if only on one occasion, based on information supplied by environmental activists in interviews.

[a] "Other local resources" captures nonmaterial sources of support (such as donated office space, computer equipment, or services from any source) and money from membership fees.

socialization and experiences, they are more willing and more able to exploit some funding opportunities than others. Organizational similarity arises out of leaders' varying interest in and ability to take advantage of a similar resource stream, resulting in similar choices as to whether to seek support primarily from local, state, or transnational allies.

Table 4.3 outlines the primary sources of support for environmental organizations as reported by the activists themselves. The figures related to foreign funding stand out most dramatically. All professionalized organizations, with one exception, have received financial support from foreign grant programs or transnational partnerships, while fewer than half of grassroots organizations have received foreign funding, and none of the government affiliates.[10] Although information on the amount of funding is not available in every case, interview data also revealed that grassroots organizations are much more likely to have received relatively small grants—generally the equivalent of $1,500 or less—than professionalized groups. Government funding is also unevenly distributed. All government affiliates, with the exception of one political party, acknowledged receiving financial support from the state, while only 38 percent of grassroots and 30 percent of professionalized organizations had done so. One point of agreement across organizational types that emerged in interviews is

---

10. Some sources claim that environmental groups are more likely than other Russian social organizations to have received a foreign grant (see, for example, Henderson 2003, 45). Anecdotal evidence supports this claim. While overall only 27 percent of Primorksii Krai social organizations claimed to have received a grant, my sample showed that almost 60 percent of environmental organizations in the region had received grant funding (*Zapiski c Dal'nego Vostoka* 1999, 30).

the growing significance of cash flows for social organizations in Russia. Sergei Pashchenko speaks for many activists when he remarks:

> Here money has started to have value. Earlier I had my salary and that was all—our scientific instruments and equipment were free. Now money is becoming for us as it is in the West. If there is money, you can buy instruments, or you can hire a lawyer in your defense.[11]

Another environmentalist joked that the old Soviet-era saying "Better a hundred friends than a hundred rubles" now needs to be reversed to reflect the growing value of money over connections in society.

Although monetary resources are increasingly influential, connections and nonmonetary resources are still the mainstay of most environmental organizations. All three types of organizations depend upon local resources, including in-kind donations from other community institutions or commercial enterprises, small membership fees, and donated services such as free advertising in local newspapers. Perhaps because they are closer to environmental problems, local and regional government officials often passively assist social organizations by allowing activists to use state-owned premises to house their offices—some with explicit permission but many on an informal basis. These premises, usually in institutes and schools, often include a telephone and basic office equipment. Most environmental organizations, and grassroots groups in particular, also depend on volunteer labor to carry out their projects and activities.

What emerges from this data is that while there is significant overlap in funding, the primary-resource dependency of each organizational type is different. Grassroots organizations depend upon local funds, professionalized organizations rely on transnational support, and government-affiliate organizations rely on state resources. Reliance on various sources of funding is not, however, merely a matter of chance—an organization just happens to catch the government's attention or succeeds in a grant competition, for example. Environmental leaders of different professional backgrounds are more or less disposed to seek out different types of resources and more or less able to take advantage of opportunities to access them.

---

11. Pashchenko interview.

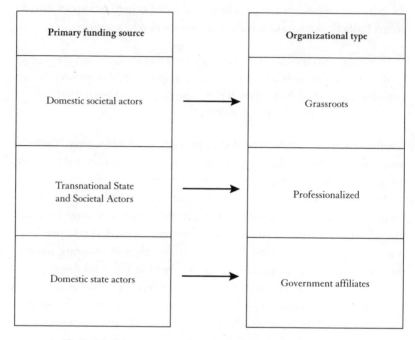

Figure 4.1. Primary-resource dependency of three organizational types

The importance of leadership preferences and abilities is underscored by a remarkable homogeneity of environmental leaders' professional backgrounds within each organizational type. Grassroots organizations tend to be led by educators (primarily women), from the kindergarten (*detskie sady*) to pedagogical-institute level; professionalized organizations are most often led by scientists, particularly biologists, and other academics who work in universities and research institutes; finally, most government-affiliate organizations are headed by bureaucrats or scholars who were loyal Communist Party members during the Soviet era. In sum, then, the breakdown of professional backgrounds of leaders in the three types of environmental organizations is as follows:

Grassroots organizations: Educators
Professionalized organizations: Scientists
Government-affiliate organizations: Bureaucrats

Professional socialization filters the signals from Russia's current economic and political landscape, highlighting some opportunities while obscuring others. Professional experience also tends to correlate with environmental activists' beliefs about the previous and current regimes and their ties to networks and institutions. Their past experiences also make leaders more aware of and more likely to have access to different kinds of resources: community institutions for grassroots environmentalists; scientific institutes and universities for professionalized activists; and bureaucratic resources for government-affiliate groups. Ultimately, leaders with similar professional backgrounds tend to gravitate toward the organizational niche in which their knowledge, skills, and connections are most likely to enable organizational survival. As demonstrated in later chapters, environmental leaders across organizational types exhibit different ideas about the most pressing issues for environmental activism and different assessments of appropriate and inappropriate behavior for social organizations. These varying orientations toward state and society amount to, in effect, different visions of what civil society organizations should do and can do in Russia today. Thus environmental leaders' socialization in their preactivist professions serves as a proxy for the Soviet legacy, a legacy that has diverse meanings depending on the social groups in question.

Professional training and experience continue to be relevant in part because many environmental leaders still work part-time in their primary places of employment. Activists understandably are anxious about committing to nonprofit work full-time because of to the instability of funding for these organizations. In addition, one's professional position was important in accruing nonmonetary resources during the Soviet period, and these advantages sometimes persist into the present period. Ledeneva notes that it was common during the Soviet years for an individual to view his or her occupational position as a type of resource. Professional positions fulfilled basic needs but also allowed individuals to gain status as a kind of gatekeeper of key resources for friends and acquaintances, resources that could be exchanged for less-concrete necessities such as contacts and information (1998, 125–26). While the importance of state resources may lessen as Russia's private sector develops, many activists still carefully guard information about opportunities, laws, regulations, and funding, seeing it as a valuable resource. In addition, the reconsolidation of state authority in many areas of governance under Putin and Medvedev may reinforce the importance of cultivating and using connections to state actors.

Leadership, Scarcity, and Strategies of Sustainability

The sections below examine each of the three organizational types in detail in order to explain how resource scarcity and leadership preferences combine to shape varying organizational forms.

Grassroots Organizations   Meeting a grassroots environmental activist often means taking part in the time-honored Russian tradition of sitting around a table with a cup of hot tea and discussing environmental issues as family life or work continues in the room next door. Grassroots environmental leaders share treasured mementos of past activities including photographs of environmental festivals and summer camps and children's art on environmental themes, testifying to the enthusiastic, if small, group they have gathered around the organization. Grassroots organizations tend to be relatively fluid and informal groups lacking office space; their activities are often intertwined with the day-to-day lives of their leaders and members.

Grassroots groups are the least known environmental organizations, and they generally work on projects at the community level; therefore they are the most difficult to locate. Not only are they less likely to appear in NGO directories compiled with the support of foreign donors, they are also less likely to produce official public-relations material advertising their activities. Grassroots groups are smaller and more locally rooted than their professionalized and government-affiliate counterparts—often membership is based on preexisting social networks and extends only to a small family group, circle of friends or colleagues, or even a single individual. Grassroots groups' actual impact on the community may be broader than other green organizations, however, as they attempt to draw community members into their projects and activities.

Grassroots groups address environmental issues that fall within three broad areas: environmental education; community well-being (health, safety, and recreation); and eco-spirituality. In the 1990s, a few small green political parties also fell into the grassroots category due to their informal organizational style. Across these variations in theme, grassroots organizations are united by their focus on local interests. For example, in Bryansk and Vladimir "Save the Springs" movements have mobilized small groups of local citizens, often elderly residents, to meet informally in order to restore the areas surrounding natural freshwater sources. Many Russians believe that these springs possess sacred healing power, and citizens have asked the government to officially preserve these areas and protect them from illegal garbage dumping. As a result, several springs have been declared regional monuments. In Vladivostok, the *Ozero* (Lake) initiative group, founded by concerned parents, organized the cleanup of a local pond where children often swim, convinced local industries in the vicinity to change their waste-disposal practices, and then lobbied the local administration to plant trees in the area. In Bryansk, the Egida Society for the protection of animals began as a club for dog lovers. Noting the growing stray-pet population in the city and the threat to sanitation posed by the animals, the group organized to take in hundreds of stray animals each year.

The Druzhina student environmental group at Vladimir's Pedagogical Institute is in many ways a typical grassroots organization. According to its leader, Dmitrii Evseev, the group was started in March 1999 by a group of students after a local environmental activist encouraged them to attend a conference of student nature inspectors.[12] Druzhina's primary mission is to patrol nature preserves, looking for poachers, but they also plant trees, clean up parks, and collect signatures for petitions to save local springs. Several years after its founding, the group had ten active members and fifty interested students who participated because "they love being in nature." Druzhina is not registered, does not have a bank account, and relies on the volunteer labor of students. Institute officials occasionally allow the students use of a lecture hall in exchange for help in its arboretum and also donated a room in the basement of a dormitory, but the students have not been able to purchase materials to remodel the room. They described their situation as precarious, fearing that institute officials may "try to get rid of them." The group relies on students' personal computers and e-mail accounts for communication. They completed one grant application, proposing that some members attend a summer program for student

---

12. Dmitrii Evseev, author interview, Vladimir Druzhina, Vladimir, May 23, 2000.

environmental inspectors, but they were not successful. Evseev expressed uncertainty about the group's future as he is not sure who will take over when he graduates.

FORM: Grassroots environmental organizations are less likely to be legally registered than other green groups. Those activists who lead unregistered organizations cite the time and expense involved in the registration process and its limited advantages, especially since many grassroots groups have no need of a bank account—the primary benefit of legal status.[13] Individuals engaged with eco-spirituality were particularly prone to respond that registration is too complicated and has few benefits. The lack of registration generally does not indicate how active a grassroots group is, however. While an organization may only "exist on the level of consciousness" (a euphemism offered by one activist to describe his group's inactivity) in spite of their registration,[14] others are actively engaged in local projects without seeing the need to register.

Some grassroots organizations avoid the need for registration by developing an informal sponsor relationship with a professionalized NGO or another institution. To cite a few examples: the Youth Section of Chemical Safety worked under the wing of the group For Chemical Safety in Bryansk; in Vladivostok the environmental-education organizations Nadezhda and In Defense of the Sea operated under the auspices of a naval museum and a natural history museum respectively; the League to Save the Steppe of Novosibirsk worked informally out of the offices of Ekoklub; and the eco-spirituality organization Green Attitude is not registered, but its partner organization, the Bryansk Ecological Union, is. The sponsor provides the grassroots group a *krysha*—or roof—shielding it from official scrutiny and the complexities of the registration, banking, and tax systems. Sponsorship, of course, could be severed by the sponsoring organization,

---

13. In this sample, one professionalized group also remains unregistered and cites similar reasons for its status. Sergei Pashchenko of Siberian Scholars for Global Responsibility, argues that registration can be a burden. "Even though you have nothing in your bank account, the tax inspector sends a pile of papers every quarter. You aren't able to say: I simply don't have anything. You have to answer, you have to go and defend yourself. In that sense, it is overwhelming." His organization has been able to share the bank account of and receive grants through another social organization, the Center for Public Health, obviating the primary need for registration (Pashchenko interview).

14. Anonymous environmental activist, author interview.

and occasionally personality conflicts and disputes over resources end this type of relationship.

Grassroots groups are the least likely of all green organizations to have official premises: 60 percent of grassroots activists simply work out of their home or from their desk at their primary place of employment. Others have been given space informally in educational institutions. Grassroots organizations are extremely unlikely to have paid staff members (only 10 percent paid one or more individuals) and generally eschew formal titles and hierarchies, aside from a clear leadership role for one individual. They also are less likely to have office equipment and computers. While 50 percent of grassroots activists say that they have regular access to a computer, only slightly more than 20 percent own their own machine (compared to 94 percent of professionalized activists who possess a personal computer or organization computer). Their lack of technological sophistication corresponds to grassroots groups' lower likelihood of having an e-mail account, Web page, or international contacts.

While the more informal organizational style of grassroots groups could be seen simply as a sign of less-successful strategies of organizational development, many grassroots activists in fact prefer working within a less structured, less hierarchical, and less resource-dependent type of organization. Evgeniia Pender of the St. Petersburg group Mir (Peace) said that she would rather develop networks of like-minded individuals than gather members together into one big organization.[15] Mir and other eco-spirituality groups avoid all organizational hierarchy. Iliia Smelianskii of the initiative group the League to Save the Steppe saw the economic advantages of a more informal organizational style, arguing "Initiatives and initiative groups are a lot better [than formal organizations]. We don't need to 'feed' a bookkeeper."[16] Smelianskii pointed out that in the past there were two other Novosibirsk organizations working to protect the steppe ecosystem, but they ceased to exist after they failed to secure grant funding; by keeping its activities small and affordable, his organization avoided that fate, albeit ultimately only for several years. It also is not the case that grassroots organizations are simply more recently established than professionalized

---

15. Evgeniia Pender, author interview, Mir, St. Petersburg, May 4, 1999.
16. Iliia Smelianskii, author interview, League to Save the Steppe, Novosibirsk, December 9, 1999.

groups or government affiliates. While some grassroots groups were founded quite recently, approximately one-third of those surveyed were established during the perestroika period or in the early 1990s.

LEADERSHIP AND RESOURCES: Grassroots organizations most commonly are led by educators—usually elementary-school teachers but occasionally teachers from pedagogical institutes or universities; directors of kindergartens; librarians; and curators of museums. Seventeen grassroots environmental leaders interviewed work as teachers or had worked as teachers in the past, while four grassroots organizations were led by students from postsecondary institutes. Other grassroots leaders are employees of the local government administration, journalists, small-business owners, or pensioners. The majority (twenty-four out of forty-two) of leaders of grassroots environmental organizations are women, in part reflecting the high number of women who work in the educational sector.

These educators and others draw upon their ties within the community to locate the resources their organizations need to survive. Since they generally do not maintain office space, staff, or technological equipment, grassroots groups require less financial support than professionalized or government-affiliate groups. Limiting their material requirements is part of grassroots environmental organizations' survival strategy, as noted by one representative of an eco-spirituality organization:

> How do these organizations survive? In practice these organizations have all the resources that they need. They find premises by personal agreement and they do not pay rent. They are assigned a small space in a library or some kind of office in an institution where they can meet regularly.... Someone takes them in, helps them—they do not use the formal process. The resources that they need are very minimal.[17]

The most common response of grassroots environmental activists to the question of how they fund their organizations is that their work is based "on enthusiasm." Indeed, grassroots activists commonly cite enthusiasm and optimism as their greatest resources. More than 70 percent of grassroots groups have volunteers from the community; one grassroots

---

17. Kuliasova interview.

representative even asserted "organizations are stronger when everyone works for free."[18]

Grassroots environmental activists have become expert at recycling pre-existing institutions and networks for the purpose of environmental activism. The strategy of reusing the resources of state-owned institutions for social activism is particularly appropriate in post-Soviet societies that are still coping with the legacy of the Communist Party's monopoly on organizational resources. Contrary to the general depiction of Soviet-era institutions as relics of authoritarianism, approximately 40 percent of grassroots groups are based, often unofficially, in state-owned educational and cultural institutions, such as schools, libraries, museums, dormitories, kindergartens, Houses of Children's Creativity, former Pioneer summer camps, or nature preserves (*zapovedniki*). As Tatiana Vassilieva, the leader of the Bryansk children's environmental organization Ladushka, commented, basing an environmental organization in an established community institution "makes it easier to attract attention and publicity, to survive."[19] More intangibly, these ties transmit legitimacy to the social organization within the local community since the group appears to be an extension of a valued local institution.

Nonmonetary support from the local community also sustains grassroots groups. In Vladivostok, the Laboratory for Environmental Education has been given space in a commercial tourist firm and access to e-mail through its affiliation with the larger professionalized organization Green Cross. Other grassroots environmental activists use computers at NGO resource centers. In-kind donations can be valuable for groups' specific activities as well as general operations. The Novosibirsk group Save the Ob! has found a lab that is willing periodically to donate free analyses of Ob River water, enabling the group to continue both its monitoring program and its children's environmental research competition; Save the Ob! also relies on a local museum to provide space for meetings. Commercial organizations often are willing to offer prizes or refreshments for charitable events, children's educational competitions, and summer camps, as long as activities are not overtly political. The group Nadezhda counts on the local *Trudovaia Slava* newspaper to publicize its educational events to

---

18. Tatiana Vassilieva, author interview, Ladushka, Bryansk, April 25, 2000.
19. Vassilieva interview.

the community. The Russian Scouts in Vladivostok are able to continue their summer-camp program through connections to people and organizations that donate space at other established children's camps. The microzapovednik project at elementary school No. 7 in Sosnovii Bor outside St. Petersburg relies on a sympathetic school director and local foresters who are willing to give free lectures to students. The Egida animal-protection organization in Bryansk has received a remarkable number of in-kind donations. In addition to free advertisements in a local paper and free radio time from a supportive radio host, the organization has completely remodeled a derelict building provided by the local administration, creating a veterinary office and animal shelter using only donated construction materials from local businesses.

Monetary resources are obviously more fungible than donated materials and services but are difficult for grassroots groups to obtain. In a rare example of membership fees, the Bryansk Ecological Union asks for ten rubles a month (roughly equal to thirty cents) from approximately ten to twelve members. The leader of the group admits that not everyone is able to pay and that some months they do not receive any fees at all. The St. Petersburg Society of Greenpeace Supporters was one of the few grassroots groups studied that occasionally received donations from the public, but initially many of these funds come from foreigners residing in the city. In its early years, the society also had some difficulty determining exactly how they could officially accept these donations because of the complex bookkeeping issues that surround this type of income. Grassroots leaders cite questions of accounting and taxation as one of their most persistent problems with receiving financial contributions.

Given the dearth of local resources, some grassroots organizations have turned to commercial activities to supplement their funding. In one of the more unusual fund-raising strategies, the animal-protection society Egida organizes an annual off-road jeep race for local enthusiasts, charging an entrance fee for drivers. The Russian Scouts (unlike the similar Pioneer children's clubs started in the Soviet era) do not receive any funding from their members or the local administration but do have some income from the sale of their journal. The leaders of the environmental-education organization Ladushka considered cultivating mushrooms to cover their expenses but decided that it would be too time consuming. Instead they turned to selling small artificial Christmas trees, and in the future they hope to sell souvenirs and seedlings to raise funds. In fact, making souvenirs to sell to tourists is a common practice of many children's groups. Other grassroots groups talk vaguely about producing some sort of ecologically "clean" products to sell, but few activists have any commercial experience, and Russia continues to present a challenging environment for small businesses. In a few instances, a sympathetic businessperson uses his or her commercial enterprise to fund a social organization. In St. Petersburg, the business Christmas, a publisher and purveyor of scientific equipment, supports two environmental organizations, Soyuz and the Federation for Ecological Education.

City and regional governments also occasionally provide small amounts of funding for grassroots environmental organizations, previously through their Ecology Funds, before the federal-level environmental fund was closed in 2002 and many regions effectively did away with their funds as well, or absorbed the funds into their general budgets. Thirty-eight percent of grassroots groups have received money from the government at some point, although the amounts tend to be small. Educational organizations are the most likely recipients. For example, AVES in Novosibirsk received funding from the mayor to support its educational olympiad program. Several groups, however, indicated that they were suspicious of the "dishonest politics" that go into the distribution of government funds and said that only "tame (*ruchnye*)" social organizations—those that support the government—are likely to receive that money.[20]

Finally, 40 percent of grassroots organizations had received one or more small grants, often characterized as seed grants by foreign donors.[21] For example, Save the Ob! received funding from the Siberian Center for the Support of Civic Initiatives to make a short film, Nadezhda was given a small grant from ISAR-FE for a summer biology program, and the Vladivostok Russian Scouts received money to buy a computer from the Eurasia Foundation. In spite of these successes, grassroots groups tend to participate in grant competitions infrequently. Leaders ascribe their reluctance to pursue grant funding to their lack of information about available grants,

---

20. Anonymous environmental activist, author interview.

21. Groups pursuing environmental education are most likely to receive this funding. Donors are unlikely to give funding to eco-spirituality organizations, and most have rules against granting funds for political activities, effectively ruling out small green parties.

their limited understanding of the terminology and types of project that compose a successful grant application, and their lack of organizational infrastructure (such as registration, a bank account, and a bookkeeper) to support grant funding. Natalia Knizhnikova of Green Attitude said that she thought of applying for grant funding several times but didn't because she found it difficult to fill out the forms and thought it unlikely that her group would receive funding. Antonina Kuliasova, a St. Petersburg sociologist and activist, asserted that most grassroots "do not receive any kind of grants." The reason for this, Kuliasova said, is that

> they are not able to write the applications. Some groups would like to write grants [*pisat' granty*], but they are not able to write grants—not because in principle they could not write them—but because they have a different style. They have a style of conversation, a style of exposition of the material, which is different than that demanded by applications for grants.[22]

Galina Kuchina of Save the Ob! echoed Kuliasova's comment: "We don't have any financial resources besides those we receive if we win a grant, but we win very little and very rarely. We are capable of working, but we aren't able to arrange ourselves as donors would like."[23] Tatiana Krylova of Egida noted that in her organization "they don't even dream of grants" and that "they don't have the time or the terminology" to engage in grant seeking.[24] Some activists have more ideological reasons for not applying for grants; for example, a Bryansk environmentalist commented that the lack of grant support is a virtue for her group because they are happy to work at the local level on local resources.[25]

Staff members at ISAR-FE, an NGO resource center and environmental group in Vladivostok, noted another obstacle to organizations seeking grants: while it is relatively easy for environmental organizations to get small grants to start a project, it is more difficult to get money to continue the group's activities.[26] Donors also occasionally expressed disappointment in the NGIs, or nongovernmental individuals, that they find at the grassroots level. As one European aid official noted, every now and then she

22. Kuliasova interview.
23. Galina Kuchina, author interview, Save the Ob!, Novosibirsk, December 10, 1999.
24. Tatiana Krylova, author interview, Egida Animal Protection Society, Bryansk, April 25, 2000.
25. Vassilieva interview.
26. Nataliia Proskurina, author interview, ISAR-FE, Vladivostok, November 1, 1999.

thinks she has discovered an interesting new organization, but it often turns out to be simply "a Website, a man, and his dog."[27] Finally, there is fierce competition for small grants. The leader of the organization Krug (meaning "Circle") related that her group developed an environmental-education project entitled "Home" and received a small amount of grant funding to support it. The group applied for a follow-up grant but was unsuccessful, later discovering that the donor had received more than six hundred applications and selected only a handful of projects to fund.[28] Other activists expressed bewilderment at why their applications were unsuccessful. A Novosibirsk environmentalist concluded that her group's projects weren't funded because they were focused on local concerns and "of course foreign funds represent foreign interests."[29]

FUTURE SUSTAINABILITY: Grassroots organizations rely on resources from local communities. Given this situation, their sustainability depends to a certain degree on Russia's economic growth and stability. It also depends on the continuing support of their local constituencies. The embeddedness of grassroots organizations in Russia's educational and cultural institutions provides them with crucial resources; however, it also means that the systemic problems of underfunding for state social services plague grassroots organizations. For example, teachers tend to receive very low salaries, and in the 1990s, when some regional governments fell into wage arrears, they occasionally were not paid at all. Thus they are a challenging clientele for grassroots organizations' fee-based educational services, such as teacher-training conferences or environmental-education journals. In Vladivostok, the teachers' association Krug organized a survey of its members and discovered that only five teachers out of ninety could afford to pay for educational seminars. Anton Semenov of ISAR-FE and Galina Chan of Krug feared that their educational programs were limited by teachers' financial situations. Liliia Kondrashova of the Resource Information Center (RITs) agreed:

> In general we cannot be the kind of organization that is self-financing. We cannot do paid services. This is the main difference between us and organizations in the U.S. . . . The financial situation is so complicated now. We had

27. Karen Widess, author interview, TACIS, Moscow, April 20, 2000.
28. Galina Chan, author interview, Krug, Vladivostok, November 18, 1999.
29. Anonymous, author interview.

a project on Kamchatka to conduct a seminar. In the project, we had money so that we could travel there, so that we can make all of the materials available for teachers, so that we can pay the teachers simply to get around the city because they do not have money, so that we can feed them lunch and a coffee break because they do not have money. We are not able to say to them, You should pay.... Self-financing in this economic situation is impossible.[30]

In addition, access to technology in schools, libraries, and museums remains low. Internet connections in the school system are still rare, presenting another obstacle to the development of grassroots groups. Unless a teacher has another means of accessing e-mail or the Internet, perhaps through another job or at home, he or she is unlikely to be able to participate in online educational projects designed for his or her benefit.

Grassroots organizations' preference for smaller projects and more limited goals and their reliance on volunteers in some ways make their groups easier to sustain, setting them on a path of organizational development that may remain viable under fluctuating economic conditions, although these features also limit the scope of their activities. Grassroots activists have been ingenious in reusing the limited organizational resources that exist in Russian cities by drawing on their personal networks and community institutions. The activities of grassroots environmental groups suggest that citizen activism doesn't need to be embodied in a new organization form but can also be found in the creative reuse of past practices and institutions. The future of grassroots organizations is likely to depend on Russia's growing middle class, the level of public concern about local environmental issues, and citizens' willingness to cooperate in order to resolve local problems.

Professionalized Organizations   Of the three types of environmental organizations in Russia, professionalized organizations are most similar to environmental NGOs we are familiar with in the West. Professionalized groups are likely to appear in official NGO directories, to have office space and Web pages, and to disseminate materials publicizing their work. Offices bustle with ringing phones and the sound of incoming faxes, while

---

30. Liliia Kondrashova, author interview, Resource Information Center, Vladivostok, October 19, 1999.

staff members or volunteers labor over clearly defined projects and engage in public-relations work. Of course, since they are environmentalists, the dress code still tends to be informal, but professional behavior, organizational hierarchy, and modern office equipment are clearly in evidence. Leaders of professionalized groups were often willing to speak authoritatively about the environmental movement or the NGO community as a whole. Many activists, as former or current academics, had their own theories about the development of Russian civil society and their role in the process. They also frequently were outspoken about their frustration with the government and foreign donors alike, the two groups with whom they most commonly interact.

Russia's professionalized environmental organizations are engaged in a wide variety of ambitious projects. To offer a few examples: the St. Petersburg Coalition Clean Baltic works with its Scandinavian counterparts to develop regional solutions for transboundary pollution; the Phoenix organization in Vladivostok advocates the protection of the Amur tiger; and the group Siberian Scholars for Global Responsibility in Novosibirsk investigates the extent of radioactive pollution throughout Siberia. One of the most successful professionalized environmental groups in Russia is the Center for Russian Environmental Policy (CREP) based in Moscow. Founded in 1993 by a group of scientists, including Aleksei Yablokov, former science adviser to President Yeltsin, CREP directs research projects to assess environmental risk, prepares environmental-policy alternatives that often build on the experience of other countries, and disseminates these proposals to relevant government committees. CREP's studies have tackled issues such as chemical pollution in Russia, the state of the country's Arctic environment, and the development of environmental law in Russia. The organization is well developed—it has a board of directors, office space in Moscow, and a permanent staff—and is supported by a number of public and private foreign funds, including the W. Alton Jones Foundation, the MacArthur and Mott Foundations, USAID, and several foreign embassies. Professionalized organizations with similar objectives exist in other regions, such as the Fund for Wildlife in Khabarovsk.

Form: As legally registered nongovernmental organizations, professionalized organizations represent a fundamentally new institutional form in Russian society. Registration is not always easy for these groups, sometimes

for political reasons. Oleg Bodrov, the leader of Green World based in Sosnovii Bor, just outside St. Petersburg, recounted his group's experience in
the 1990s:

> We tried to do it [to register], but...the organization arose as a result of a
> conflict with the authorities. It is necessary to register in the city offices. We
> tried to do it, but we didn't succeed because we were in a situation of con-
> flict. For that reason we didn't really register until 1997. We finally regis-
> tered with the Justice Department in Leningrad Oblast'—not in Sosnovii
> Bor, but in the regional offices.[31]

Bodrov believed that "there is no real advantage to registration. We work
as we worked from the start. But there is an advantage in cases in which
we are communicating with donors [*fondy*]. In order for them to support
our projects, it is important that we have a bank account." Indeed, most
donors interviewed, even prior to the 2006 NGO law, confirmed that they
fund only legally registered organizations.

A number of activists from professionalized groups recount that they
first were motivated to formally register their organization, often in the
mid- to late 1990s, in order to apply for funding from a foreign donor. Consequently, in what became a rite of passage for many professionalized leaders, environmentalists attended conferences or training programs funded
by foreign donors at which Russian activists were instructed on how to register their organizations and how to apply for grants.[32] Through these conferences and training programs, leaders of professionalized organizations
become embedded in a larger network of social organizations and a transnational funding system at an early stage of their development. For example, Liudmila Zhirina, the leader of the Bryansk group Viola, remembered
that in 1991 three people from her organization attended a Socio-Ecological Union conference.[33] There they learned how to register their organization and met many Western donors. Several years later, Viola hosted a
similar conference and passed along their experience and expertise to the

---

31. Bodrov interview.
32. USAID estimates that it alone has trained more than 13,500 Russian activists working on
different social issues. As one observer noted, training can be seen as a "tax" that activists need to
pay for receiving grant money (Bruno 1998).
33. Liudmila Zhirina, author interview, Viola, Bryansk, April 28, 2000.

leaders of another Bryansk organization, Erika. Leaders of professional-ized organizations take pride in their ability to negotiate the complex rules surrounding legal registration, to establish a bank account, to complying with frequently changing tax law, and to work with funding agencies; they consider it a sign of their professionalism and ability to get things done.

Professionalized organizations are more likely than grassroots groups are to have paid staff members, to adopt a formal organizational hierar-chy, and to rent office space. They also tend to possess more technologi-cal capacity than other green groups in Russia. More than 90 percent of professionalized environmental groups own or have regular access to a computer, and all professionalized groups in the study use e-mail to com-municate. Technological capabilities facilitate international contacts. Al-exander Karpov of the St. Petersburg Society of Naturalists noted the role of technology in his organization's development, crediting their first in-ternational partnership program to the fact that the society purchased a modem, set up an e-mail account, and was able to communicate regularly with other groups.

Russia's professionalized environmental groups are not mass-membership organizations—in other words, they do not rely on membership fees for their continued development, and recruitment of new members is often low on their list of priorities. The lack of concern with membership is re-lated to the facts that many Russians are not able or willing to pay even modest membership fees and that widespread social distrust and avoid-ance of political action make finding new members a difficult and time-consuming task. In Novosibirsk, Ekoklub—a long-standing organization founded in the early 1990s and based upon an even older Druzhina student environmental group—concluded in the late 1990s, after much experi-mentation, that "membership fees are not possible in Russia right now,"[34] Instead, professionalized organizations tend to be more akin to interest groups or think tanks in the West.

When pressed, most leaders of professionalized organizations counted their staff and those who collaborate on their projects as "members." This is especially true of scientific organizations. For example, the Amuro-Ussuriskii Center for Bird Diversity in Vladivostok claimed nineteen

34. Aleksandr Dubinin, author interview, Ekoklub, Novosibirsk, December 9, 1999.

members after eight years of organizing. In fact, these "members" are predominantly scientists who participate in their efforts to track endangered bird species, including two doctors of science, four doctoral candidates, and various research assistants. Several professionalized organizations maintain a list of "collective members," or institutional affiliates. For example, Green Cross of St. Petersburg has seventy collective members, mostly commercial enterprises.

LEADERSHIP AND RESOURCES: Many leaders of professionalized organizations are members of a social elite, having risen out of the intelligentsia, particularly from the biological sciences. Of the professionalized groups studied here, nineteen out of thirty-three organizations have leaders with advanced degrees in the natural or social sciences. A 1997 report evaluating USAID's support for environmental organizations confirmed the highly educated status of Russia's early environmental leaders, concluding that 65 percent of participants in the environmental movement had a higher education and an astounding 23 percent were either candidates or doctors of science (the former equivalent to U.S. Ph.D. recipients and the latter holders of an even higher degree) or were pursuing a graduate degree (Institute of Natural Resources Management 1997, 20). The leaders of professionalized green groups also frequently have ties to Soviet-era scientific organizations that promoted nature protection—in particular, the Society of Naturalists (*Obshchestvo Estestvoispytatelei*) and the Druzhina movement.[35] These individuals, socialized in the institutes of higher education in the Soviet era, place great faith in professional expertise and scientific objectivity. Environmentalists from professionalized organizations also tend to have an ambivalent attitude toward the current regime. Many were adamantly, if privately, opposed to the Soviet regime, yet they are dissatisfied with the performance of post-Soviet governments in protecting the environment.

This segment of the population has been hard hit by decreasing state funding for education and research. For many professionalized activists, the impetus for forming a social organization arose in the early 1990s when

---

35. Professionalized activists are somewhat less likely to be previously affiliated with the All-Russian Society for Nature Protection (VOOP), generally considered to be a "tame" organization by the late Soviet period (Weiner 1999, 195–200).

scientific institutes and universities were unable to continue funding research projects or in many cases even to pay basic salaries. Nongovernmental environmental organizations became a vehicle for some members of the scientific community to continue their research, even as state-owned institutes effectively closed, and to air their concerns about the environment. As Evgenii Sobolevskii, the leader of the Vladivostok organization Ekolog, noted, he is motivated by two goals: he founded his organization in order to preserve endangered species in the region but also so that his team could continue their research. Pointing to his research equipment, Sobolevskii pointed out, "All of this technology we have been able to buy on account of grants, because the institute does not finance our instruments. It only gives us the lowest salary."[36] Other social organizations got their start after scientific institutes abruptly stopped paying salaries, including the Institute for Sustainable Natural Resource Use, the Society for the Promotion of Sustainable Development, and Siberian Scholars for Global Responsibility. The Baltic Fund for Nature, Green World, and EkoDom have all attracted underemployed academics to their ranks. Arising partly from the problem of chronic underfunding in Russian higher education, these organizations have introduced talented people with professional qualifications into the green movement.

The founding of the Amuro-Ussuriskii Center for Bird Diversity is an example of this trend. Nataliia Litvinenko recounted the organization's history:

> The year 1991 was a very difficult one for science. It was a transitional period from Communist Russia to what we have now. And so the institute stopped paying regular salaries.... We wanted to continue our studies. That was the founding goal of our laboratory and nature protection activities. They let go of half of the institute. Later they took us back, but at first there was no money, no money at all, and nothing to do. They let us go—me because I was too old and Seriozha because he was too young. It was practically a complete dissolution. But we needed to survive. And we organized the Center.... We advertised that we could show the rare birds of Primorskii Krai, and [foreign] bird-watchers came to us.[37]

36. Evgenii Sobolevskii, author interview, Ekolog, Vladivostok, October 28, 1999.

37. Nataliia Litvinenko, author interview, Amuro-Ussuriskii Center for Bird Diversity, Vladivostok, October 20, 1999.

After organizing expeditions for foreign bird-watchers and researchers for several years, the leaders of the center realized that as a social organization they could apply for grants that would allow them to continue their research work. Yuri Shibaev recalled, "The institute didn't object. We were able to continue our work, not at the level we had earlier, but all the same we could continue with our studies."[38] Eventually they came to receive funding in two ways: approximately half of the time they propose projects to granting agencies, and the rest of the time they are asked to participate in ongoing international projects. The development of the Center for Bird Diversity has slowed due to the death of its leader, Natalya Litvinenko, in 2001, but her colleagues have continued to do research and collaborate internationally under its auspices.

Continued use of their academic office space, communications technology, and office equipment is common among professionalized organizations that remain based in universities and institutes. Other groups, including Ekoklub in Novosibirsk, have been able to hold onto the room their Soviet "parent" organization originally occupied, in Ekoklub's case a university dormitory room that traditionally belonged to the Druzhina organization. Ekoklub also has been allowed to use the university's Internet server without charge. In addition to the continued use of office space in scientific institutes, professionalized environmental organizations rely on some in-kind donations from the local community. Liliia Kondrashova of RITs in Vladivostok recalled that her organization was approached by a printing firm and offered some paper remnants that the firm had planned to discard.[39] RITs used the paper to make a small environmental calendar that included the organization's contact information. They then distributed three thousand calendars to the general public. In a similar effort to solicit in-kind donations, the St. Petersburg Urban Gardening Club persuaded commercial organizations to donate sand, rocks, and soil for their rooftop gardening project.

Professionalized organization leaders' commitment to their original research goals, and their need to maintain their staff, occasionally lead them to offer their services as paid consultants. Some organizations have had

---

38. Yuri Shibaev, author interview, Amuro-Ussuriskii Center for Bird Diversity, Vladivostok, October 20, 1999.

39. Kondrashova interview.

limited success charging fees for their services, including the St. Petersburg Society of Naturalists, which provides research and expertise under a program called Ecoservice, and Zov Taigi (Call of the Taiga) in Vladivostok, which runs a commercial printing business for environmentally friendly clients alongside the publication of its environmental journal. These groups tout themselves as models of how organizations can combine grants and self-financing to ensure sustainability. Yet several social organizations that have tried offering paid services have seen increased scrutiny from tax inspectors, even when the proceeds were used to support their social work. Other groups have tried to set up a separate legal entity to avoid this problem, but maintaining two organizations has divided their time and energy. Most environmental leaders agree that self-financing has been difficult under unstable economic conditions; several leaders of professionalized organizations point to their inability to finance themselves by offering paid services as one of the biggest differences between Russian and Western nongovernmental organizations. Ideological concerns also play a role in limiting the attractiveness of commercial work. After a decade working in the NGO sector, preceded by a career in academia, one professionalized activist worries that his group would lose an important element of its mission by seeming to give up their nonprofit status, particularly in a climate of pervasive corruption in the private sector.

Government officials generally have not been inclined to award money from city or regional budgets to professionalized organizations. Although professionalized environmental leaders pointed to the lack of government funding as one of many hindrances to the development of the environmental movement, they also noted that government officials tend to be "conservative" and "inflexible." Even when the Ecology Fund money was available, professionalized activists were skeptical about how it was distributed, most believing that it was used for the administration's own bureaucratic expenses. A St. Petersburg activist said, "We don't ask about the fund. As soon as you pronounce the word 'fund,' [local officials] immediately start to say 'No, no, no, we don't have any money!'"[40] A leader whose organization had received some money from the local administration complained about the small amount of government awards, noting that "you

40. Sergei Stafeev, author interview, Transboundary Environmental Information Agency, St. Petersburg, April 7, 1999.

can't do anything big with them."[41] In general, the leaders of professionalized groups value their autonomy, often connecting their ability to critique regional and local governments to the fact that they do not receive
any funding from the authorities.

Foreign funding has been the biggest source of revenue for most professionalized organizations throughout the post-Soviet period. Sergei Stafeev
of TEIA spoke for many professionalized activists, stating, "Unfortunately,
right now in Russia nonprofit organizations do not have any sources of financing except help from Western funds and participation in cooperative
projects with their colleagues. Neither the government nor the university
can finance us." All of the professionalized organizations studied, with the
exception of one group that had applied for funding but was unsuccessful,
had received financial support from grant programs run by foreign donors.
When asked to characterize his organization's funding sources, the leader
of one of the most active organizations in the St. Petersburg region confirmed that they "rely 100 percent on grants." In addition to grants from
private U.S. foundations, the majority of the group's funding comes from
the Swedish and Norwegian Ministries for Nature Protection. While the
group can claim a number of local supporters, it does not receive money
from members. The organization's success at winning grants exceeds that
of most other groups—they estimated that they are awarded about 25 percent of the grants they apply for. Representatives of the group attributed
this success to a process of trial and error by which they have become better
acquainted with the donor community and have learned which donors are
likely to be interested in them and their projects. After more than a decade
in operation, the organization is also a known quantity for donors and has
developed a well-deserved reputation for completing its projects.

The significance of external funding is not only related to the amounts
available but also to the organizational and cultural expectations that come
along with it. Natalia Proskurina of ISAR-FE commented, "Funders
bring with them more than simply money, but also a culture, a way of
working. We had this culture in Russia before the revolution, but then
lost it completely."[42] Different donors have different priorities and funding restrictions. Most donors do not support administrative expenses that

---

41. Zhirina interview.
42. Proskurina interview.

are not directly related to specific projects, and do not cover individual stipends or salaries, publishing costs, or general operating expenses having to do with technology or office equipment. Overtly political and religious activities are also often prohibited. Activists participate in training, hoping to learn the secrets of effective grant writing and organizational survival.[43] In addition to technical expertise, training conveys certain attitudes about appropriate organizational strategies.[44] For example, granting agencies stipulate conformity with certain organizational norms, such as the preparation of quarterly reports and evaluations and the use of Western accounting standards.[45] Early success in attracting resources, information, and partnerships increases a group's chances of participating successfully in grant programs in the future, illustrating the path-dependent nature of organizational development.

It is not surprising that professionalized groups are most successful at accessing foreign funding.[46] Professionalized environmental activists tend to have a more cosmopolitan outlook than other environmental leaders

---

43. Some activists express frustration with more informal obligations to donors. Hosting Western visitors and volunteers can take a significant amount of time and energy. For example, the leader of a St. Petersburg group noted that he spends almost half of his time communicating with Western donors and Western NGO counterparts, contributing to donor reports, and elucidating his group's relatively successful experience. Some social activists also argue that Western organizational practices are not suited to their local setting.

44. Desirable characteristics for social organizations can be extrapolated from donor targets for organizational development. For example, the USAID *NGO Sustainability Index* (1999, 10–11, 16) lists the following characteristics of increased "organizational capacity": a core of professional leaders and trainers; a well-developed mission statement; a board of directors and staff, with a clear division between the two; organizational roles, not just personalities; financial-management structures; fund-raising ability; and familiarity and conformity with legal and tax issues.

45. Bernadine Joselyn of the Eurasia Foundation characterizes this as training Russian NGOs "how to think '*proyektno,*'" or in a project-based fashion. She comments that it is a matter of teaching Russian activists "what is a goal, what is an outcome, what is a work plan—the who, what, why, how, when piece that Russians, culturally, historically, are not very good at or they have not had much experience with. They are going to solve the world's problems and they take this global or very philosophical approach. It's very hard to get them to be really concrete" (author interview, Moscow, March 24, 2000).

46. There is much anecdotal evidence pointing to the fact that activists' ability to develop close relationships with donor representatives working in Russia was highly correlated with successful grant applications in the early 1990s. Donors had little experience in Russia and relied on friendly relations with activists who acted as "translators" of Russia's complicated political and social sphere. While understandable, this practice led to the even-greater importance of charismatic and well-connected leaders within social organizations and increased the value of foreign-language ability.

based on their membership in a transnational community of scientists. They frequently communicate with colleagues from other countries, fitting relatively comfortably in the transnational milieu where higher education and a command of foreign languages are the norm.[47] This context affects the decisions professionalized groups make about who they take on as staff and members. As one leader commented, "The members of our organization need to have higher education . . . and they need to know how to use technology. Preferably they need to know foreign languages."[48] Professionalized environmentalists value their relationships with foreign donors not only for the resources they provide but also because they allow them some independence from the state. Many professionalized activists take care to note that their funding sources showed that their groups are not beholden to state officials.

Receiving grant funding, while a boon financially, entails logistical difficulties for professionalized groups and has become increasingly complicated in recent years. Accounting often requires a new layer of staffing within the group in order to accurately pay taxes related to grants and produce the reports required by the Ministry of Justice. This is why the first paid staff person in most organizations (and the last person to go without a salary, even between funding cycles) is the *bukhgalter,* or bookkeeper. Professionalized organizations also need a capable staff to carry out the projects that they have proposed to donors, requiring them to offer salaries that can compete with what the private sector has to offer. The former leader of Ekologos in Vladivostok commented, "All organizations are looking for a good cadre, and consequently they are looking for grant money so they can provide good salaries."[49] In addition, professionalized organizations are more likely to have the financial obligations of office space than other green groups, so securing continuous funding is a high priority for that reason as well.

This pattern of organizational development sets up a circular dynamic as the advantages of transnational resources and the demands of

---

47. A number of environmentalists cited their knowledge of English as a great asset, while others noted their lack of foreign languages as a drawback.

48. Vladimir Aramilev, author interview, Institute for Sustainable Resource Use, Vladivostok, November 17, 1999.

49. Valentina Kubanina, author interview, Krug and Ekologos, Vladivostok, November 4, 1999.

organizational maintenance reinforce each other, each further increasing the need for the other. Grant recipients need a higher level of organizational development to manage the funding, but then they require additional grants to maintain their new level of institutionalization. In emulating the NGO model, leaders of professionalized environmental groups are motivated both by their own desire to follow a strategy shown to be effective by environmentalists in other parts of the world and by the encouragement of foreign donors promoting a particular organizational form. But for most environmental organizations—with the exception of branches of international organizations such as Greenpeace and WWF—the organizational capacity of the NGO model remains more of an aspiration than an achievement.

FUTURE SUSTAINABILITY: When asked whether their organizations were likely to be sustainable in the future, most leaders of professionalized NGOs were optimistic. They cited a number of advantages. Professionalized organizations are the most highly institutionalized environmental groups. Leaders almost universally described themselves as true "professionals," noting their experience and reputation for completing projects. They gained a technological edge over other green groups early on; accessing the Internet and e-mail and possessing an organizational Web page all allow professionalized activists to enter a broader transnational community where they may be able to locate resources, gather supporters, and develop partnership relations with international organizations. In terms of the amount of financial support, professionalized organizations have had the most successful strategy of mobilizing resources in the early post-Soviet period.

If Russia's recent steady economic growth leads to the emergence of a middle class, professionalized groups may benefit from new supporters, although cultural barriers to charitable giving are likely to erode slowly. Philanthropic traditions were destroyed during the Soviet period. Thus far Russia's tax code does not offer tax incentives for charitable donations (Shuvalova 2006; Gambrell 2004).[50] In spite of unfavorable regulations,

---

50. In fact, throughout the 1990s the tax code did not differentiate between commercial and noncommercial organizations, resulting in an overall tax rate of more than 35 percent for many social organizations. This tax status underscores the low value that the government places on the

however, corporate philanthropy in Russia may be growing (Krestnikova and Levshina 2002). Banks were among the first commercial organizations willing to support social organizations, although they are most likely to support artistic and cultural projects. In Bryansk, the organization Erika received money from a bank to support environmental education in local schools. A coalition of WWF branch organizations received some funding from Mezhkombank for their Ecoregions project.[51] However, the climate for corporate philanthropy cooled noticeably in the wake of the trial of Mikhail Khodorkovsky, the former head of the Yukos oil firm and an oligarch who provided support for political parties and social organizations, in 2005. Many observers link his arrest for tax evasion and fraud and subsequent sentence to nine years in prison to his support for groups perceived as opposed to the government polices. Some environmental organizations are experimenting with new fund-raising strategies, such as soliciting donations from the public for specific environmental campaigns. Only the largest groups have the resources to invest in the outreach required.[52]

There is one way in which increasing resources could undermine the sustainability of professionalized organizations, however. Growth in the funding available for purely scientific research could lead to a reduction in environmental advocacy work. For example, in 1999 the Vladivostok group Ekolog received a new opportunity to research gray whales and bird populations affected by oil drilling in Sakhalin. "The organization [Ekolog] is not working right now. At this moment I am fully occupied, frankly, with scientific work, and so right now I have very little time for social activism [*obshchestvennuiu rabotu*]," Sobolevskii remarked, adding,

---

activities of social organizations. A group of social organizations began a campaign to change their tax status in the late 1990s (Dzhibladze 1999a, 1999b), but it wasn't until the Putin administration overhauled the entire tax system that the rate was lowered in 2001.

51. Ironically, one possible source of future funding for environmental protection is natural-resource corporations, such as Russian petroleum companies that have some Western shareholders. For example, the company TNK-BP promised to spend $1 billion on environmental protection over a decade, and LUKoil announced that it would spend a similar sum on environmental-safety programs between 2004 and 2008 (Agency WPS 2003).

52. In 2002, the Moscow office of the World Wide Fund for Nature sent out an appeal to more than two hundred thousand addresses in Moscow, St. Petersburg, and Yekaterinburg informing recipients of the organization's activities and requesting donations of 600 to 3000 rubles (approximately $20 to $100) to protect Russia's wildlife. A WWF representative said that 0.5 percent of those who received letters (or one thousand people) responded positively—not a large number, but significant in terms of resources (Varshavskaya 2002; Interfax 2002b).

"Social activism demands a lot of time."[53] If many opportunities to undertake scientific projects reappear, professionalized leaders are likely to spend less time on public outreach and education; their research could serve as the basis for future advocacy projects, however.

Professionalized organizations' strategy of mobilizing resources thus faces a glaring obstacle to their likely sustainability: namely, variation in the amount of foreign assistance going to Russia in general and to environmental goals in particular. Reliance on external funding subjects professionalized groups to the vicissitudes of foreign-policy issues over which they have no influence. For example, in the 1990s groups receiving funding from the European Union found their funds frozen due to the European Parliament's objection to Russia's war in Chechnya. Environmentalists also find public support fluctuating with international events, such as the strong surge in anti-Americanism during the U.S. bombings of Yugoslavia in 1999, the deterioration of relations related to U.S. support for Ukraine's Orange Revolution in 2004, and tension between the United States and Russia following the conflict in Georgia in 2008. In recent years, as funding for civil-society and democratization programs decline, a growing percentage of funding comes from transnational environmental organizations. Some environmental organizations have felt that grant funding is increasingly difficult to find.[54] Representatives of the Amuro-Ussuriskii Center for Bird Diversity joked about their lack of recent grant success: "We write grants but don't receive any. They have stopped loving us (*rasliubili*). America has stopped loving us."[55] They feared that donors are losing interest in Russia's problems. When a professionalized organization fails to win a round of grant funding, its existence is in jeopardy. For example, the Novosibirsk organization Social Ecology was sponsored by the Open Society Institute for the first few years of its development. When the group had to compete with other professionalized organizations, however, it struggled to maintain its status, office space, and staff and to live up to

---

53. Sobolevskii interview.

54. The scarcity of grant funding prompted a sort of grim humor among social organizations. A magazine for the NGO community ran a cartoon in which two men each hold one hand of a third man who is dangling over a cliff, and one says, "It seems to me that we have supported him long enough. Now it's time to let go so that he learns to be independent." *Byulleten' Moskovskogo ISAR*, no. 6 (Summer 1998):20–21.

55. Litvinenko interview.

the ambitious projects that the staff had devised during its early success. Lacking financial resources, the employees of the organization began to pursue other professional opportunities.

Government Affiliates   Approaching a state institution with faded slogans from the Communist era exhorting workers and peasants to greater achievements may be the first sign that one is encountering a government-affiliate organization. The quiet hallways, often with a guard at the door and a registration desk for visitors, signal an environmental organization that has been able to obtain permission to occupy space in regional or local government offices. At the entry to the organization, one may encounter the unusual luxury of a secretary ensconced behind a heavy desk who serves as a gatekeeper for the organization's leader. When you finally gain access, the secretary adopts the traditional use of first name and patronymic to present the organization's leader, an individual surrounded by the accoutrements of Soviet-era officialdom. Yet this is not a state agency or government bureau but a legally registered social organization representing a new hybrid type of activism in Russia.

Form: Government-affiliate organizations are highly institutionalized in the sense that they are the most likely of all environmental organizations to be legally registered, to have a paid staff, and to adopt formal organizational hierarchies. They are only slightly less likely than professionalized groups to have their own office space. Government affiliates fall between grassroots and professionalized groups in terms of their access to technology.

Environmental organizations that are government affiliates seek legitimacy through their close ties to state officials and the endorsements of well-known scientists and politicians. Government affiliates often maintain collective members or large mass memberships. Members may include all of the industries in a certain sector of the economy (for example, industrial waste producers are members of the Association Clean City in St. Petersburg) or a number of research institutions or schools (as is often the case for branches of the All-Russian Society for Nature Protection). These memberships generally do not extend much beyond a list of names. For example, the Vladimir Society of Hunters and Fishers claims almost twenty thousand members, all of whom applied to the organization for a sporting license but who have no other role in the organization.

One such government affiliate is the political party KEDR (an acronym meaning "Cedar" in Russian), the Constructive Ecological Movement of Russia, which then changed its name to the Russian Ecological Party "The Greens" in 2002.[56] KEDR originally was organized by a federal-government official from within the Epidemiological and Public Health Ministry (*Gosepidnazdor*). The party had been quite large relative to the proliferation of small green parties in the 1990s—in 1999 the group claimed 221 members in St. Petersburg, although at the federal level it has polled less than 0.5 percent of the vote in parliamentary elections. The party, which has been affiliated with the organization Movement KEDR, works closely with federal and regional governments. In interviews, professionalized environmentalists suggested that the party is a government organization in all but name.

Although government-affiliate organizations are legally registered as social organizations, other environmentalists occasionally charge that they are "in the pocket (*v karmane*)" of the state. However, most of these groups are not organized by the state per se, but were formed by individuals with state affiliations who are concerned about the environment. The founding of several government affiliates, including the All-Russian Society for Nature Protection (VOOP), preceded the current regime. Although their independence during the Soviet period was highly circumscribed, they now claim autonomy from state and government institutions.

LEADERSHIP AND RESOURCES: Six out of ten leaders of government-affiliate organizations have experience working in state or party posts. Their backgrounds range from experience as oblast first secretary to administrative jobs at a state university and bureaucratic positions in the former public health and ecology ministries. Government-affiliate leaders are also more likely than other environmentalists to occupy positions in the state administration at the same time as they conduct their nongovernmental work. For example, the leader of the All-Russian Society for Nature Protection (VOOP) in Vladimir simultaneously held a seat in the government's Ecology Commission. Almost all leaders of government affiliates express their primary aim as assisting the government in carrying out environmental

---

56. See http://www.greenparty.ru/main_en.php.

protection, and they claim that their activities are proof that laws mandating public participation in policymaking are fulfilled.

Leaders of government affiliates generally have a supportive relationship with government officials, continue to use government-friendly rhetoric, and offer the opinion that environmental protection is a state function that society should support not challenge. Several government-affiliate leaders noted that Russia's current system of environmental protection is adequate; it just needs to be implemented more effectively. In the opinion of Ilias Gadzhiev, the leader of Novosibirsk's VOOP, there were some problems in the Soviet era, but now social organizations no longer need to oppose the state since it has environmental protection well in hand. This view represents a fairly common belief among the leaders of government affiliates that the current Russian government can be relied upon to act in the interests of the public without the need for criticism from societal groups.

Government-affiliate organizations rely on small resource flows from the state, previously from city and regional Ecology Funds, and also discretionary funds from state officials. For example, branches of VOOP in Vladimir and Novosibirsk receive money for rent, telephone, and computers under the auspices of these government funds. In spite of their heavy reliance on government support, representatives of government affiliates describe their organizations as independent from the government, deeming the Ecology Fund to be an apolitical social fund that is fairly divided among worthy social organizations. Gadzhiev of the Novosibirsk VOOP stated: "This organization itself is a social organization. It doesn't receive any funding from the government. Only that from these funds that I told you about—those extra-budgetary [ecology] funds."[57] Other greens, however, charge that the distribution of the Ecology Funds was extremely politicized and express resentment that these funds were primarily used to support organizations that maintain a "special relationship" with local officials. Even the proposed use of government funding to construct a House of Nature (*Dom Prirody*) in Vladimir is looked upon by other greens as an investment that will benefit only VOOP; other environmentalists do not expect to be allowed to use the building.

---

57. Ilias Gadzhiev, author interview, All-Russian Society for Nature Protection, Novosibirsk, December 3, 1999.

Nonmonetary government support is a mainstay of these organizations as well, including office space, office and communications equipment, and occasionally staff. Yet even government affiliates cannot count on a secure flow of financial resources. In the past, the regional branches of VOOP were well funded by mandatory membership fees and government funds. Now support from regional and local budgets given on an annual basis depends upon maintaining close connections with government officials. While government-affiliate organizations are more likely than other green groups to claim that businesses, notably banks, give them charitable contributions, their leaders also express the least interest in and knowledge of fund-raising or grant seeking. When asked about fund-raising, Galina Esiakova of VOOP-Vladimir commented, "It is just not correct" to ask the public for money.[58] Representatives of the organization Movement KEDR insisted they were not interested in grants and would not accept them even if they were available.

FUTURE SUSTAINABILITY: Leaders of government-affiliate organizations base their expectations of future sustainability on their long history as an organization (in the case of VOOP), larger size, and greater stability than other environmental organizations. Certainly, steady flows of government funding to these organizations indicate that government affiliates have carved out a relatively stable niche. However, local authorities may also lose interest in government-affiliated organizations. The Siberian Fund for Ecology had been well supported by the Novosibirsk regional administration for a number of years, but in 2000 it lost the government funding that had allowed it to pay staff salaries and to arrange conferences for university academics, leaving only three people in the organization working mostly as volunteers. Remaining staff members turned to running educational programs for children in an effort to keep the group going. The danger of losing government sponsorship also looms if a government affiliate steps outside the boundaries of what state officials consider appropriate behavior. In general, however, since government affiliates rely more on the administrative apparatus of the state rather than elected officials, they are not as vulnerable to perceived political missteps. Government-

---

58. Galina Esiakova, author interview, All-Russian Society for Nature Protection, Vladimir, May 22, 2000.

affiliate organizations may never fulfill their potential because of the government's lack of interest in environmental issues but they play an increasing role in Russia's social sector. Although government affiliates represent the smallest category of environmental organizations in this study, their significance in social activism in Russia appears to be growing in other issue areas. The most notable example is the state-sponsored student group Nashi that received significant support under the Putin administration (Konovalova 2007).

Each organizational type faces threats to sustainability that are inherent in their reliance on a particular resource stream. There is also an important shared threat to environmental organizations' maintenance and survival—the loss of its leader. As we have seen, several factors have combined to reinforce a leader-centric model of social organizing, including the desire for autonomy that is a reaction to experience with Soviet mass-mobilization groups and the need to build personal relationships with donors, but this tendency leaves groups vulnerable when that key figure can no longer offer his or her reputation and contacts to the group. Many organizations have difficulty surviving the loss of their leader. The Russian Society of Ginseng Growers in Bryansk oblast fell into disarray after its president passed away. The acting leader admits that the organization had difficulty continuing its work, although in the past it boasted 380 members. In a similar story, the Club of the Green Movement in Vladimir, once one of the stronger organizations in the city, virtually stopped its activities after its leader died in the late 1990s and its members were unable to find anyone to be accountable for the organization. A representative of the group, who asked not to be named, commented, "We had a very good leader and at one point we were a very strong organization, but when our leader died the organization never really worked after that."[59] Valentina Kubanina of Ekologos said that, in her opinion, the experience of her organization as a group that "depended on one leader and when that person disappears the organization starts to fall apart" was "sufficiently typical."[60] After a series of acting leaders, they have not found anyone willing to take on the liability of the bank account and to sign for the organization, especially since they are unable to pay a new leader without more grant funding.

---

59. Anonymous Club of the Green Movement representative, author interview, Vladimir, 2000.
60. Kubanina interview.

Resource Scarcity and Intramovement Dynamics

Each of the organizational types discussed above has found a relatively—and temporarily—stable resource stream on which to base its development. Yet the overall scarcity of resources has other effects on relations within the environmental movement. Foreign funding, in particular, has exerted a particularly strong influence on relations within the movement, unintentionally reinforcing certain preexisting tendencies, including the lack of cooperation among green organizations, and encouraging new behaviors, such as environmentalists' tendency to affiliate themselves with multiple organizations.

Competition and Suspicion

While foreign funding has helped to create opportunities for many Russian organizations that might otherwise be struggling, it also inspires competitive, and occasionally acrimonious, relations within the green movement, most frequently among professionalized organizations.[61] Donors are quick to note the benefits for Russian social organizations of the competition for grants.[62] Liudmila Vikhrova of USAID, for example, argued that she sees the capacities of NGOs increase dramatically when multiple donors are active in a region.[63] Bernadine Joselyn of the Eurasia Foundation office in Moscow agreed: "I tend to think that the idea of competition is healthy and good. If at an early stage of third-sector development, you have a lot of players at the table, it helps create healthier organizations at the end than if you have one or two that from the beginning are hot-house developed."[64] But Russian environmentalists have their own opinions about the consequences of foreign funding for the movement. Igor Ogorodnikov of EkoDom in Novosibirsk commented: "There is competition

---

61. Sperling (1999) documented this tendency among organizations in Russia's women's movement.

62. A senior USAID official in Moscow argued that there may be too many social organizations in Russia and that organizations need to compete more for the foreign resources they receive. This official compared the proliferation of NGOs to the large number of newspapers in Russia, each unable to maintain a financially viable readership, and to the great number of political parties that do not actually represent society's interests. She argued that each of these sectors needs to be consolidated in order to be more viable in the future (Susan Reichele, author interview, USAID, Moscow, April 21, 2000).

63. Liudmila Vikhrova, author interview, USAID, Moscow, April 3, 2000.

64. Joselyn interview.

among organizations that have a similar theme, for resources and for donors (*grantodatelei*), of course. And since we have a limited number of
donors, and many groups don't have the opportunity to leave for a different
region, competition arises."[65] While generally in favor of competitive grants,
Yuri Shirokov of ISAR-Siberia noted that competition can make for un-
friendly relations within the movement, as groups try to distinguish themselves to donors by arguing, "We are the most green, the most aware; we
know everything and these other groups are just upstarts."[66] Some environmental groups have been reluctant to cooperate on grant applications for
fear that by sharing information and projects they would lose their competitive advantage or devalue their contribution in the eyes of donors.

As each environmental organization, regardless of type, struggles to
maintain itself by securing scarce resources, it is not surprising that within
the movement some mutual suspicion exists as to how groups are managing to support themselves. Grassroots and professionalized organizations
tend to be suspicious of government affiliates. Pavel Vdovichenko, a Bryansk activist, proudly noted that his organization has survived for almost
fourteen years. He asserted, "I work not because there is money; I have
money because I work," and, "No one has fed us (*nikto nas ne kormil*)." But
he also expressed skepticism as to how other groups survive. He estimated
that only 10 percent of NGOs are really active and that "most of them
probably live in someone's pocket."[67]

Those organizations that receive foreign or government funding are
the most likely to be scrutinized, not just by the authorities, but by other
activists as well. Organizations that have been particularly successful at
exploiting a niche and securing longer-term funding may be criticized or
shunned by less well-endowed groups. One of the most well-known environmental organizations in Bryansk is frequently cited by other activists as
an example of an organization that has built a very positive international
reputation and has won many grants but does not have many local projects and is not responding to local concerns.[68] Some groups have responded

---

65. Ogorodnikov interview.

66. Yuri Shirokov, author interview, ISAR-Siberia, Novosibirsk, December 2, 1999.

67. Pavel Vdovichenko, author interview, Radimichi, Novozybkov/Bryansk, April 26, 2000.

68. In fact, several activists noted that they have altruistically tried to "save" foreigners from
becoming involved with this organization.

to suspicions from within the movement about their income by being as open as possible. When confronted by rumors about their grant income, the leaders of Erika said, "We didn't hide the amount of the grants and widely broadcast our activities, building connections with the media and suggesting mutually productive cooperation with others."[69]

Professionalized environmental organizations that receive grants have been accused of opportunism by observers inside and outside the movement. Representatives from NGO resource centers acknowledge that there are some organizations that have been founded only to receive grant money and not to solve local problems, but they insist that there are very few organizations with this motivation. In fact, most donors believe that it is unlikely that social organizations are founded simply to obtain foreign funding. It is simply too difficult to register and to write effective grant applications, and a successful outcome is too uncertain, to encourage many opportunists. Most environmental leaders comment without prompting that they would never enter a grant competition just for the money since their reputation is too valuable and they know that foreign donors share information about organizations. Inevitably, however, a leader does have to take the organization's future development into account when applying for foreign funds, considering what kinds of technology, training, or partnerships can be justified under the project that also will assist the organization's future development. This is not so much opportunism as a type of strategic planning for the organization's maintenance and expansion. Most grants are given for a single project and for a limited period of time. Grants generally cannot be used for an organization's operating expenses, and therefore it is difficult for environmental groups to retain staff and continue their activity between grants. The leader of a very successful professionalized environmental organization based in Khabarovsk acknowledged that with each grant he applies for, he also considers what type of office equipment or technology might be most useful to the group and works them into the proposal.[70] Another activist, who asked not to be named, noted that sometimes groups need to present their work in a certain way so that it fits with donor demands, "but really they are only focusing 10 to 20 percent on what the grant is for and the rest on their own

69. Aleksei Chizhevskii, author interview, Erika, Bryansk, April 24, 2000.
70. Aleksandr Kulikov, author interview, Fund for Wildlife, Khabarovsk, November 24, 1999.

interests." He also said that all organizations use some grant money to pay staff members, even if that technically is not allowed under the terms of the grant, noting, "Without that, how could they survive?"[71] These practices represent activists' efforts to exert more control over the organization's resources and to maintain a more balanced and continuous organizational development than grant funding will normally allow.

Multiple Affiliations

Individual activists have to come up with ways of dealing with the scarcity of resources on a personal level as well. First, environmentalists often maintain their professional positions as scientists, government officials, or educators while simultaneously acting as the leader of a social organization. Second, and more notable, is the tendency of individual environmental activists to affiliate themselves with multiple green organizations, sometimes even occupying leadership roles in several groups simultaneously.[72] These organizational affiliations represent more than just a proliferation of names. In most cases, each of the multiple organizations has an official registration and is listed independently in NGO directories.[73] An activist affiliated with several organizations is even likely to have multiple business cards representing his or her different professional roles. In an interview setting, this can lead to humorous and confusing encounters in which several different business cards are offered to the interviewer and the interviewee responds differently to questions depending on which group he or she is representing at that time.

At first glance, it may appear that these multiple affiliations represent nothing more than the opportunistic behavior of impoverished

71. Anonymous environmental activist, author interview.

72. This practice of multiple affiliations is also noted by Kouzmina and Yanitsky (1999, 185). It is interesting that this adaptation takes the form of multiple organizational affiliations rather than a decision to operate as an independent activist as in green movements in other parts of the world (see, for example, Diani [1995] on Italian environmentalists). In Russia, however, organizations seem to have more legitimacy than individual activism. Funding incentives reinforce this pattern.

73. Note that for many activists, getting an organization listed in an NGO directory is often the first step to organizing a group, not the culmination of the organization process; it represents an effort to generate contacts and funding. As a result, Russian NGO directories, to a degree, represent a collection of unfulfilled ideas and unrealized organizations.

environmental activists. Certainly a greater number of "legal faces" may lead to more opportunities to seek resources and develop partnerships. Yet arguably the strategy of affiliating oneself with several different organizations is also a response to Russia's peculiar mobilizational environment, not just a desire for personal or professional aggrandizement. In particular, it is a logical reaction to donors' preference for funding new organizations and new projects rather than providing continuing support for one organization over several years.

Multiple affiliations also may represent activists' need to compromise temporarily on their personal environmental interests in order to stay active in the movement or, put another way, to cast a wide net to see what kinds of activism are sustainable under current conditions. For example, Natalia Knizhnikova, the leader of Green Attitude (an eco-spirituality group) and the Bryansk Ecological Union (a group that attempts to monitor government action on environmental issues), described her activism in a way that freely intermingled her role in the two organizations. Asked why she has two organizations, she replied, "Green Attitude represents my heart, but the Ecological Union, my reason."[74] In this case, the relative success of the latter organization, which was registered in 1999, has all but subsumed the older Green Attitude, an organization that remains unregistered and has few members. Knizhnikova acknowledged that Green Attitude showed less potential for future development so she committed herself to more pragmatic activism even though she did not enjoy the work as much.

A leader of an organization may have many potential project ideas and cast about for public or donor interest in one of them, dividing into several organizations if necessary. As mentioned above, the commercial organization Christmas in St. Petersburg funds two small environmental groups, Soyuz and the Federation for Ecological Education. A representative from Christmas acknowledged that the organizations overlap almost completely. Even activists in government-affiliated organizations are not immune to the tendency to develop multiple affiliations. The leader of VOOP-Vladimir started a new organization called the Center for Ecological Education from within the VOOP offices. Given the uncertainty of Russia's political and economic environment and the relative newness of

---

74. Natalia Knizhnikova, author interview, Green Attitude and the Bryansk Ecological Union, Bryansk, April 28, 2000.

the third sector overall, activists committed to pursuing some sort of environmental agenda, and to maintaining their own livelihood, face incentives to develop a broad approach in order to continue to work as green activists. Maintaining multiple affiliations seems to have assisted environmentalists in identifying viable strategies of organizational development and experimenting with new models without jeopardizing their livelihood or their activism.

Achieving Internal Goals: Organizational Sustainability

When scholars ask whether a social movement as a whole, or a particular social organization, is "effective" or "successful," their query often sidesteps the question of effective or successful at what specifically? Social organizations have numerous goals, including changing attitudes and policies in their issue area and making their political and economic environment more favorable to social activism. We have labeled these different aims of organizations substantive and transformational goals. In order to achieve these political and social goals, however, many organizations are first concerned with a more fundamental goal: the organization's maintenance and sustainability. When asked about the future, almost all of the Russian environmentalists interviewed discussed their desire to continue their work and expand their organization. They recited similar hopeful litanies for the future: more money, more connections, and more projects. Liudmila Komogortseva of the organization For Chemical Safety, is typical in summarizing her goals as the leader of the organization: "It's very simple: that the organization exists and is active" (as quoted in Khalii 1998, 11). Many professionalized activists also hope that their organization can expand beyond their region. In fact, the leader of only one group studied, the St. Petersburg Society for the Protection of Krestovskii Island, said that the organization would cease to exist if it achieved its goals. "When we win," Boris Kulakov declared, "we will be able to live a peaceful life."[75]

A follow-up survey carried out between June 2005 and July 2006 was designed to assess whether environmental groups had been able to survive

---

75. Boris Kulakov, author interview, Society for the Protection of Krestovskii Island, St. Petersburg, April 20, 1999.

and how their environmental activism had changed over time. The representatives of twenty-eight social organizations replied with information about the status and activities of their groups. In two cases, activists offered updates about another organization, increasing the number of organizations I was able to follow up on to thirty.[76] Responses came from all regions studied and included thirteen professionalized organizations, fourteen grassroots organizations, and one government affiliate.[77]

Recognizing that the responses are almost certainly biased in favor of those groups that continue to work actively, it is interesting to note that of thirty organizations covered, eight groups were no longer operating—seven of which were grassroots organizations—and two other groups acknowledged that they were not as active as they had been in the past. In cases in which the organization had ceased to exist, environmental concerns still occupied former leaders professionally. Four groups were on hiatus while their leaders pursued academic work related to environmental themes. Two former leaders continued to pursue environmental advocacy in other organizations when their groups had failed to sustain themselves, and one activist had taken a position in an international environmental group based in Norway after his internationally funded group had come to the end of its mandate. The final group, a student organization, had failed to persist after its members graduated. For those organizations operating at a lower level than in the past, one activist was pursuing environmental filmmaking, and in the other case, the original leader had died.

Of the remaining twenty organizations, half reported that they were working at the same level as in the past, and half said that they were more active than they had been previously. Professionalized groups appeared to be particularly resilient. Six organizations of the total thirty had survived the departure of their original leader. This fact somewhat mitigates concern about the "strong leader" model of environmental organizations. All of these organizations were professionalized groups, and in each case a member of the organization took over the leadership position. In two of

---

76. Given the changing political situation in Russia and the lack of face-to-face contact that allows for a full discussion of confidentiality options, respondents were guaranteed anonymity. Therefore no organization names are attached to material from the 2005–2006 survey.

77. The two organizations for which information was spontaneously given were grassroots organizations.

those six cases, the leader who had departed had started a new environmental organization that was operating successfully. The emergence of new organizations is another sign of the ongoing dynamism of the environmental movement.

In terms of resources, nearly all activists once again cited the lack of financing as one of the major obstacles to their work. Most environmental leaders continued to have second jobs in order to support themselves. A professionalized activist based in Bryansk noted that she and another staff member who had previously been employed full-time by their environmental organization had taken teaching positions in the local university to make ends meet.[78] Respondents' assessments of available resources for environmental activism were remarkably consistent across organizational types. The overwhelming consensus was that funding from foreign donors was much less available than in the past and that a number of funding institutions were no longer working in Russia. Activists used phrases such as "it has noticeably declined," "foreign funds no longer exist," and "they have closed in Russia" to describe the current status of foreign support. In spite of this, most professionalized organizations continued to cite foreign funding as their primary or only source of financing. In two cases, professionalized groups had been internationally recognized for their work and continued to receive a relatively steady flow of funds, and in the other cases groups appeared simply to manage with fewer resources than the past.

Government funding was also judged to be the same or less than in the past, although not by as large a margin. Two environmentalists who said that government resources for social organizations were more available in general qualified their remarks by stating that most of those funds are not directed toward environmental groups. Several respondents noted the loss of city and regional Ecology Funds as damaging for green organizations. A Vladivostok environmentalist stated that ecological fines were still collected in the region, but the authorities were spending the money on other problems.[79] Indirect state support in the form of donated office space in community institutions continued to be available for many groups. A grassroots organization in Vladivostok had found space for its activities in

---

78. Environmental activist AA, July 14, 2005.
79. Environmental activist B, July 13, 2005.

a museum and was able to register on that basis,[80] while a number of other groups reported that they retained their borrowed premises. A Novosibirsk activist revealed the downside of relying on goodwill for office space, however, reporting that her organization had moved fifteen times in eighteen years of operation.[81]

Respondents were split down the middle about whether more funding was available from the public and private firms. An activist who argued that there was an increase in funds from these sources qualified his remarks by saying that the funds that did exist were very small and represented an "increase" only in the sense that nothing had been given in the past.[82] Activists noted that most commercial firms did not want to be associated with "democracy, human rights, or the environment,"[83] and they were "too dependent on exploiting natural resources."[84]

Overall, the survey indicated an increasingly challenging resource environment for activism. The effects of the tightening financial situation were evidenced by the closure of one-quarter of organizations responding to the survey. Somewhat unexpectedly, among the organizations surveyed, grassroots organizations were the hardest hit, while most professionalized organizations had found a way to survive, whether by operating with less funding, no longer paying salaries, joining transnational campaigns, or diversifying their activities—in some cases, beyond an environmental agenda. Grassroots organizations, on the other hand, appeared to be victims of one or more factors: their leaders' more part-time approach to their careers as activists; the dearth of political opportunities for effective collaboration with regional and municipal governments; or the public's continued skepticism about social organizations and their role in the public sphere.

Examining the three types of organizations that make up Russia's environmental movement highlights patterns of resource dependency. Environmental groups' different organizational forms are directly related to the fact that they responded differently to the incentives of the mobilizational

---

80. Environmental activist BB, July 22, 2005.
81. Environmental activist G, July 22, 2005.
82. Environmental activist D, November 30, 2005.
83. Environmental activist AA, July 14, 2005.
84. Environmental activist U, July 18, 2005.

field for social activism in post-Soviet Russia. Using their professional ties and past experiences, leaders seek resources in the networks where they are most comfortable and most likely to be successful—primarily in the transnational level, state, or societal arena. Over time, leaders' choices about how to acquire scarce resources creates dependencies within the movement that, in turn, set new constraints on how organizations develop. Professionalized organizations rely on funding from foreign donors, particularly given their lack of membership support and difficulty in charging fees for their services. External funding allows groups to gain access to a world of transnational ideas and partnerships and offers an alternative to Russia's inhospitable economic and political environment. However, these opportunities may widen the preexisting divisions between professionalized activists and other environmentalists. Grassroots organizations have achieved a measure of sustainability by relying on volunteer labor and sponsorship from larger organizations, but they are limited in the size and scope of their operations. Government affiliates have found a small but steady flow of resources from local authorities, but the size of this niche is limited due to the government's lack of interest in environmental issues. The loss of government support would be devastating for these organizations since they have failed to engage with private actors. Given the tenuous nature of each strategy, many activists have chosen to affiliate with multiple organizations in order to increase their chances for future success.

How environmental groups achieve the goal of organizational maintenance influences not only the type of organization they develop but how (and how well) they go about achieving their substantive and transformational goals as well. These three organizational types crystallize certain features of Russia's mobilizational field, demonstrating how activists have responded to shifting political and economic incentives of the post-Soviet period. Once established, these organizations shape varieties of activism and political behavior. Thus these organization types, and the strategies they employ, have profound implications not only for environmental organizations' ability to mobilize resources but also for their effectiveness in pursuing environmental protection and social and political transformation.

5

STRATEGIES FOR DEFENDING
RUSSIA'S ENVIRONMENT

A tiger-preservation organization in Vladivostok; a group studying the lingering effects of radioactivity from the Chernobyl nuclear accident in Bryansk Oblast; a neighborhood association cleaning a local pond in the historic city of Vladimir. What do these groups have in common? First, they all consider themselves to be environmental, or *ekologicheskie*, organizations. Their primary goal is to address Russia's environmental crisis. Second, they all face a political system generally dismissive, if not hostile, to their concerns. Third, they all seek a stable flow of resources that will allow them to continue their activism. Russia's state-dominated, institutionally unstable, and economic growth–oriented government has generated significant obstacles for the environmental movement. In response to these common challenges, however, organizations have formulated diverse strategies of environmental activism which are more apparent at the regional level than in Moscow. A close examination of Russia's environmental movement reveals variation in the goals and tactics of green organizations in the regions, variation related to different visions of what environmental activism means in contemporary Russia.

Grassroots organizations focus on environmental education and local green issues. Professionalized groups address issues of national and international significance. Government affiliates help the state fulfill its environmental protection commitments. As we have seen, acting under conditions of resource scarcity and limited political opportunities, environmental leaders use their beliefs and experiences from the Soviet period to make choices about their organizations and allies, choices that have implications for their ability to achieve their environmental goals.

This chapter examines the range of green activism at the regional level. First, the specific projects and activities pursued and the tactics used by grassroots, professionalized, and government-affiliate organizations are described. The chapter then demonstrates that the different types of environmental activism engaged in by these groups are influenced by how leaders respond to their Soviet experience and new incentives in Russia's mobilizational field. Next, it considers elements of regional political environment that limit the effectiveness of environmental organizations. Finally, the chapter addresses the implications of these trends in activism and organizational form for the movement's effectiveness at environmental protection.

Strategies of Environmental Activism: The Three Organizational Types

Environmental movements are by nature diverse and heterogeneous coalitions. In part, this is because "environmentalism" is a big tent, encompassing questions of preservation, recreation, human health, sustainable growth, and ethical behavior. The Russian green movement is typical in that it is not unified by one overarching goal. In Russia, however, the general condition of heterogeneity within the movement is compounded by the severity and diversity of the ecological issues that environmentalists face, which, in turn, are partly due to the Soviet legacy of severe industrial and urban pollution alongside vast areas of protected or undeveloped lands now under threat of degradation. Russian green activism also is influenced by the starkly different discourses of environmentalism that emerged during the country's history, including the conservation-focused movement of the Soviet era, the prodemocracy mobilization of the perestroika years, and varied responses to the instability of the early post-Soviet period.

In view of the diverse environmental problems and many strategies for addressing them, it is useful to ask the questions: What is it that these groups actually do? Which issues have they chosen to tackle? What tactics do they employ to achieve their goals? In order to determine the content of contemporary Russian environmentalism, I asked activists to describe their goals, their main activities and projects, and how they go about their work.[1] What my interviews show is that the type of green activism groups engage in tends to correlate with strategies of organizational development. In other words, grassroots, professionalized, and government-affiliate organizations tend to articulate different visions of what environmentalism in contemporary Russia should be.

The activism pursued by grassroots, professionalized, and government-affiliate organizations varies in several ways: they address different issues, use different tactics, and choose to collaborate with different partners, whether local, international, or government (see Table 5.1). In terms of issues addressed, grassroots groups are concerned with environmental

TABLE 5.1. Varieties of Environmental Activism

	Grassroots	Professionalized	Government affiliates
Projects	• Environmental education and teacher support • Local environmental issues • Eco-spirituality	• Biodiversity conservation • NGO support • Sustainable development	• Environmental enforcement • Biodiversity conservation • Environmental education • Green politics
Tactics	• Contact with individuals • Disseminate information • Lobby the government	• Lobby the government • Disseminate information • Scientific research and monitoring • Cooperate on international projects • Publishing	• Use bureaucratic channels • Scientific research and monitoring • Lobby the government • Contact with individuals
Partners	• Local educational and cultural institutions	• International donors and partners	• Government agencies and bureaucrats

1. Interviews were semistructured, and questions were open ended. Activists were allowed to list multiple activities from both the past and present.

education, local environmental issues, and eco-spirituality; professionalized groups work on conservation, sustainable development, and NGO support; and government affiliates try to enforce environmental laws, while also working on conservation, education, and green politics generally. Organizations differ tactically as well. While lobbying the government is a strategy of all three groups, it is most frequently undertaken by professionalized groups. Professionalized groups also tend to focus on scientific research and monitoring to provide evidence of environmental harm; grassroots groups rely on contact with individuals to change attitudes, and government affiliates work through bureaucratic channels.[2] Finally, the partners with whom environmentalists collaborate also vary: grassroots organizations work with local community members in educational and cultural institutions; professionalized organizations frequently cooperate with international partners; and government affiliates work closely with government agencies and bureaucrats. The following section presents brief descriptions of several groups in order to illustrate these tendencies. For each organizational type, these descriptions are followed by an analysis of the factors that shape environmental activism.

Grassroots Organizations

The activities of three grassroots environmental organizations illustrate the diverse projects undertaken by these groups and, at the same time, some of the goals and tactics that they have in common. These summaries also demonstrate that resource availability and leadership preferences shape strategies of activism.

In Defense of the Sea   The Vladivostok organization In Defense of the Sea started in 1996 in a local museum of marine ecology. According to Anna Gulbina, the leader of the organization, the group grew out of a series of summer classes on ecology and biology that proved very popular among local children.[3] The goals of the organization are "to widen the circle of children who receive environmental education and to inspire the attitude that

---

2. Professionalized groups are likely to employ a greater number of tactics to achieve these goals than the other two types of organizations—in fact, roughly twice as many as the average number of tactics used by grassroots groups.

3. Anna Gulbina, author interview, In Defense of the Sea, Vladivostok, November 16, 1999. See also Erastova 1999.

they are caretakers of the island [where the museum is located], so that they are not just unthinking tenants—'this is mine!'—but they understand that they are responsible for the island as caretakers." The museum supports the group by providing space for classes and other activities, and local biologists and naturalists have volunteered to lead courses. Gulbina said proudly, "It is all done on enthusiasm. These people come simply because they enjoy it."

Although it is not a registered social organization, In Defense of the Sea has applied for and received several small grants through the museum. A small grant from the Open Society Institute allowed them to mount an exhibition and play about marine ecology in local schools. After being invited to present the play in towns throughout the region the following year, they failed to win further grant support and were not able to continue the project. In Defense of the Sea also received a Peace Corps grant to put on a summer camp for disabled children from around Primorskii Krai.

Although the organization has a generally positive relationship with the local authorities and officials have attended many of their events, they have been frustrated in their efforts to have regulations against illegal tree cutting on the island and other environmental infractions enforced. They have written letters to the Committee on Ecology and local newspapers, with no result. Gulbina remarked: "They [the local authorities] are poor, and so they in fact do not help us.... They come to us with groups of people and boast about us, saying, How wonderful, we are such a good group, but nothing else." In Gulbina's view, the government offered them passive but not concrete support. Bit by bit, however, she believes that the authorities are coming to rely on the children as informal environmental monitors on the island; members of their group distribute information on rare plants and animals to tourists, warn visitors against damaging the local ecosystem, and generally try to raise awareness. Government officials turned to the organization as an informal consultant for several groups that wanted to set up camps on the island.

Kukushkin Pond   The Kukushkin Pond group of Vladimir was founded thanks to the energy and devotion of one local resident, Marina Ivanovna Aleshechkina.[4] In the mid-1990s, Aleshechkina worked for a furniture-making cooperative that occupied a previously abandoned apartment

---

4. Marina Aleshechkina, author interview, Kukushkin Pond, Vladimir, May 24, 2000. See also Kaliuzhnova 1998.

building on Kukushkin Pond, near the center of the historic city. The previous tenants had thrown their garbage and broken appliances into the pond, and the cooperative continued to use the area as a garbage dump. Inspired by an article about the environmental damage caused by polyurethane and other chemicals, Aleshechkina convinced her employers to "do something good" and change their waste disposal practices, but the business closed before they could follow through with their plans. Although Aleshechkina then retired, she decided that she "didn't want a quiet life.... I had a dream that that corner of Vladimir should be beautiful."

Aleshechkina researched the area and found that the pond had been a local recreation site since the 1850s. Gathering supporters from within the neighborhood, she wrote an open letter to the local administration and contacted officials about cleaning up and establishing a path around the pond. At first the group found favor with the raion (neighborhood) administration and was given a small office in a local government building. That changed, however, when the group found itself in disagreement with the owners of private garages near the pond that would have to be moved in order for the cleanup to begin. The garage owners also petitioned the government. According to Aleshechkina, after that, "no one [in the administration] listened to us. How sad that the administration listens only to one side!" She continued:

> And then we understood: while we don't have legal standing, no one is going to pay attention to us. And so we registered in February 1996. Inexperienced, naive, without support from anyone influential, we started our existence. We analyzed the reasons why the pond had died and we seriously studied the issue of waste. Who was guilty for the death of our pond? Everyone! The nearby banya [bathhouse] and hospital threw all their waste into the pond and nearby residents also used it for waste so the issue of everyday waste became the center of attention of our activities. (Kaliuzhnova 1998, 1)

The group started a project to change the public's attitude toward household waste. In 1997 they won an Open Society Institute competition for the best informational material produced by a social organization, but then they lost most of the award in the economic crash of August 1998. The bank subsequently threatened to close their account for lack of funds.

Aleshechkina expressed frustration with local politicians. "Garbage is the disgrace of our city and we think that if our deputies would act, as their Moscow colleagues have, to change all the local taxes so that they can gather and dispose of the waste, then the city would become cleaner and more beautiful" (Kaliuzhnova 1998, 1). Kukushkin Pond still pursues its original objective, although in my interview Aleshechkina related that the city architect has told them that "in their priorities, reviving the ponds in the city is tenth or twentieth because the city doesn't have any money." Members of the organization are prepared to clean up the pond "on enthusiasm"—asserting that "we understand that the government doesn't have any money and we are prepared to revitalize the pond and to bring together volunteers, apply for grants, and work for money ourselves." To continue, however, they need official permission. While they wait, they continue to carry out educational and informational campaigns about the proper disposal of household wastes, activities for which they have not received any more grant support.

Mir   The St. Petersburg eco-spirituality organization Mir (Peace) was founded in 1988 as part of an effort to restore religious buildings on the island of Valaam in Lake Ladoga, north of the city. Mir is made up of a loose group of approximately seventy-five acquaintances. The group refers to its members as "friends" of the organization, and also draws in many "guests" to its events. Mir's representative (the group has no leader as such since they attempt to avoid any hierarchy within the organization), Evgeniia Pender, noted that in the course of its history, the group has changed its form and adjusted its goals several times in order to meet the needs of its members.[5] Mir's environmental program developed in response to members' experience camping near their restoration sites and their spiritual response to the unique natural environment of the island. The organization's goal is to "establish a new principled relationship with nature that is not based on consumerism." Their activities include summer "eco-schools" that provide a natural-world retreat for city residents and conferences held by the group in a basement room in a St. Petersburg apartment building. Mir also encourages members to work on literary and musical tributes to the natural world. Through the individual experiences of the group's supporters, activists hope to slowly change the public's attitude toward nature

---

5. Pender interview.

and thereby resolve other pressing environmental problems. Pender commented, "We are not interested in utilitarian questions.... Any understanding of ecology has to be spiritual. The person himself or herself has to change."[6] Mir's survival is based entirely on the volunteer labor of its members and the materials that they contribute to the restoration sites and other projects. As the group's events have become more popular, Pender has suggested that they develop a network of smaller groups rather than expand Mir itself for fear of losing the benefits of close contact with a small like-minded community.

Issues and Tactics of Grassroots Organizations   Grassroots organizations' environmental activities are directly related to the interests and needs of local populations. By far the most common activity of Russian green organizations is conducting environmental education programs for children.[7] These programs appear in many forms: they may be part of a school curriculum or after-school program or be organized around summer camps and nature expeditions. For example, each summer the Radimichi organization of Bryansk Oblast hosts an environmental program for children called Novocamp and also leads children on expeditions along the Desna River to pick up litter and publicize environmental issues. The environmental education program "Near Voznesenskii Bridge" at a St. Petersburg House of Children's Creativity runs three different projects designed to raise children's environmental awareness, including "Our Canal" in which children monitor water quality in the neighborhood, "Clean City" in which they learn about consumption and waste, and "We Help Our Little Brothers," a program about stray animals. Some grassroots organizations also support environmental education by offering training seminars for teachers, publishing environmental teaching materials, or housing small libraries that are available to teachers. The Vladivostok organization *Krug* (Circle) gathers primary-school teachers throughout the Far East in

---

6. Ibid.

7. Representatives from NGO resource centers agree that environmental education is the most frequent activity of smaller green organizations throughout Russia. Representatives from the ISAR-Far East office confirm that the most common projects of environmental NGOs are environmental camps, holidays (*prazdniki*), expeditions, conferences, seminars, and children's circles. Many organizations also pass out environmental information to the government or the public (Marina Kazakova and Anton Semenov, author interviews, ISAR-FE, Vladivostok, November 1, 1999).

seminars to show them how to integrate information about the environment into their lesson plans.

While environmental-education programs occasionally are offered by professionalized organizations and government affiliates, grassroots organizations are the most likely to pursue this type of activity. Of the twenty-five environmental-education programs mentioned in interviews, seventeen of them were coordinated by grassroots groups as compared to five by professionalized organizations and three by government affiliates. More than half of all grassroots groups pursue environmental education in some form.

In addition to environmental-education programs, grassroots organizations also address other issues of local concern. Of the forty-two grassroots organizations represented in interviews, ten work to preserve local nature areas or bodies of water. For example, the Novosibirsk group Save the Ob! tries to raise public awareness about the water quality of the city's major river, and Novomir, also of Novosibirsk, helps apartment-building residents clean and refurbish their courtyards (*dvory*) by offering free seedlings and volunteer labor. Four grassroots organizations work on health issues, such as managing the lingering effects of the Chernobyl accident in Bryansk, and two groups shelter and advocate for stray-animal populations. Six grassroots organizations promote eco-spirituality (*ekologicheskaia dukhovnost'*) and environmental ethics based on religions such as Buddhism or the teachings of Russian artist and philosopher Nikolai Rerikh.[8] These groups are not organized around discrete environmental projects but instead work on raising environmental consciousness and preserving sacred lands such as Valaam and Altai. For example, Green Attitude (*Zelenyi Nastroi*) of Bryansk has created and distributed five nature films designed to promote meditation and relaxation and to encourage greater awareness of nature. A St. Petersburg–based group plants cedars wherever possible because they believe that the cedar is a sacred tree. A related phenomenon is the growth of eco-villages in Russia, small rural settlements where groups of people try to live in an environmentally sustainable fashion.[9]

---

8. Eco-spiritualists claim that there are many more groups of their type but that they tend not to be included in directories of environmental organizations and have few ties with other green groups (Kuliasova interview; Ivan Kuliasov, author interview, Center for the Development of Perception, St. Petersburg, April 13, 1999).

9. Leonid Sharashkin of the Moscow office of the World Wide Fund for Nature estimates that there are now four hundred communities operating as eco-villages in Russia (Johnson 2002).

In addition to sharing a focus on local issues, grassroots groups are tactically similar as well. What projects sponsored by grassroots organizations have in common is their largely apolitical nature and their determination to resolve local problems through practical, hands-on activities. Grassroots groups also display a remarkable similarity in their belief that contact with individuals and experiences in nature are key to raising environmental awareness and resolving environmental problems. More than two-thirds of grassroots organizations cited engagement with individual citizens as one of the primary means by which they work toward their goals. They attempt to change people's attitudes through information, education, and group activities. As the leader of the Bryansk educational program Ladushka noted, "By teaching [children] ecological culture and the love of nature, the result will be conservation and better health."[10]

Other tactics of grassroots groups include disseminating information about environmental problems to the local population and regional and municipal authorities (40 percent of these groups). Fewer groups (19 percent) lobby the local government. Some groups combine these tactics, as did the League to Save the Steppe of Novosibirsk, which gathered information on the precipitous decline of the steppe grasslands and sent it to the regional Committee on Ecology to promote new legislation to preserve the ecosystem.

Another common tactic is to reuse and reinvent Soviet-era traditions and infuse them with environmental content, such as educational olympiads, *subbotniki* (days of volunteer labor), or children's holidays and entertainments (*detskie prazdniki i spektakly*). The educational and cultural arenas offer an array of Soviet institutions and practices ripe for reinvention. The Novosibirsk organization AVES has revived the practice of educational olympiads, giving them an environmental twist. Svetlana Gizhitskaia, the leader of AVES, noted:

> In fact, our organization is strongly connected with past traditions. Why? Because in spite of the fact that it is commonly thought that Russia's non-profit sector started to develop during perestroika, this is actually not the case.... Those organizations that existed during Socialism—the Komsomol,

---

10. Vassilieva interview.

the Pioneers—even though they were unitary, even though 80 percent of them were, of course, ideological (and with that no one can disagree), all the same they were very good schools of social activism [*obshchestvennoi raboty*]....For example, take the subbotnik. Maybe it was established as a holiday for Lenin, but through it schoolchildren felt that they were responsible for their neighborhood—that it became clean as a result....You could put the accent not on what Lenin said, but simply on the fact that the neighborhood became clean.[11]

Gizhitskaia continued by adding, "Because we had this experience, we naturally used it. Thanks to that, we were able to determine what we would work on without any 'orders from above,' you could say." Other organizations, such as the Center for Ecological Initiatives in Novosibirsk, mimic the activities of the Pioneers, the Communist-era children's organization, replacing the older group's ideological content with environmentalism. Ivan Kuliasov of the Community for Spiritual Revival in St. Petersburg gave another example: "Even President Yeltsin wrote in his biography about how he himself plants potatoes. Most Russians plant potatoes."[12] The challenge is to connect a tradition—a practice that is already part of Russian society's "repertoire of contention," such as vegetable gardening—to broader environmental questions.

Many representatives of grassroots organizations take pains to emphasize that they are "not radicals" and "not extremists." These groups generally are content to have a neutral relationship with the government.[13] Political officials occasionally make appearances at children's events and educational contests to pass out awards, but otherwise they generally do not interact with organizations working on environmental education. Groups lobbying for the preservation of local sites may address the government more directly but in doing so try to ensure that their interactions are nonconfrontational and nonideological, based firmly on existing laws or the health and safety of the population.

---

11. Svetlana Gizhitskaia, author interview, AVES, Novosibirsk, December 6, 1999. During the Soviet period, a subbotnik was a Saturday of "voluntary" community labor. For more on this tradition, see Friedgut (1979, 277, 283–84).

12. Kuliasov interview.

13. Although some grassroots organizations are small green political parties, they generally do not compete for power and instead serve as political debating societies.

Professionalized Organizations

The brief histories of three professionalized groups illustrate common patterns of activism among these organizations. The first two cases, Green World and Phoenix, demonstrate the common tactics professionalized activists use to work toward their goals. The third organization, Erika, is characteristic of another fairly common phenomenon among professionalized organizations: the simultaneous pursuit of multiple goals and projects and a de facto role as a resource center for other social organizations. In each of these cases, foreign funding has also played a significant role in the group's development.

Green World   The organization Green World was founded in 1988 in the city of Sosnovii Bor near St. Petersburg. The group began when citizens successfully protested the local administration's plan to cut down the pine trees (*sosny*) that give the city its name.[14] After this victory, Green World began to undertake projects that included monitoring water quality and radioactivity levels in the region. Almost immediately Green World came into conflict with the local authorities who did not want the group to publish a map of polluted areas, calling the information "closed" to the public. These officials refused to legally register the group, a status they only achieved in 1997 when Green World registered at the regional level. In spite of its lack of legal registration, the group was able to receive a number of small grants in its early years. The leader of the group, Oleg Bodrov, remembered their first grant of $1,300 from the Washington, DC–based donor ISAR in 1994, remarking, "It gave our group a chance. We felt that we were needed. Before that we only had endless conflicts, everyone reacted to us as an enemy.... [Receiving this grant] was perhaps one of the most important events in the life of our organization."[15]

Green World's most well-known and controversial activity is monitoring the Leningrad Atomic Energy Station (LAES), located in Sosnovii Bor. Key to their role as watchdog of the LAES has been one member of the group, Sergei Kharitonov. A longtime member of Green World, Kharitonov was an employee in charge of storing spent fuel at the LAES. In

---

14. Bodrov interview.
15. Ibid.

1995, Kharitonov and Green World protested that the LAES was trying to store more waste than it was designed to hold, and in 1996 the group publicized Kharitonov's photographs of the facility's cracked concrete walls. Kharitonov was fired in 1997 after publishing an article critical of the station's safety procedures. He then sued the LAES for illegally firing him and was reinstated later that year but was restricted to the plant's locker room for the next two years (Badkhen 1999a). Kharitonov eventually applied for asylum in Finland because of his activities as a whistle-blower (Alimov 2005).

Green World's monitoring efforts have been supported by the Ministries of the Environment of Finland and Sweden, the U.S.-based Center for Safe Energy, the Open Society Institute, and Siemens. As Green World has become more successful and well known, its range of projects has also expanded; in 2000, for example, the group's activists undertook fourteen individual or joint projects. The group has become increasingly interested in the conservation of the Baltic Sea ecosystem as a whole and now looks upon all of its projects as regional in scope. Bodrov commented, "We need to look at the problem not only as residents of the South bank of the Finnish gulf, but as a big bioregion, the Baltic region. And it's important to form our policies in the area of atomic energy not at the local level, but in the framework of the Baltic bioregion."[16] As part of these efforts, Green World has pressed for an independent environmental evaluation of the construction of a port in nearby Ust-Luga. Green World is now one of the most well-known environmental organizations in Russia.

Phoenix   In 1994, the Washington, DC–based human-rights and environmental organization Global Survival Network (GSN) set up an investigative network to expose violations of laws designed to protect the Amur tiger in Russia. Assisted by funding from the World Wide Fund for Nature, GSN and the (former) Russian Ministry of Ecology organized Operation "Amba" in order to stop poaching and limit trade in endangered species. International donors paid the salaries of ten (and later twenty-two) rangers, mostly former military men, who were trained in antipoaching techniques and given vehicles and technology to support their work. The

---

16. Ibid.

action was taken as an emergency measure to halt the precipitous decline in the tiger population. In 1998, GSN sponsored the creation of a Russian NGO called Phoenix in order to continue its tiger work.[17] Karin Elliot, a GSN representative based in Vladivostok, stated:

> Since all parties involved with Amba believed that the primary responsibility for funding the program was Russian, they launched Phoenix to function as a stopgap Russian fundraising mechanism for Amba and other biodiversity conservation organizations until Russian government funding is available.... The organizers believe that, as an indigenous organization, Phoenix will be able to more credibly solicit funds from international donors, the Russian government and the Russian business community as well as assume a leadership role in the Primorskii Krai tiger preservation effort. (Elliot 1998)

From this beginning, Phoenix became an independent Russian social organization and has significantly expanded its conservation work under the leadership of Sergei Berezniuk. Other projects include the creation of a rehabilitation center for bear cubs orphaned due to poaching and a program to reintroduce them to the wild; programs to preserve the Amur leopard and to address illegal logging; the creation of a wildlife education center near a nature preserve; information exchange with international conservation groups; and sponsorship of an annual celebration in Vladivostok to honor the tiger and educate the public. At this point, Phoenix's programs continue to be primarily funded by international donors. While Phoenix maintains cooperative relations with the government—and indeed their work depends on these ties—the Russian government has been unable to fund or take over the group's antipoaching efforts.

Erika   The Bryansk organization Erika was founded in 1993 by a group of individuals interested in environmental awareness and education. Its first two projects, Eco-School and an Information Service for Environmental Education, won grant support from the U.S. NGO ISAR. As one of Erika's coleaders, Aleksei Chizhevskii, recounted, "Almost all of the

---

17. Karin Elliot, author interview, Global Survival Network/Phoenix, Vladivostok, October 22, 1999. Information about the history of Phoenix also comes from personal communication with Sergei Berezniuk, July 13, 2005.

grant funding was spent on equipment: a computer, printer, fax-modem—with that our new life began!"[18] The group's leaders were somewhat surprised, however, when their next proposal to ISAR failed to win support. After attending a seminar on NGO development in Moscow, the group decided to turn its attention toward more "practical" work. Its next project, funded by the USAID Replication of Lessons Learned (ROLL) program, involved teaching citizens how to grow medicinal plants at home. Following that, both TACIS and the Eurasia Foundation funded Erika's efforts to create a library of original environmental films, and the Dutch organization Milieukontakt sponsored a campaign, coordinated by Erika, to improve water quality in the region. Through its projects, "Erika became known to a wide circle of social and government organizations." The group uses their past projects to facilitate work with some government officials "by showing them what the advantages are."[19]

Based on its own successful development and its legal and accounting experience, Erika received funding from ISAR and the Open Society Institute to offer NGO seminars in Bryansk. As Chizhevskii recounted,

> To strengthen our influence in the region we left the realm of purely environmental problems.... It was necessary to create [an NGO resource] center because of the crisis situation of the third sector in the oblast. Many registered organizations from 1991 (there were about 200—very few compared with other regions) had ceased to exist or didn't work actively. The majority had a very weak material base, did not have financial resources, and did not know how to attract them. They were isolated from each other and did not know where to go for help (Chizhevskii 1998).

Erika hosted seminars, organized an exhibition entitled "Philanthropy in Bryansk: Yesterday and Today," and began to advise other social organizations in finding grants. By 2000, the organization had ten paid employees and twenty-nine active members, mostly professors, graduate students, and cultural workers. Ultimately, the leaders of Erika believe that they have developed a very flexible organization that can oversee a wide variety of projects. While their basic interest is still in raising environmental

---

18. Chizhevskii interview. See also Chizhevskii 1998.
19. Ibid.

awareness, they "are able to work in all areas, especially in anything to do with information and technology" and offer "support services" for a variety of international projects.[20]

Issues and Tactics of Professionalized Organizations   In contrast to grassroots groups, professionalized organizations are more likely to tackle issues that are of regional, national, or international significance, and to engage higher-level government officials and transnational actors to achieve their goals. Professionalized organizations most frequently work on conservation issues, such as the preservation of the Siberian tiger, the European bison, or the Baltic Sea ecosystem. Research and conservation activities occupy one-third of the thirty-three professionalized organizations surveyed. For example, scientists from Ekolog of Vladivostok monitor the influence of the region's burgeoning oil industry on marine species. Another one-third of professionalized groups offer expertise, information, and support to smaller environmental (and other social) organizations, in effect acting as NGO resource centers. These groups, including ISAR-FE of Vladivostok, offer seminars and training for activists on issues such as public relations and fund-raising.[21] Seven professionalized groups work on issues of sustainable development and natural-resource use, including the TACIS Environmental Program in St. Petersburg that sponsored a local version of the international Global Action Program. Seven other organizations offer programs to support environmental education, including the Vladivostok Resource Information Center's environmental-education conferences and library for teachers. Environmentalists from professionalized groups tend to think that working on broader issues rather than individual local problems is a more efficient way to address Russia's environmental degradation. As Sergei Pashchenko argued, "Why study a certain parking lot when if you say, Let's move this parking lot to a neighboring piece of land, the residents of that area will start complaining as well."[22]

A key difference between grassroots and professionalized groups is that the latter embrace a broader range of tactics to achieve their goals.

---

20. Ibid.

21. In another example, ISAR-Siberia publishes a bulletin called *Medvezhii Ugol* (Bear's Den), which offers a section entitled "Gde procit' den'gi" ("Where to ask for money") and another section entitled "Kak procit' den'gi" ("How to ask for money").

22. Pashchenko interview.

A single organization may use research, publications, petitions, lobbying, and international partnership in support of their objectives. Almost half of professionalized organizations lobby the government and disseminate information about their environmental issues. For example, Zov Taigi (Call of the Taiga) of Vladivostok has used its environmental magazine to publicize regional environmental problems and to promote changes to the region's hunting regulations and other policies. The EkoDom organization of Novosibirsk researches energy-efficient housing, trains graduate students in environmentally sustainable design, and goes to government hearings to lobby political officials, "to remind them what they haven't done so that they don't forget."[23] One-third of professionalized groups monitor the government and industry, including the Siberian Scholars for Global Responsibility of Novosibirsk, which has publicized the government's failure to clean up areas contaminated by radioactive waste around the city. Other common tactics of professionalized groups include carrying out scientific research for international projects and offering seminars for government officials and specialists.

One tactic that Russian environmental groups at the regional level—professionalized and others—have not used frequently is public protest. With few exceptions, Russian environmentalists have been less likely to engage in protests or other kinds of disruptive action to draw attention to environmental concerns than greens in other countries. Greenpeace Russia is one exception as it has hosted relatively frequent protests in Moscow. Based on Russian and international news reports, however, these protests rarely attract more than twenty to twenty-five people. Activists are often briefly detained and asked to pay small fines for disturbing the peace after these events.[24] Under Putin, the government has been hostile to public protest and radical actions, often refusing permission for demonstrations even when requests complied with the law. In addition, donors tend not to fund controversial actions. These disincentives for engaging in protest leave the Russian environmental movement with a very small radical wing. For

---

23. Ogorodnikov interview.

24. In the regions, environmental protests are even rarer and less accepted by government officials. In Orel, environmentalists were forbidden to picket at the regional administration against plans to build a nuclear refinery because the administration regarded the protests as "inappropriate." Environmentalists went ahead with the event but complained, "Two hours of walking in gas masks or disguised as fish and birds suffering from pollution drew no fitting response from the administration officials, who ignored our actions" (Interfax 2002a).

Western movements, radical environmentalists have constituted a threat that has occasionally led governments to negotiate with more moderate greens. Recently, Russian environmental groups have appeared somewhat more willing to engage in protest, including demonstrations against an oil pipeline planned for construction near Lake Baikal and protests against the development of protected lands for the 2014 Olympic Games in Sochi.

Government Affiliates

Among government-affiliate organizations included in this study are branches of the All-Russian Society for Nature Protection (*Vse-Rossiskoe Obshchestvo Okhrany Prirody*), or VOOP. These groups are the legacy organizations of the similarly named All-Soviet Societies that served as state-sanctioned nature-conservation organs during the Soviet era.[25] Like other government affiliates, the organizations continue the practice of cooperating with the state administration and are loyal supporters of state policy. Two other organizations described here, the Vladimir Society of Hunters and Fishers and St. Petersburg's Association Clean City, also work closely with the authorities on issues of licensing and waste disposal.

VOOP-Novosibirsk   The Novosibirsk chapter of the All-Russian Society for Nature Protection was founded in 1946. The group's leaders throughout its history were traditionally the first deputy chairmen of the oblast soviet. According to the group's leader, Ilias Gadzhiev, "all of this has now been transferred into the hands of society," and the group is now officially registered as a social organization.[26] The Novosibirsk VOOP engages in a number of projects, each with the goal of helping the State Committee on Ecology by providing "social control" or oversight of the enforcement of environmental regulations. For example, they are frequently called upon

---

25. The fact that an organization survived the Soviet era intact, however, does not necessarily mean that it will be a government affiliate. For example, the St. Petersburg VOOP, led by Vladimir Gushchin, has become more independent. The group focuses on conservation but also works with international organizations and newer student groups and does not rely exclusively on government funding. Other Soviet-legacy organizations that are not government affiliates include the St. Petersburg Society of Naturalists and many university-based Druzhina student groups throughout Russia.

26. Gadzhiev interview.

by the government to conduct ecological assessments (*ekspertizy*) of commercial enterprises around the region, and they produce an "environmental passport" for each firm. Although their work is "officially to confirm activity by the Committee [on Ecology]," occasionally an enterprise will resist VOOP's efforts to carry out its research. In that situation, "an official from the Committee on Ecology will have to go there" to enforce the rules, according to Gadzhiev. The Novosibirsk VOOP also completes similar assessments for the oblast nature preserves and occasionally shepherds new territories through the process of achieving protected status. Once complete, the group's environmental assessments are officially confirmed by the regional administration. In order to facilitate VOOP's work, the regional administration also provides the group with office space, a small staff, and funding from the regional Ecology Fund and other state funds for equipment. The rest of their activities depend on volunteer labor.

Vladimir Society of Hunters and Fishers   The Vladimir Society of Hunters and Fishers is the only social organization in Vladimir Oblast permitted by the government to issue official sporting licenses. Thus the group claims approximately twenty-thousand members, all licensees. A portion of the license fees paid by these members goes to support the society. The group's representative and huntsman, Vyacheslav Shitov, lives on and maintains land designated as a natural monument on Voikhra Lake, near Vladimir.[27] He is also responsible for a second state property called Davidovskaia. His responsibilities are to serve as a resource for the society's members, although he does not have much contact with them except to give them official permission to use the land and to "strictly monitor the populations of animals and fish and work against poachers." In Shitov's opinion, "hunters and fishers are the biggest supporters of nature because they understand nature the most." In recent years, however, Shitov unofficially has expanded the work of the society to bring schoolchildren to the property for environmental education and has allowed a group of nudists to set up a summer camp near the lake. Shitov expresses some concern that the government will choose to sell the second property, which lacks official preserved status, in order to raise money, a prospect that Shitov would oppose.

---

27. Vyacheslav Shitov, author interview, Vladimir Society of Hunters and Fishers, Voikhra Lake, Vladimir Oblast, May 23, 2000.

Association Clean City   Association Clean City of St. Petersburg was founded in 1997 to coordinate the efforts of predominantly state-owned factories to dispose of garbage and reprocess wastes in the city—in other words, "to manage and mitigate wastes," according to the group's leader Aleksei Gurnev.[28] The founding idea behind the organization is that it is easier to lessen damage from industrial pollution through cooperative agreements with firms rather than through a punitive system of fines and regulations. As another of the group's representatives, Vladimir Gorokhov, explained, "We in part represent industry, industrialists share our views, but we exist in order to serve as a buffer, to work to build a single point of view [between industry and the government]."[29] The association's commercial members include factories collectively responsible for 95 percent of the volume of waste in the city. These members also finance the association. Ultimately, Gorokhov said that the association must "rely on the professionalism and experience of their members to change the way waste is handled." To achieve these goals, the association works closely with the St. Petersburg Committee on Ecology, still known as Lenkomekologiia, and a state academic institute, the Center for Ecological Safety.

Issues and Tactics of Government-Affiliate Organizations   In contrast to grassroots and professionalized organizations, government affiliates tend to cooperate closely with local and regional authorities. Six out of nine government-affiliated organizations stated that one of their primary goals was to assist the government in enforcing environmental regulations or to help the government fulfill its environmental-protection goals. As Vladimir Shemetov of St. Petersburg Movement KEDR and KEDR Party noted, the mission of these groups is to "engage in constructive dialogue with the local authorities" on environmental issues.[30] Galina Esiakova of Vladimir VOOP said that her group is "the only serious nature-protection organization, along with the government" in the region.[31]

28. Aleksei Gurnev, author interview, Association Clean City, St. Petersburg, April 16, 1999.
29. Vladimir Gorokhov, author interview, Association Clean City, St. Petersburg, April 16, 1999.
30. Vladimir Shemetov, author interview, KEDR Party and KEDR Movement, St. Petersburg, April 22, 1999.
31. Esiakova interview.

In conjunction with the goal of assisting the authorities, three government affiliates focus specifically on conservation. Projects undertaken by government affiliates include evaluating the environmental significance of nature preserves, working with industrial enterprises to meet current environmental standards, and publishing a newspaper highlighting the local government's ecology-related projects. Three government affiliates have become involved in the increasingly popular activity of environmental-education programs for children. Two government affiliates interviewed were green political parties who campaigned on platforms supportive of the government and fielded candidates drawn from the state bureaucracy.

Firmly ensconced in government networks, government-affiliate organizations most frequently try to achieve their goals by using existing bureaucratic channels and exerting influence on the bureaucrats themselves. Some members of government-affiliate organizations also engage in scientific research of rare and endangered plant and animal species. Finally, government affiliates occasionally reach out to the public through educational campaigns, often based in schools.

Expanding Activism over Time

Based on my 2005–2006 follow-up survey, environmental organizations were generally engaged in pursuing the same or similar environmental goals as in the past, although many had added new projects. Environmental education continued to be the most popular activity. A grassroots activist based in St. Petersburg noted that environmental and outdoor education have been embraced "as a way to save their small schools from extinction, a way to give the schools a new profile which will make them attractive to parents."[32] Five groups had begun working on projects related to sustainable development, and several groups have turned their attention to health issues. Environmental activists have undertaken new activities such as encouraging recycling among industries, setting up a "green hotline," planting trees in urban areas, promoting organic farming, and making environmental films. Other groups have diversified their activities beyond strictly environmental issues. New initiatives by green organizations that

---

32. Environmental activist R, November 7, 2005.

were only indirectly or not at all related to the environment included creating a tourist club and computer clubs for young people, organizing a business venture to provide expertise on cultivating seafood products, developing programs to combat violence against women, and designing a distance-learning program.

Those groups that had found a way to interact productively with state institutions and actors noted the benefits of pragmatic cooperation on persistent community problems at the regional or municipal level. For example, a grassroots group in St. Petersburg has been able to cooperate productively with the local government—and even won a government award—by joining their environmental goals with antipoverty work and offering outdoor education to impoverished children. At the same time, however, several activists noted that there is "no legislative base" that allows the authorities to officially contract with social organizations in order to ameliorate broader social problems. A Bryansk activist suggested, "I am sure that the city and regional authorities would work actively [with social organizations] if only they had the necessary federal legislative foundation."[33]

Professionalized activists continue to experience difficult relations with the state related both to state weakness and hostility from the authorities. Professionalized activists frequently cited the lack of relevant legislation or weak law enforcement—what one environmentalist called "the ancient disease of Russia"[34]—as an obstacle to their work. Several activists noted instances of municipal governments violating their own regulations as they engage in construction and work on infrastructure. An environmentalist working on forestry and wildlife issues complained that the legislation in those sectors has been changing frequently. An environmentalist in the Far East suggested that the federal authorities did not understand the local situation in the region or, as another environmentalist commented, "Moscow resolves all questions in its own interests."[35] A representative from a group that is no longer operating summed up her account by saying, "There are no environmental policies in the government and no normal government financing [for the environment]."[36]

---

33. Environmental activist L, January 5, 2006.
34. Environmental activist Y, January 7, 2006.
35. Environmental activist D, November 30, 2005.
36. Environmental activist H, July 12, 2005.

A growing trend among Russia's professionalized environmental organizations, according to scholarship and fieldwork in Russia's regions, is participation in international environmental campaigns aimed at Russian state or commercial actors. Environmental organizations vigorously campaigned for Russia's ratification of the Kyoto Protocol (Henry and Sundstrom 2007) and have played a significant role in the effort to press Russian forestry firms to adopt international certification standards for sustainable forestry (Tysiachniouk 2006; Kotilainen et al. 2008). Environmentalists surveyed, all from professionalized organizations, continued to cooperate with Scandinavian partners on antinuclear activities, participate in international efforts to protect the Siberian tiger, and provide research on regional biodiversity to international organizations. A Vladivostok activist argued that his personal knowledge of local actors has been invaluable in understanding the obstacles to international sustainable forestry campaigns in Russia.[37] This strategy of international cooperation appears most successful when an organization is well established in the field prior to joining a transnational campaign and has credibility among local actors. Russian activists seem to have less success when trying to initiate campaigns. A Bryansk activist who reached out repeatedly to international organizations' offices in Moscow and abroad, asking them to condemn President Putin's veto of Russia's first law against animal cruelty, received no response. In her opinion, international activists, even those working in Russia, are too busy "defending Greenland whales and African elephants" to worry about animal endangerment occurring in Russia's regions.[38]

Strategies of Activism: Legacies and New Incentives

If the slogan of the environmental movement is to "think globally, act locally," it appears that in Russia there is a division of labor among environmental organizations; professionalized groups focus on the first half of this mandate as they address issues of transnational significance, often supported by foreign funding, while grassroots and government affiliates

---

37. Anatoly Lebedev, author interview, Bureau of Regional Outreach Campaigns (BROC), Primorskii Krai, October 2007.
38. Environmental activist L, January 5, 2006.

gravitate toward the second half of the slogan, with grassroots groups working with small groups of citizens on community problems and government affiliates collaborating with bureaucrats on state environmental policies. These activists express different ideas of what it means to be an environmentalist and how to conduct social activism in post-Soviet Russia.

Environmentalists navigate Russia's field for social mobilization using their beliefs and past experiences. These are what influence their decisions about which activities, resources, and allies it makes sense to pursue. Activists intentionally seek those supporters who adopt a like-minded approach toward environmentalism. Ultimately, the nature of the organization's primary resource provider, not just the amount of resources, influences varieties of environmental activism as activists try to balance their own interests with the need to accommodate the interests of critical supporters. Early choices by environmentalists about which issues to address and with whom to cooperate reinforce these tendencies, leading to the emergence of different types of activism. All environmental grievances are not created equal, however. Some environmental issues are more likely to attract foreign funding, while others are more likely to be supported by the state.

The following sections consider these varying definitions of environmentalism, how resource dependencies develop and reinforce these different visions of the movements, and how activists adjust their strategies to adapt to a challenging resource environment.

What "Environmentalism" Means in Post-Soviet Russia

Russia's environmental movement has long combined what seem to be contradictory strains of thought. In particular, there is a tension between the romantic vision of the natural world associated with various back-to-the-land movements that started during the tsarist period and the more rationalist, technology-oriented approach that dominated in the Soviet era. Other tendencies within Russian environmental thought encompass different justifications for environmental concern: the environment's influence on local cultures, its role in economic development, its contribution to Russia's national identity, or its ability to transcend national boundaries and serve as a basis for internationalism. During perestroika, environmental mobilization was seen variously as a means of reforming the Communist regime, retrieving Russian sovereignty from the Soviet Union, or overthrowing Soviet power and installing a new democratic government. In the current period, professionalized organizations tend to use frames and rhetoric borrowed from the transnational environmental movement—for example, the language of biodiversity and sustainable development—while government affiliates and grassroots organizations are more likely to call upon Soviet, tsarist, or religious ideas about the environment—ideas as diverse as the "rationalization" of natural-resource use or a "noosphere" linking the biological and spiritual worlds.

Activists' interpretation of environmentalism is filtered through their past professional affiliations, which also shape the range of "acceptable" allies and tactics. The teachers, scientists, and bureaucrats who typify the leadership of grassroots, professionalized, and government affiliate organizations respectively emphasize different elements of environmentalism. Grassroots leaders focus on "human ecology" and community development, professionalized organizations hew more closely to the original scientific meaning of the term *ekologiia* and are concerned with macrolevel goals such as sustainable development, and government affiliates prefer to focus on traditional ideas of conservation and rational resource use.

Grassroots Leaders   For the educators, students, and others who lead grassroots organizations, environmentalism offers a means of reforming the school curricula and revitalizing community networks. To achieve these goals, grassroots leaders often reuse traditions from the Soviet period to spread environmental ideas, drawing members of the general public into familiar events or familiar settings, such as local museums and schools. Svetlana Gizhitskaia, a leader of AVES, an environmental-education organization in Novosibirsk that runs ecology olympiads around the region, pointed out that these traditions attract the support of local residents and local officials. Gizhitskaia commented on her group's success at convincing the local administration to sponsor some of their educational events:

> [Local officials'] support is connected to our traditions. You see, the city committee always sponsored student olympiads. It all started from that.... If we hadn't had that tradition [of sponsorship], it's not clear what would have happened to our olympiads.[39]

---

39. Gizhitskaia interview.

Other leaders, recalling the Soviet tradition of subbotniki, or voluntary weekend labor, were likely to express the opinion that achieving environmental goals is just a matter convincing community members to work together in order to improve their quality of life.

Many grassroots activists articulated ideas that are a continuation of the romantic strain in Russian environmentalism, emphasizing nature's ability to transform human consciousness. Ivan Kuliasov, a St. Petersburg activist, said, "By changing a person's orientation toward the value of the environment, we can change the way they live, the way they feel about themselves."[40] Grassroots leaders' focus on local issues and individual transformation has been less likely to attract either transnational or government attention, but they create opportunities for participation in small community groups in a way that other organizations do not.

Professionalized Leaders   With backgrounds in higher education, most professionalized environmental leaders embrace a scientific approach toward the environment, using their familiarity with scientific principles and language to foster international partnerships. Professionalized leaders generally believe that those with the proper training "know what is best for the environment" and should play a dominant role in environmental protection. These scientists and academics also tend to have a pragmatic approach to the issues they address and to the form their organizations take, first surveying available political and economic opportunities. Vladimir Aramilev of the Institute for Sustainable Natural Resource Use in Vladivostok recounted the history of his group:

> Before [registering] we had a meeting. We engaged in a discussion with our colleagues and at that time came to understand that a social organization was needed…that there was an "ecological niche" in Primorskii Krai that was not occupied…. To put it briefly, this niche was for projects on the conservation of rare animals, the use of nontimber forest products, the use of biological resources on the principles of sustainability.[41]

Aramilev and his colleagues then built their organization based on this assessment. Engaged in research projects to develop new approaches to

---

40. Kuliasov interview.
41. Aramilev interview.

nature protection and seeking transnational support, professionalized environmentalists are less likely to look to the local community or the Russian government for support, but instead focus on like-minded partners, nationally and internationally. There is often a disconnect between professionalized organizations and the local population. For example, a WWF-Vladivostok report on foreign assistance for environmental issues demonstrated that most foreign funding in the region goes to environmental education and protection of rare species, while public surveys of Russians in the Far East showed that residents most desired money for fire prevention, ecotourism, and traditional resource use—the three least funded items.[42]

Government-Affiliate Leaders   Most leaders of government-affiliate organizations believe that the government has identified an appropriate balance between environmental protection and economic growth. In the opinion of Ilias Gadzhiev, the leader of Novosibirsk's All-Russian Society for Nature Protection (VOOP), social organizations no longer need to oppose the state; consequently there has been a natural reduction in the level of environmental mobilization in Russia. Gadzhiev commented, "The environmental movement has lessened in scope and intensity [since the perestroika era] because the government established committees to deal with those questions."[43] The leaders of government affiliates claim that the current Russian government can be relied upon to act in the interests of the public without the need for criticism from societal groups. They eschew foreign funding because they see the need for uniquely Russian solutions to Russian problems. Naturally, with their limited range of issues to address and government-friendly rhetoric, government support has gravitated toward government-affiliate organizations.

---

42. "Analiz finansovoi bazy prirodookhrannykh initsiativ, sushchestvuiushchikh v ekoregione," (draft given to the author by Yulia Fomenko, WWF-Vladivostok, November 1999). While there appears to be passive support for tiger conservation, a vocal minority is opposed to the programs owing to the facts that small villages compete with the tiger for wild game and that tigers occasionally kill local residents. Vocal advocates of "control" of the tiger population have lobbied government officials, and more importantly local citizens, while professionalized groups have pursued research and monitoring and largely failed to build ties to area residents. Only belatedly, several years after the tiger-protection programs began, did greens start to reach out to the public with tiger celebrations and education programs.

43. Gadzhiev interview.

Dependencies and Activism: Domestic
and Transnational Resources

The need to find financial support shapes the choices leaders make about
the type of activism their groups engage in, directing them toward some
issues and away from others. The most attractive funding incentives are
those that reinforce environmental leaders' own vision of what environmental activism in Russia should be. Thus, the three distinct strategies of
pursuing environmental activism characterized by grassroots, professionalized, and government-affiliate organizations are linked to leaders' ongoing efforts to align their environmental concerns with those of key resource
providers. Environmental activists are not motivated only by maintaining
a flow of resources to their organizations; most activists work long hours
for little or no compensation. Environmentalists are in subtle yet real ways
limited in their issues and tactics by their dependence on different resource
providers, however. Dependency is a risk for social activists worldwide but
is particularly likely to occur where social actors are severely impoverished
relative to state actors and transnational resources are more readily available than domestic resources.

Government affiliates depend on state resources. Grassroots organizations primarily rely on local resources. The constraints generated by these
dependencies are clearest in the case of government-affiliated organizations that work only on issues that have been clearly sanctioned by the local
or regional administration. While they may occasionally come into conflict
with state-owned commercial firms or agricultural operations, government affiliates rely on the imprimatur of the official environmental-protection agencies to justify and carry out their work. The relationship between
government affiliates and the authorities is so close that interviews with activists did not reveal any cases in which a government affiliate had come
into conflict with local or regional officials.

Grassroots organizations face a somewhat different situation. Clearly
the motivation for their projects emerges from the concerns of the local
communities—whether those concerns have to do with the education and
well-being of children or the health, safety, and recreation of the public at
large. Maintaining their local focus is critical to maintaining the support of
local volunteers and educational and cultural institutions. Moving beyond
pragmatic local issues—for example, shifting their attention to broader,

more complex environmental issues or coming into conflict with the government by pursuing more politicized goals—risks estranging grassroots groups from key elements of their support: the active participation of small but committed social networks and the tolerance of the local authorities.

Professionalized organizations are largely dependent upon funding from non-Russian donors. Therefore, they find themselves operating in a different incentive structure. As Western activists have long known, the changing agendas of funding institutions are an inevitable feature of the fund-raising landscape. Over time, certain issues and tactics become increasingly prevalent among grant-funded organizations. These issues and tactics often overlap significantly with the interests of professionalized activists, but they also serve to reinforce the goals and tactics of the transnational environmental movement over purely local concerns. The changing incentive structure of foreign funding may encourage a shift in the priorities of Russian green groups that are attempting to survive in an unfavorable domestic political and economic milieu.

The priorities of foreign funders are oriented most commonly around global environmental issues such as conservation, biodiversity and the protection of endangered species, sustainable development and natural-resource use, global climate change, and nuclear energy.[44] Programs centered on the preservation of large mammals such as the Siberian tiger or the Amur leopard in the Russian Far East or unique natural environments such as Lake Baikal have been very popular within the transnational environmental movement. Certain funders are also interested in their own security and health issues, such as the Scandinavian governments' support for Green World's monitoring of the Leningrad Atomic Energy Station.

Environmentalists are aware that some issues are more likely to be funded than others. Artamonov of the St. Petersburg Society of Greenpeace Supporters explained the situation in a matter-of-fact way, "Of course, they [donors] don't pay for everything. They pay for those actions they are most interested in. Concretely—in the experience of our organization—I can

---

44. Liudmila Vikhrova said that in establishing its funding priorities, USAID tries to determine need in cooperation with Russian state agencies. USAID's first responsibility is to develop priorities with Russian government institutions because all USAID money is given as part of a bilateral agreement. Vikhrova noted that the U.S. government has its own priorities—for example, biodiversity and climate change are popular programs for Russia because they are issues that can only be addressed on a global scale (Vikhrova interview).

say that, without a doubt, the Finns are very interested in the conservation
of forests on the Karelian peninsula. They want to be able to come here for
recreation."[45] Bodrov of Green World also offered a measured evaluation
of the influence of donor funding:

> Sponsors support only those projects which they think are necessary. An or-
> ganization may have many projects, but only those [projects] which people
> from abroad understand to be the most important will be supported. In that
> sense, there is an influence [on our projects], but at the same time I would
> say that there is no real pressure that I feel.[46]

Pavel Vdovichenko of Radimichi recognized, "They [our foreign part-
ners] don't always agree with me, or I with them....We often have different views of what is needed."[47] Other greens whose concerns have not
been funded by grants expressed greater frustration. Lev Kolomyts, acting leader of Ekologos of Vladivostok, complained, "There is no money
for some issues. No one works on urban ecology. You can't get any money
for working on industrial centers. People know that the cities are dirty,
but what can they do? We need a very big project on this....We need to
address, not just monitor, pollution."[48] The focus of grant competitions
changes frequently, leading environmentalists to try to read donor preferences before writing their applications. Social organizations must try to
adapt to these changes in order to ensure their own success and survival.
Dale Miquelle, an American who represented the Hornocker Institute in
the late 1990s and who has worked on conservation in the Russian Far East
for many years, acknowledged the situation:

> It's true that the tiger is a very charismatic large cat and it grabs the atten-
> tion of foreign donors. In general, this is useful because many other species
> and ecosystems can be protected by tiger-focused programs. However, some
> high biodiversity areas that should be conserved don't overlap with tiger
> habitat, so the goals don't always match. For example, tigers do quite well in

45. Dmitrii Artamonov, author interview, St. Petersburg Society of Greenpeace Supporters,
St. Petersburg, April 27, 1999.

46. Bodrov interview.

47. Vdovichenko interview.

48. Lev Kolomyts, author interview, Ekologos, Vladivostok, November 12, 1999.

areas that have been logged, while other species are decimated. Regardless, money for the tiger is a fact. The trick is to try to merge different conservation goals, to strategically use the tiger as an umbrella species for protecting other things. It's just a fact of life.[49]

Opportunities for foreign funding also influence grassroots environmental organizations that engage in occasional grant seeking. While grassroots groups are less likely to apply to grant programs overall and more likely to receive very small amounts of money, they also are trying to infer donors' preferences, often with less success than their professional counterparts. A representative from Bell of Chernobyl in Bryansk wondered why donors seem to have become less interested in Chernobyl: "Things are very difficult and we are considering ending some of our programs although we have worked on them for seven years. Funding organizations are less interested in Chernobyl now.... Maybe we should focus on antinuclear work or perhaps purely on health?"[50] Participation in grant competitions is a difficult issue for grassroots and government-affiliate organizations since reorienting their activism could potentially estrange them from their domestic supporters.[51]

In addition to determining the kinds of environmental grievances that are addressed in Russia—or those, at least, that will receive significant financial backing—foreign funding has influenced the development of professionalized environmental organizations in several other ways. These tendencies have included incentives for grant-seeking groups to pursue multiple projects simultaneously and incentives to "scale up" the organization's level of activism.[52]

---

49. Dale Miquelle, author interview, Hornocker Institute, Vladivostok, November 3, 1999.

50. Representative, author interview, Bell of Chernobyl, Bryansk, April 23, 2000.

51. Many ideas for small (*melkie*) projects never do find grant support. When asked for examples of the types of projects they are not able to fund, a representative of an international organization in Vladivostok offered up a proposal from a local schoolteacher that failed to find funding. In the application, a group of teachers and students from Gimnasiia No. 1 suggested carrying out an environmental inspection of their neighborhood. They would grow seedlings for trees and bushes, plant them around the community, and nurse them through their first years. The total cost of the project was $950, just fifty cents per plant, plus some extra money to support the cultivation of the seedlings. The cost was too high to attract local support, but too small for transnational donors.

52. Some of these phenomena have been noted in several works on NGOs and foreign assistance. For a critique of the "projectization" of civil society, see Sampson (1996), and for the pressure to scale up, see Fowler (1997).

Multiplying Projects   Grant competitions are designed almost exclusively for discrete environmental projects, often involving seminars, conferences, a fixed period of environmental monitoring, the preparation of a report, or a single public event. These project-based incentives make it difficult for professionalized organizations to institutionalize themselves. Oleg Bodrov acknowledged that international funding plays a role in the development of green organizations: "There is an influence thanks to the fact that *organizations* are not supported ... but separate *projects* are supported. If they would support an individual organization then they [people within the organization] would use the support as they consider necessary."[53]

Funders' orientation toward projects also affects the nature and number of activities a group undertakes. Many professionalized groups either engage in a series of projects on a wide variety of themes over the organization's history—in a sense following the interests of donors or hoping that breadth will lead to security—or undertake a number of projects simultaneously in order to ensure, as much as possible, a steady flow of resources to the group. These strategies are the rational response of activists who are trying to regularize resource flows to their organization and ensure their continuing ability to work on important environmental issues. The Bryansk group Erika typifies the first strategy—frequently changing the issues they address. When asked why they have worked on such a wide range of issues—from education to medicinal plants to water quality to film to NGO support and philanthropy research—one of Erika's leaders commented that they were "keeping [their] options open," but he also acknowledged that many of their projects end when funding ends because they are not sustainable by other means, even though the Erika remains interested in the ideas behind the projects.[54] This jack-of-all-trades approach has been relatively effective for the group. They are now well known in their region and among donors, having shown that they can propose clear projects and carry them out—or as their leader Chizhevskii put it, donors know the group "can adjust to the different needs of different projects."[55] For many environmentalists, a "have-registration-will-travel" approach

---

53. Bodrov interview.
54. Chizhevskii interview.
55. Other environmental organizations have pursued similar strategies, including ENSI of Novosibirsk and the Society for Sustainable Development in Vladivostok.

allows them to continue to work actively in the movement under changing conditions for mobilization.

Scaling Up   In the late 1990s and early 2000s, there was a trend among the donor community for building NGO resource centers in Russia's regions. Donors suggested that their more-effective grant recipients scale up their activities and become trainers of other Russian social organizations.[56] Erika's transformation into a default NGO resource center, offering seminars and consultations to other social organizations, is representative of a relatively widespread phenomenon among professionalized organizations that began in the late 1990s. The idea of funding regional NGO resource centers throughout Russia gained significant donor support as a means of resolving Russian social organizations' problem of sustainability, but these centers themselves struggled to survive because of the lack of domestic funding to support their work.[57]

In recruiting existing organizations that have the potential to develop into resource centers, donors frequently looked to professionalized environmental groups. These green groups represent some of the most well-established and highly institutionalized organizations in the region, and they have the strongest record in grant seeking.[58] ISAR-FE (a Vladivostok organization affiliated with the Washington, DC–based ISAR), not only made the transition from its start as an environmental organization to becoming almost exclusively an NGO resource center, the group also contracted with USAID to create a network of resource centers throughout the twelve regions of the Russian Far East. What has been a gain for the NGO sector as

---

56. Joselyn interview; William Pryor, author interview, United Kingdom Department for International Development (DFID), Moscow, May 29, 2000.

57. The Moscow offices of the Eurasia Foundation, Ford Foundation, C. S. Mott Foundation, and the Open Society Institute cooperated on the development and strengthening of NGO resource centers around Russia. In 2000, they supported 14 centers (Joselyn interview, and Shannon Lawder, author interview, C. S. Mott Foundation, Moscow, May 19, 2000). Bernadine Joselyn of the Eurasia Foundation acknowledged that resource centers are a completely Western concept, not indigenous to Russia, but argued that they are a good way for foundations to try to aid as many NGOs as possible when they do not have resources or time to help many smaller social organizations. In that sense, resource centers are very cost effective for Western donors. For the organizations that became resource centers, the shift implied moving up a notch in the NGO food chain and becoming more regularly funded, but this funding generally did not continue beyond one or two years, after which the resource center was supposed to become sustainable.

58. Kazakova interview.

a whole, however, is often a loss for the environmental movement as some of the most capable groups move away from green activism.[59]

Though transnational funding presents activists with powerful incentives, donors do not impose issues on Russian greens, and Russians do not propose projects simply because they are likely to be funded. There are clear advantages to transnational mobilization. It offers professionalized organizations freedom from the domestic authorities who are often dismissive of or hostile toward environmental activism. For example, it would be difficult for the group Green World to continue to confront officials at the Leningrad Atomic Energy Station as directly as they do without the moral and financial support of Baltic-region governments and NGOs who share their concerns.

Activists have become increasingly aware of problems related to transnational funding. Since the mid-1990s, a few Russian environmentalists have doubted the wisdom of relying on external funding to develop the movement. Yuri Shevchuk, a leader of Green Cross in St. Petersburg, is one such critic:

> The "Western Greens"…do not know what plants and animals are protected in the region, or what the composition of sewage from the typical pig farm is.…To put it simply, they do not know anything that is beyond the scope of their main professional line. Therefore, their advice might often prove to be speculative and practically inapplicable. (Shevchuk 1995, 44)

Noting donors' fondness for small grants to fund environmental education, a Vladivostok activist worried that "feel-good" ecological education

---

59. In other cases, scaling up can be a benefit to both the organization and the movement. The Resource Information Center (known by its Russian acronym RITs) is a Vladivostok-based environmental-education group that caught the attention of the USAID ROLL program with its comprehensive program for teachers in the Far East. RITs had earlier attracted grant funding to support its library of educational books and videos, and its group training seminars for teachers. Then, through ROLL, RITs received funding to act as an environmental-education resource center in the Far East, with a mandate to create smaller centers in Magadan, Sakhalin, and Kamchatka, thereby spreading environmental-education programs to regions that had lacked them. The transition to resource center can lead to more sustainability but can also jeopardize existing support. For example, RITs used some grant money to refurbish their office space, earlier donated by the local House of Children's Creativity, turning it into a lively center for environmental education. As the organization's income has become more apparent, however, the House of Children's Creativity has asked the group either to pay rent or relocate. Simultaneously donors are encouraging the group to move on to self-financing, although their client population is unlikely to be able to pay (Kondrashova interview).

is creating "cognitive dissonance" for Russian children who have to live in the real world and who then feel guilty for "doing what they must to survive in a system that won't allow them to be ecological."[60] A leader of a Russian green party based in St. Petersburg worried that donors direct too much of their funding toward wildlife rather than toward "real problems here and now in Russia."[61] The representatives of Erika said that they would "like to find some way to use environmental information, not only to gather it."[62] Finally there is a general concern that after two decades spent identifying what has gone wrong with the Russian environment, too little time has been spent publicizing what is good and valuable, leading the public to take a very dismal view of the potential for positive change.

Regional Political Opportunities: Obstacles to Environmental Goals

While leaders' decisions play a crucial role in determining issues and tactics, it is the opportunities and limitations of Russia's domestic political environment that influence the ultimate effectiveness and success of organizations. The obstacles to environmental mobilization at the national level are reproduced to varying degrees throughout Russia's regions. In general, regional activists echoed Aleksei Yablokov's concern about the "de-ecologization" of Russia and identified three key challenges to their work: unfavorable attitudes and institutions, the state's concern for growth and security, and the need for political allies.

Attitudes and Institutions

Environmentalists in Russia's regions lament the unreconstructed attitudes of the authorities toward the environment. The belief that Russia's vast natural environment has an unlimited ability to absorb waste, for example, explains why environmental concerns are given low priority by government officials. In 1999 St. Petersburg greens sounded the alarm that a toxic-waste pond at the Syas Pulp and Paper Mill, north of the city,

---

60. Kolomyts interview.
61. Svetlana Belaeva, author interview, Northwest Green Party, St. Petersburg, April 26, 1999.
62. Chizhevskii interview.

had started to leak into a river that contributed to the city's water supply through Lake Ladoga. Yet rather than ordering an investigation, Aleksei Frolov, chairman of the state environmental committee for St. Petersburg and the Leningrad oblast, asked, "What do 700,000 cubic meters of waste mean to a lake as big as Ladoga?" (Badkhen 1999b). Commenting on a similar problem with overflowing liquid waste at the Krasnii Bor chemical-waste reprocessing plant, also near St. Petersburg, Kirill Fridman, an official with the local branch of the State Sanitary and Epidemiological Service (*Gossanepidnadzor*) said, "Nature can bear anything.... There is no reason for alarm" (Badkhen 1999c).

Referring to Bryansk regional authorities' careless attitude about environmental protection, Valerii Soloviev, a bureaucrat and environmentalist, lamented "the collapse of all of our work" in the post-Soviet period: "The oblast has operated for five or ten years without effective environmental control.... We are back to the place we were twenty years ago."[63] In Novosibirsk, an environmentalist commented that the official environmental-protection service for the region is "90 percent dead" and that of 120 original staff members, only fifteen to eighteen remain.[64] Viktor Kutsenko, head of the Natural Resource Ministry's Ecological Control Department, acknowledged that the number of environmental inspectors had been reduced by one-third after the dissolution of *Goskomekologiia* (Lambroschini 2001).[65] A Vladimir bureaucrat employed by the Committee on Ecology offered his opinion on Russia's lack of an independent environmental protection agency, "Ideally there would need to be independent nature protection from natural-resource use, but it seems we haven't developed to that point (*dorosli do etogo*)."[66]

Even as they push for new environmental legislation, environmentalists are keenly aware that existing laws often are not implemented or enforced. St. Petersburg activist Ivan Kuliasov described the basic problem: "There are so many presidential decrees each year, but the fact is that, even so, the administrative authorities do not carry them out. The president does not

63. Valerii Soloviev, author interview, Bryansk Ecological Union, Bryansk, April 24, 2000.

64. Pashchenko interview.

65. Enforcing environmental laws related to natural resources is increasingly dangerous work. Overworked and underpaid nature-preserve workers are often injured on the job by poachers or unsafe equipment.

66. Yuri Leontiev, author interview, State Committee on Ecology, Vladimir, May 23, 2000.

have authority over the administration; the administration does not have authority over the people."[67] While some federal-level environmental organizations have used legal battles and the courts to work toward their goals, greens at the regional level have been reluctant to become enmeshed in the judicial process. Bodrov of Green World noted the perils of using the court system:

> It's a problem, on the one hand, that our infrastructure—the judicial organs and lawyers—this system has not been developed as in the United States, for example, and for that reason it's difficult to organize an effective case. On the other hand, we don't have a tradition in society in which we would resort to a judicial investigation in order to resolve a conflictual situation. We don't have that kind of tradition, and because of that, to take part in a legal case is seen in society as something criminal.... A legal suit remains, as in the Soviet period, something negative, connected to criminal offences, and not like a system that permits the discovery of the truth.[68]

Sergei Pashchenko of the Siberian Scholars for Global Responsibility stated: "Although we duel with [polluters] in lawsuits and we have brought cases many times, it is not a very effective method, especially in Russia where judgments depend on who your lawyer is, who your acquaintances are.... Here it is 'easy to swim among the laws.'"[69]

Economic Growth and State Security

Environmentalists in the regions recognize that concern for economic growth pushed environmental issues off the political agenda, particularly in the 1990s. Although the Russian economy grew steadily from 1999 to 2008, the global economic crisis once again emphasized the need for economic development in Russia. Valerii Soloviev of Bryansk, an environmental activist and a bureaucrat in the regional State Committee for Environmental Protection, cited a common reason that environmental issues are not addressed at the regional or local level: "[Government

---

67. Kuliasov interview.
68. Bodrov interview.
69. Pashchenko interview.

officials] see ecology as obstructing industry at a time of economic weakness."[70] In the 1990s, challenges to environmental protection were related to the post-Soviet economic crisis. Representatives of the Amuro-Ussuriskii Center for Bird Diversity recalled their experience interacting with Primorskii Krai government officials: "When we approach them and say to them that cranes are dying, that we need to establish a nature preserve, they say, 'Our potatoes are rotting in the field, and you come to us with your cranes!'"[71] Since the late 1990s, natural-resource extraction has played an important role in economic recovery and growth. Dmitrii Artamonov, a leader of the St. Petersburg Society of Greenpeace Supporters, noted obstacles to the group's efforts to protect forests in northwest Russia: "There are serious problems related to our forest campaign, namely that there is a very strong connection between our commercial organizations which harvest timber and those government structures that are supposed to monitor them. There is no independence between them."[72]

Russian officials also are still grappling with the economic ramifications of the disintegration of the Soviet Union. Oleg Bodrov of Green World expressed frustration that the government has built two Baltic Sea ports in the St. Petersburg region—one at Primorsk to service the end of the Baltic Pipeline System (BTS) and one at Ust-Luga to transport coal—that will significantly damage waterfowl habitat. Since the Soviet period, Russian petroleum products and coal have been shipped through the independent states of Estonia and Latvia, yet Russia spent more than $500 million on the port projects in order to circumvent the Baltic states. Bodrov asked, "Why do we need these ports? There are ports in Latvia, Lithuania, and Estonia that we don't want to use. We don't want to feed our oil to the Estonians, Lithuanians, and Latvians....It is all based on political motivations."[73] When asked by members of the press if these ports were necessary, President Putin replied, "Russia simply cares about its security and independence" (*RFE/RL Newsline* 2001).

---

70. Soloviev interview.
71. Litvinenko interview. A few seconds later this activist sighed and said, "Well, potatoes are important," expressing her own ambivalence about the possible trade-off between economic and environmental issues.
72. Artamonov interview.
73. Bodrov interview.

The Search for Allies

Russian environmentalists in the regions often have more success at finding allies among state agencies than greens operating at the federal level.
The state bureaucracy is not monolithic; it is made of up diverse individuals, some of who are concerned about the environment. When an organization can find an official to cooperate with, the relationship can prove
crucial to the group's development, but these connections tend to be idio-
syncratic, based on sympathetic individuals rather than formal incentives
for officials to work with social organizations. Officials lower down in the
bureaucracy generally appear more interested in cooperating with environmental organizations than higher-ups do, especially if the project will
cost them little in terms of manpower and funds. Anatolii Sosnin, head of
the St. Petersburg Society for the Protection of Animals, recounted how
his group found an ally in the local administration after establishing the
city's first animal shelter:

> After two months [the first, temporary shelter] was completely over-
> crowded.... It became dirty. It was necessary to clean it all out. Our board of
> directors invited the head veterinarian of the city to come, the director of the
> city's veterinary service. That was decisive. I would say it was our smartest
> step because with his help a year later we received—on his instructions!—a
> big piece of land, completely fenced in, and a small building from the turn
> of the century.... They gave us that place, and that started the second period
> [of our organization's development].[74]

Finding a sympathetic official is often a matter of recognizing and seiz-
ing an opportunity. Liudmila Komogortseva, the leader of the Bryansk
organization For Chemical Safety, says that her group had difficulty raising awareness about the effects of chemicals on the public health within
the Committee for Ecology and the regional legislature. Then the regional
procurator's five-year-old granddaughter had a reaction to pesticides after
eating cucumbers from local greenhouses. Hearing about the group's activities, the procurator subsequently invited Komogortseva to give a lecture
on the theme of local food safety. After that, a local newspaper published

---

74. Anatolii Sosnin, author interview, St. Petersburg Society for the Protection of Animals,
St. Petersburg, April 6, 1999.

a long article on the group's activities, and they gained a great deal of publicity (Khalii 1998, 9).

Ekoklub of Novosibirsk cooperated with the regional Committee on Ecology on a project called "Operation Black Stork," a competition to discover where rare and endangered birds nest within the region, with the secondary goal of trying to preserve those sites. Citizens were asked to send in a form to the committee if they knew of any nesting sites; if their findings could be verified, they received an award of sixty rubles. Ekoklub received more than thirty forms from around the region. Sympathetic committee officials helped Ekoklub publicize the event in regional newspapers. The group's leader, Aleksandr Dubinin, said that the project not only helped raise awareness about endangered species but also helped the organization become acquainted with environmental-protection officials and landowners. Although the committee decided not to protect all of the nesting sites, they agreed to make the event an annual one.[75] However, cooperating with the state is not always a positive experience for greens. The leader of a Novosibirsk organization said that the group ended their relationship with the regional Committee on Ecology after they realized that the committee was exploiting them for free labor in reworking the regional ecology plan and would not support their activities after that project was complete.

Finding allies within the local or regional authorities, or at least gaining officials' attention, appears to be somewhat easier for groups in regions where power is dispersed between the regional and city administrations or between the regional executive and legislature. For example, some St. Petersburg environmentalists noted that earlier they had been able to use the divisions between the legislature and Governor Yakovlev to their advantage, in particular by finding legislators from the Yabloko Party in the city's Duma who were willing to oppose the governor. The benefits of decentralized power are clearest in Novosibirsk, however, where the oblast governor and city mayor competed for authority throughout the 1990s and early 2000s. Several Novosibirsk activists suggested that city officials were more open to cooperation with environmental groups than those at the regional level, but the real benefit appears to be each official's desire to show

---

75. Dubinin interview, and Dubinin 1998, 33–36.

that he is more concerned about social issues than his competitor. For example, since 1996 the Siberian Center for the Support of Civic Initiatives, an NGO resource center in Novosibirsk, has hosted an annual fair for social organizations. Since 1998, the fair also has included a grant competition for NGO projects, with initial funding for the grants from the Open Society Institute. In 2000, after the mayor and governor attended the fair during their campaigns for reelection, they attempted to outdo each other in a show of support: Governor Viktor Tolokonskii signed a resolution to support five social organizations who had participated in the fair, and Mayor Vladimir Gorodetskii budgeted for 550,000 rubles (approximately $23,000) for future grant competitions (Maslennikova 2000b).[76]

Taken to extremes, of course, the fragmentation of political power is not helpful to greens, especially if it prevents the implementation and enforcement of environmental laws. Environmental groups in Vladivostok complained that the political battle between the region's governor and the mayor of the city left the city administration paralyzed. Many greens compared Primorskii Krai and Vladivostok unfavorably with the neighboring region of Khabarovsk where Governor Victor Ishaev has dominated the political system since 1996; under his control the region has developed a new forest code and a new approach toward environmental education. Political infighting and the relative weakness of some state agencies hamper environmentalists' work. Vladimir Aramilev of the Vladivostok Institute for Sustainable Natural Resource Use noted that while his group has good relations with the regional Committee on Ecology, the Society of Hunters and Fishers, and the Natural Resources Ministry, those groups fight among themselves, making it difficult to come to an agreement with them. Aramilev argued that if the authorities were stronger—more organized and less penetrated by corruption—they could implement a program to protect the Siberian tiger while also compensating people for livestock losses due to the predator.[77]

---

76. Other Novosibirsk groups also benefited from electoral campaigns. Galina Kuchina of Save the Ob! said that she was invited to appear on a television program on water pollution and health in the region because the local authorities were trying to demonstrate their environmental concern during the election campaign. When the organization EkoDom temporarily fell out of favor with regional officials over a dispute about the regional government's failure to pay for housing construction, the organization was able to continue to work at the municipal level.

77. Aramilev interview.

Some regional environmental organizations also face a dilemma when deciding whether to work at the regional or federal level. This has been a particularly pointed issue for those engaged in tiger conservation in Vladivostok. For example, Vladimir Aramilev believed that his organization needed to build cooperative ties with officials at the federal level in order to have an impact, especially since nature preserves are managed through the federal administration in Moscow. Yet the politicized environment in Primorskii Krai and the dictatorial tendencies of the region's governors have meant that organizations need permission to carry out their research from the regional administration as well. Representatives of the Hornocker Institute found it prudent to obtain permission from the Primorskii Krai Department of Natural Resources to work within the region's nature preserves, although officially they are only required to have permission and capture permits from Moscow. Operating at both levels is more difficult for Russian groups that lack the prestige and resources of their international counterparts. The Amuro-Ussuriskii Center for Bird Diversity proposed preserving a habitat for endangered migratory birds by declaring a national park on Lake Khasan in Primorskii Krai, but the group was stymied by the governor's unwillingness to cede more of his territory to Moscow's administration, which would occur by default if the area was given *zapovednik* (nature preserve) status. Only after years of wrangling did Governor Nazdratenko agree to establish a regional nature park in the area, a level of nature protection under regional jurisdiction and a lower status than the center had hoped.

Achieving Environmental Goals?

The task of assessing the overall effectiveness or success of the environmental movement in Russia is difficult, not only because of the need to conceptualize "success" and address questions of causality and intentionality, but also because of the diversity of the movement's goals. These difficulties are evidenced by the fact that so few authors have taken on the challenge of evaluating the effectiveness of environmental movements.[78]

---

78. Exceptions to this rule include several evaluations of antinuclear movements around the world, an issue area tending to have quite clear and narrow goals—the closure of nuclear power

In the Russian case, for example, air and water quality in Russia have improved significantly on certain environmental indicators in the first post-Soviet decade. These improvements cannot be attributed to the activities of the country's environmental organizations, however, since they have occurred in a period when environmentalists were largely excluded from policymaking and had little influence on government or industry. Instead, improved environmental quality was the result of the country's severe economic recession and industrial contraction in the 1990s (Oldfield 2005).

Any measurement of Russian environmental organizations' progress toward their goals is also limited by the short duration of their existence. The Russian environmental movement has operated freely for less than two decades, and many environmental groups were founded quite recently. Given these theoretical and practical obstacles to arriving at a clear evaluation of movement, this section will only examine what the implications of current patterns of activism are for effectiveness. One insight gained by comparing the three types of environmental organizations in Russia is that access to greater resources does not translate directly into greater effectiveness for an environmental group. As the previous chapter demonstrated, greens have been quite successful at identifying resource niches and expanding the movement through the development of a number of formal organizations. Yet effectiveness at achieving internal and substantive goals is not necessarily correlated. Effectiveness also is facilitated or limited by the issues chosen, tactics employed, relationships developed with other actors, and constraints in the domestic political environment.

There are trade-offs inherent in activists' strategic choices. One might expect that professionalized groups, many of which are securely funded by international donors, would prove to be the most effective at achieving their environmental goals. Professionalized groups' outspoken advocacy directly challenges the government's inaction on many environmental issues; their inability to mobilize local support has hindered their environmental work, however. Professionalized environmentalists have been most successful at monitoring environmental violations and chronicling the state's lack of enforcement of its own environmental laws. They have formed connections with international groups and taken advantage of the Internet and e-mail to

---

stations and dismantling of nuclear weapons (Kitschelt 1986; Kriesi et al. 1995; Dawson 1996). Dieter Rucht's evaluation of Western environmental movements' overall impact is one of only a few (1999).

broadcast their concerns.[79] Thus far, however, environmental organizations have made only modest progress in areas such as encouraging the creation of additional protected lands and contributing to environmental policy. These accomplishments have occurred outside any sort of formal participatory process and cannot be taken as signs of a shift toward the consistent application of the rule of law in the area of environmental protection.

Regional and municipal governments have been most amenable to environmental organizations' participation when it is confined to a kind of expertise-and-agreement role in which environmentalists, as apolitical scientists, offer a stamp of approval to government policies. Even when environmentalists agree to play this role, however, achieving environmental goals continues to be hampered by weak implementation, lax enforcement, and an unreformed legal system. The government may also disregard their expertise. Scientists from the Amuro-Ussuriskii Center for Bird Diversity were invited to participate on a government panel, but found their recommendations ignored: "They don't listen to us. We have been trying to ban spring hunting for many years. It is forbidden in all civilized countries. It is incomprehensible! So we wrote them, consulted with them, explained, wrote a statement, proposals. We got nothing from them."[80]

Grassroots and government-affiliate organizations may be effective at achieving their goals in part because of their more limited aspirations. Several grassroots activists pointed to the fact that twenty-two schools in Vladivostok have established environmental-education programs as a clear sign of their impact. Grassroots groups called attention to numerous environmental camps, olympiads, and other activities that have become much-anticipated annual events in the community. The majority of grassroots activists also pointed to the enjoyment of the children and adults who participate in their programs. Government affiliates' strategy of not challenging but promoting the government's environmental-protection procedures may serve to keep environmental issues on the political agenda, at least at the local and regional level. For example, a 2002 survey conducted by the president's own surveillance department in conjunction with

---

79. Pashchenko declared, "E-mail is our weapon!" He said that he now sends his evaluations and reports by e-mail directly to the head of a local chemical plant so that the director cannot deny having seen the results of their studies (author interview).

80. Litvinenko interview.

representatives from regional-level agencies (with the cooperation of many regional VOOP members) highlighted the weakness of the state's enforcement of environmental legislation (Petrov 2002). If government affiliates do not exactly transform the environmental debate, many of them do work to prevent further erosion of government attention to green questions.

Other activists warn that environmental organizations cannot compensate for the state's weak environmental protection strategies. For one, the transnational funding that has supported many of these projects is not indefinite. Evaluating antipoaching efforts in the Far East, Dale Miquelle cautioned: "Have [Russian environmentalists] made progress in the last seven years? A lot of what has been done for the tiger is simply stopgap. There is no substitute for real federal funding on an annual basis. It is the Russian government's responsibility to maintain protected areas. That is as it should be."[81]

Environmentalists have convinced many members of Russia's government elite that environmentalism is, if nothing else, a worthy public relations issue. In St. Petersburg, Yakovlev's administration, in cooperation with a local university, published a journal called *Ecology and Education*. Each issue started with a letter of support from the governor. Governor Nazdratenko of Vladivostok also had his picture prominently featured on a brochure designed to lure ecotourists to the region's natural sites. At the beginning of his term, President Putin even expressed to a foreign audience his interest in becoming an environmental activist in the future: "I've often thought what I should do when my term expires.... It is a noble task to support the ecological movement. At least I wouldn't be sorry to spend time on it" (Hoffman 2000). While Putin's remark may have been a throwaway line designed to distract attention away from his consistently antienvironmental policies, the comment does indicate that the Russian president is aware that environmentalism is a vocation likely to bolster his international image.

The post-Soviet years have witnessed the neglect of environmental issues in Russia—a disheartening landscape for activists who hoped to strengthen environmental protection, not witness its dismantling. The

---

81. Miquelle interview.

environment is still not high on the political agenda of the presidential administration or the Duma. Greens do not have the positive power to promote new policies, and they are unable, by themselves, to prevent erosion in the institutions and implementation of environmental protection. As at the federal level, environmentalists have had relatively little impact except to bear witness to the state's inattention of the environment and to record and publicize the need for further environmental protection. Their greatest achievement has been in promoting environmental education and raising awareness about specific issues.

Yet far from simply struggling against the closed political opportunity structure of Russia's federal center, the Russian environmental movement in the regions has embraced diverse goals, activities, and tactics. Grassroots groups tend either to operate below the radar of government officials or to cooperate with government officials at the lowest levels on events that are perceived as innocuous or beneficial for the local community. Building upon state institutions—even schools and museums—does necessitate strategic choices by grassroots environmentalists that may lead them to rule out activism on politically or economically sensitive issues, however. Government affiliates are in a contradictory position. They could have a unique ability to influence government policy from within, if not below, but they may be easily co-opted by government officials. Professionalized organizations' experience sheds light on some of the dilemmas of foreign funding. Professionalized groups have adopted a transnational environmental agenda that has left them well funded but estranged from local communities. While none of these environmental organizations could be called truly effective under Russia's current political conditions, the interaction between the organizational type and the broader political context varies—a fact that has significance for the movement's future development and success.

Identifying and comparing the varieties of activism within Russia's environmental movement suggest some important conclusions. First, the types of activism pursued by grassroots, professionalized, and government-affiliate organizations result from the reinforcing incentives created by the preferences of leaders and critical funders. Activists' vision of what environmentalism means is influenced by their professional backgrounds, as is their access to and ability to exploit different funding sources. Given the constraints of their political and economic environment, activists of all stripes make rational choices to mobilize particular resources in order to achieve their environmental goals. Environmentalists are neither puppets for Western interests nor victims at the mercy of state actors. They are not the passive recipients of a funder's agenda. Instead it would be more accurate to say that they have a menu of choices before them and are engaged in active selection of options that meld their own interests with the survival of their organizations. Still the limitations inherent in all sources of funding—domestic and transnational—do have implications for their overall effectiveness at achieving their substantive goals. Second, effectiveness at achieving internal and substantive goals is not necessarily correlated. An environmental group can achieve sustainability but still struggle to achieve its environmental protection goals in the challenging political environment of Russia's regions, where there remain significant obstacles to environmental protection.

6

ENVIRONMENTALISM AND STATE-SOCIETY RELATIONS IN RUSSIA

Environmental activism is not only a way to reckon with Russia's poor environmental conditions but also a way to inject new ideas, identities, and interests into the political arena. Green activism offers a potential path for increasing public participation in the political process and demanding government accountability. Indeed, supporters often frame the contributions of social organizations in terms of their role in developing civil society. Social organizations' efforts to change the political and social system in a way that increases participation and renders future activism more likely to be successful are referred to as transformational goals. This chapter demonstrates that the same factors that shape environmental organizations' sustainability and varieties of activism also affect the way these groups choose to interact with state and societal actors. These choices, and the kind of state-society relations that result, then influence environmental organizations' ability to achieve their transformational goals.

Environmental activism, in Russia and globally, often combines demands for a response to specific environmental problems with agitation for broader social, political, and economic change. Around the world, environmentalists have expanded their activism to encompass political demands ranging from sovereignty to feminism, human rights, social justice, and cultural and religious revival. As we have seen, Soviet-era scientists defending the environment were motivated in part by the desire to preserve a role for scientific expertise in the politicized realm of Soviet policymaking (Weiner 1999). During the perestroika years, environmental rhetoric was used by nationalist movements in the Soviet republics to critique the Communist Party–dominated administration (Dawson 1996). It is therefore not surprising that transnational actors interested in promoting democracy in the former Soviet Union identified environmental organizations, along with other social groups, as likely conduits for the public demand for a more transparent and responsive government, and ultimately as vehicles for civil society development and democracy promotion.

Social organizations, such as environmental groups, are thought to contribute to the development of civil society and democracy through their role as intermediary organizations. The activities of social organizations may serve to broaden the meaning of citizenship by fostering debates related to the public interest and by demanding that the state consult citizens when making policies. However, to posit that social organizations may play this role in civil society is not to say that these groups always directly or self-consciously try to develop civil society. Some environmentalists are quite deliberate about their role in building *grazhdanskoe obshchestvo* (civil society), while others concentrate only on environmental goals. Yet in the process of constructing social organizations and addressing environmental problems—to the degree that it involves mobilizing citizens, advocating for the public interest, and demanding accountability from the government—environmental organizations are pressing for a more democratic process.

Any effort to transform state-society relations takes place within the constraints of the preexisting political and economic environment, however. Ongoing trends toward liberalization or centralization will influence what social actors can achieve in terms of transformational politics. In addition, social actors, such as environmentalists, will have diverse reactions to similar political conditions, depending on their particular goals and past experiences interacting with state and societal actors. For these reasons, we once again see that the variation in organizational type within Russia's environmental movement has a profound effect on these groups' abilities to act as intermediary organizations in the political arena.

Environmentalists exhibited different attitudes toward the Soviet regime—attitudes that frequently shape their expectations of the current regime. They use their past experiences, in part, to answer the following questions: Who is our opponent? Who are our allies? Who is our constituency? Environmentalists' understanding of the current political situation also varies in ways that influence their desire and ability to play a democratizing role in the political system. Grassroots groups hope to restore order and optimism in society; professionalized organizations refer to "critical engagement" models of state-society relations from the West to envision Russia's future; and government affiliates claim to improve the efficiency of current governance without jeopardizing the status quo.

This chapter looks, first, at how environmental organizations interact with the public and the state, the two primary aspects of their intermediary role. Measuring actually existing social organizations against a theoretical ideal is inherently unfair. Yet an assessment of their intermediary role is a useful exercise for identifying which functions civil society organizations are playing in practice and how this differs across types of organizations. The evidence reveals that each organizational type tends to focus on only a small part of its potential role as an intermediary. While government affiliates try to make the most effective use of existing laws and practices, they do so without consulting social groups about their needs and preferences. Grassroots organizations generate new opportunities for participation but often avoid direct interaction with the authorities. Professionalized organizations attempt to hold the state accountable and monitor its activities but do so without first building support in Russian communities. This section also shows that these three types of organizations remain largely disconnected from each other within the environmental movement as a whole. Next, I examine how the Russian government has reframed environmental activism as a threat to the country's interests, further constraining greens' ability to play an intermediary role. Finally, I consider evidence from the campaign against the import of nuclear waste that demonstrates that environmentalists recognize their past constraints and have attempted to broaden the significance of their work. The chapter concludes with an assessment of environmentalists' effectiveness at achieving their transformational goals.

Environmental Organizations as Intermediary Groups

Shifting our analysis from activists' advocacy for environmental protection to their quest for political transformation, we ask not only whether environmentalists have influenced the Russian government's specific environmental policies and practices but whether environmental organizations have been able to affect the larger political process: how policies are made, how the public interest is debated, how the public participates in politics, and whether the state is compelled to respond to public concern. This section considers environmental organizations' ability to play the role of state-society intermediaries by examining the two halves of that role—engagement with citizens and engagement with the state. From this perspective, it becomes clear that Russian environmentalists have struggled with both sides of the equation. Each type of green organization contributes to part of this intermediary role but faces its own unique challenges in influencing evolving state-society relations in Russia. Thus, the evaluation of Russian environmental organizations as weak is accurate (Crotty 2006), but this analysis reveals that the nature of this weakness varies among organizations. Varieties of weakness arise out of activists' choices about navigating an unfavorable political and economic environment.

As discussed in earlier chapters, Russian environmental organizations confront a public that has been preoccupied with economic concerns or has been alienated by past experiences with politics. As a consequence, when environmental organizations have been able to secure support from foreign or state sources, they generally have had little incentive to reach out to and mobilize the public. Grassroots, professionalized, and government-affiliate organizations also have adopted different strategies of interacting with the state. Environmental leaders are polarized by past experiences with the Soviet state and their evaluations of the current regime. Following Hirschman's (1970) characterization of human responses to dissatisfaction, environmental groups have three possible responses to the political sphere: loyalty, voice, and exit. Activists can support and cooperate with the state administration; they can oppose and critique state practices; or they can remain neutral—in effect exiting the political arena.

Grassroots organizations have built strong ties to local citizens, but—with few exceptions—have avoided interacting with the government altogether or have confined their lobbying efforts to apolitical issues related to community well-being. In general, the educators who frequently lead grassroots organizations have a less politicized attitude toward state and society than professionalized activists. They tend to act in nonconfrontational or neutral ways in the public sphere, preferring to address issues that are pragmatic rather than political.

The leaders of professionalized environmental organizations often openly announce their desire to transform Russia's political system into one that is more open and democratic. Activists from professionalized organizations, particularly those in St. Petersburg, frequently described themselves as building civil society or the third sector, a language that they have adopted from foreign donors and from their own academic experience. Professionalized environmentalists interpret their role in civil society primarily as holding the government accountable. These groups act as watchdogs for the natural environmental and as critics of current environmental policy. In fact, professionalized environmental organizations, along with human rights groups, have been the most ardent critics of the federal and regional authorities (Weiler 2004; Pustintsev 2001). However, professionalized groups' relationship with average Russian citizens is less developed. Many professionalized activists have not seen much benefit in the time-consuming and often frustrating task of gathering local supporters when they have had the opportunity to carry out urgent environmental projects funded by foreign donors.

Government-affiliate organizations' role in civil society development is more difficult to label; they are fewer in number and their leaders are more reluctant to share their opinion of state-society relations. However, it is possible to identify some tendencies related to their role as intermediaries between state and society. Government affiliates generally have a cooperative relationship with the state. They have formal but distant ties to societal groups. Those groups that are descendants of Soviet organizations are technically mass-membership organizations, considering large groups of students or other institutions to be their natural members. While these groups generally do not provide opportunities for active participation by members, the All-Russian Society for Nature Protection (VOOP), for example, gains legitimacy from its status as one of the only environmental groups, aside from Greenpeace, with which average Russian citizens are familiar. However, government affiliates also offer the state a way to influence the development of civil society from above. Table 6.1 summarizes

TABLE 6.1. Environmental Organizations' State-Society Relations

	Professionalized	Grassroots	Government affiliates
Relations with society	Elite, disconnected, few members	Tied to preexisting societal networks	Elite, disconnected, nominal members
Relations with state	Opposition or critical engagement	Avoidance or neutrality	Cooperation

these choices, illustrating the varying strengths and weaknesses in the intermediary role of each type of organization.

What informs environmental organizations' relationships with other actors in state and society? These relationships are related, first, to environmental leaders' past experiences in the public sphere and, second, to the reliance that their organizations develop on certain flows of funding, allowing groups more or less autonomy from domestic societal interests and from the state. Leaders' preferences, relatively similar within each organizational type, result in similar assessments of appropriate and inappropriate behavior for social organizations and suggest certain relationships with state officials and citizens. These relationships are reinforced by the preferences of the groups' primary funders.

Varied Visions of Environmentalism in Civil Society

For grassroots activists, environmentalism is a means of reviving public self-confidence. Grassroots leaders are likely to have a history of working in the community on quality-of-life issues, especially questions related to children. They tend to have great faith in the regenerative power of society, in particular the potential of the next generation to address environmental problems. Natalia Smetanina, the leader of the Laboratory for Environmental Education in Vladivostok, described the role of her organization as follows, "It's a difficult situation in Russia because nobody believes in anything. The joy is gone.... They need to see good examples and to believe that the changes can be made by individuals."[1] Grassroots leaders are likely to express the opinion that it is just a matter of rolling up their

---

1. Natalia Smetanina, author interview, Laboratory for Environmental Education, Vladivostok, October 29, 1999.

sleeves and getting to work in order to get things done, regardless of government policies or social apathy. To solve environmental problems, Elena Pototskaia of Sosnovii Bor Ecological School said, "You just need to look for interested people and give them encouragement."[2]

Grassroots activists also use environmentalism as a way to "humanize" the school curricula after the political orthodoxies of the Soviet period. In a sentiment echoed by many grassroots leaders, Valerii Soloviev, who is affiliated with the Bryansk Ecological Union, said that the most important challenge faced by the environmental movement is to "raise children with a civilized relationship toward nature."[3] Environmentalism offers a way to steer the next generation through an era of political, economic, and even moral uncertainty. When they discuss why their work is needed, several grassroots environmentalists invoked the image of children playing idly in the street, without hope or purpose.[4] Eco-spirituality organizations, including Green Attitude of Bryansk and Mir of St. Petersburg, also see the natural environment as a source of energy, solace, and the regeneration of faith.

Adopting a broader view, many professionalized activists see themselves not only as domestic actors but as part of global civil society. Kouzmina and Yanitsky, Russian sociologists, have argued that Russian environmentalists escape the infelicitous domestic sphere by embedding themselves in transnational networks. They do so in order "to have a safe (stable) resource pool abroad" and "to disengage as much as possible from current political battles in Russia" (1999, 180). Russia's professionalized environmentalists have embraced transnational concepts and tactics both as a means of generating new sources of financial support and as a way to shape the future of post-Soviet society. Indeed, a number of professionalized environmentalists asserted that they are part of something larger than just the Russian green movement, a transnational environmental community of like-minded actors, a community that provides a respite from the often hostile domestic political system. For example, Oleg Bodrov of Green World said,

---

2. Elena Pototskaia, author interview, Sosnovii Bor Ecological School No. 7, Lomonosov, April 18, 1999.

3. Soloviev interview.

4. A number of these concerns (children, health, education) are what would traditionally be the purview of women in society and may reflect the number of women who lead grassroots environmental organizations.

We purchased a computer and modem and it is thanks to e-mail—which is really the most important—that we see ourselves as part of the Baltic system. Without that it would be impossible—impossible to exist in Sosnovii Bor because this town is entirely oriented around the development of atomic energy, and all of its infrastructure was created for that. And this infrastructure doesn't permit people who think differently to survive—they absolutely have to leave here.[5]

Another environmental leader commented that transnational support is valuable because it "allows us to move beyond the provinces"—in other words, to escape the constraints of their local environment.[6] Yuri Shirokov of ISAR-Siberia, a professionalized group that supports other environmental organizations, described his efforts to attract donors to the region in order to provide more opportunities for activists and to expose them to new models of activism: "We have many great people here. They simply deserve, after this bleak life, to participate in these programs." He believes that transnational ties are necessary so that "our organizations do not feel so isolated, that they are not outside the international process, the international debate."[7]

The leaders of government-affiliate organizations often were bureaucrats and party members during the Soviet era. They value order and rule following over dissent and confrontation. They also base their environmental work on the shared belief that science is outside politics. Leaders of government affiliates tend to be of the opinion that the state did a reasonable job at managing the natural environment throughout the Soviet period, and that although not perfect, it continues to have environmental protection well in hand. In the post-Soviet context they have adopted a supportive relationship with government officials.

Environmentalists from government-affiliate organizations also tend to have a somewhat more uniquely Russian approach to environmentalism than pragmatic grassroots activists and overtly democratic professionalized groups. Aleksei Gurnev of Association Clean City and the St. Petersburg branch of the Russian Green Party summed up his approach: "Representatives of the green movement can be divided into green globalists and

---

5. Bodrov interview.
6. Zhirina interview.
7. Shirokov interview.

green statists (*gosudarstvenniki*). The first believe that it is possible to sacrifice local interests for the general good; the second believe that each should fight for his own interests. We align ourselves with the second category."[8] He was careful to point out that they are not nationalists, only that they "disclaim internationalism as a myth," both in the Communist sense and in terms of new efforts to build a transnational civil society.

Acting as Intermediaries: Relations with the Public

In order to carry out their activities, grassroots leaders generally rely on like-minded networks of family, friends, colleagues, or the parents of children enrolled in their programs. For example, Kukushkin Pond of Vladimir and the Society for the Protection of Krestovskii Island of St. Petersburg have drawn on networks of neighbors to preserve green spaces in both cities. The spiritual group Mir of St. Petersburg was founded by a group of friends who spend their summers on the island of Valaam in Lake Ladoga. The St. Petersburg Society for Animal Protection relies on a network of *babushki*, or elderly ladies, to house stray animals in their homes. By starting with personal networks, grassroots activists tap into neglected groups in society. Valentina Kubanina pointed out that the most active participants in local environmental organizations are young people and pensioners, in part "because no one else wants them."[9] Anna Gulbina of In Defense of the Sea said that her group reaches out first to schoolchildren, "and through the children, perhaps, we can get through to the parents, other organizations, and the administration."[10]

Teachers in primary and secondary schools have been particularly receptive to the messages of their colleagues in grassroots environmental organizations. Alena Vlazneva of AVES in Novosibirsk recounted the ease with which her organization has found sympathetic teachers: "Schools are generally open. It seems to me that a situation has taken shape where teachers who are trying to work creatively are looking for projects like ours. They are searching for materials, and it's easy to contact them."[11] These teachers

---

8. As quoted in *Pchela* 1997, 84. Comments confirmed in author interview.
9. Kubanina interview.
10. Gulbina interview.
11. Alena Vlazneva, author interview, AVES, Novosibirsk, December 6, 1999.

are important agents of change because they are implicitly charged with transmitting norms of citizenship to the next generation. There are limits to what grassroots environmental groups can do in the schools, however. Svetlana Gizhitskaia of AVES offered as an example the time her group tried to introduce meditation as part of a study of deep ecology and alienated parents and school administrators.

The Vladivostok organization Nadezhda is a grassroots organization that has been successful at encouraging participation of local community members. Tatiana Zviagintseva, the leader of the organization, said that the group's original goal was to create a maritime museum in a small town near Vladivostok. Nadezhda then built a children's environmental-education program using the museum facilities and volunteer labor. The organization, which was unregistered for most of its development, sponsors different environmental activities. These activities include cleaning up litter in the town's green spaces, helping students monitor water quality, creating art on environmental themes, and sponsoring a young-journalists organization. Rather than pursuing one narrow goal, Nadezhda has adopted a broad definition of environmentalism, responsive to the interests of its constituency. The organization advertises its activities in area schools and through a network of teacher acquaintances. At first only about twenty students participated regularly, Zviagintseva reported, but now many more students are eager participants and their parents often accompany them to the group's activities. Zviagintseva acknowledged that the town's residents "are too poor to be environmentally aware," but said that "everyone in town seems to love the museum." She believes that the group gradually is raising environmental awareness while achieving its larger goals—"to keep children off the streets" and "to help people understand that they can do things for themselves."[12]

There is only one grassroots environmental organization among those studied that did not use the strategy of tapping into preexisting networks for volunteers and participants, an exception to this general rule that demonstrates how rarely Russians gather together to form an organization with nonacquaintances. The St. Petersburg Society of Greenpeace Supporters formed after a number of the city's residents wrote letters to Greenpeace Russia, based in Moscow, in response to a Greenpeace television

---

12. Tatiana Zviagintseva, author interview, Nadezhda, Vladivostok, November 2, 1999.

advertising campaign. Letter writers wanted to know why the organization did not have a St. Petersburg office. Dmitrii Artamonov, a leader of the St. Petersburg group, recalled:

> Our letters piled up in Moscow, and [Greenpeace representatives] decided to come here with a few people and host a small meeting for their support-ers. Here in St. Petersburg there were about eighty supporters at the meet-ing,…and we suggested, "Let's organize ourselves here." It was clear that they [Greenpeace Russia] could not give us any kind of financing, but we decided to start our organization.[13]

The St. Petersburg group was not created as an official branch of Green-peace International but rather as a club of supporters that raises its own small amount of funding locally and struggled to establish itself, operating without office space for several years. Twelve individuals carry out the or-ganizations' activities in St. Petersburg.

Grassroots organizations attract citizens because grassroots leaders un-derstand the type of environmental concerns that exist in the community and act on them, even if those concerns lead simply to cleaning up litter or planting flowers.[14] They cater to the interests of their constituents, even if their concerns seem frivolous or minor to other environmentalists. Grass-roots leaders have also realized that it is easier to draw in participants from the community when the events and organizations involved are familiar to them or are activities in which they already engage. Examples already mentioned include Pioneer-style summer camps, *subbotniki,* educational olympiads, and Soviet-style children's programs and holidays. As Svetlana Gizhitskaia of AVES remarked, "Why do we use [past traditions such as]

---

13. Artamonov interview.

14. Eco-spirituality organizations and small green parties serve a slightly different purpose in local communities—articulating alternative ideologies and new identities in society. These small groups gather to discuss a range of environmental problems and the appropriate political response to them. Spiritual groups tend to be networks of individuals numbering from twenty to fifty. The green parties that existed until the early 2000s maintained loose associations of members aver-aging fewer than ten individuals between elections and increasing to thirty to forty during the campaign season. Participants in small green parties and eco-spirituality groups appear to be in-dividuals who are more concerned with group solidarity or the sense of well-being derived from belonging to a group of like-minded people, rather than focusing on one particular environmen-tal grievance.

olympiads and *subbotniki*? Because nothing ever springs up suddenly from an empty place."[15]

In the late 1990s, the St. Petersburg Club of Urban Gardeners and its project EkoDom, (meaning "Ecohouse") demonstrated how grassroots activists can address environmental, socioeconomic, and quality-of-life issues simultaneously. EkoDom, a project led by Alla Sokol, a retired engineer, was an effort to transform a typical nine-story St. Petersburg apartment building into a model of ecological living.[16] The project, which started in 1993 and included more than fifty building residents by 1999, had two components: limiting and recycling residents' waste and growing food in the rooftop garden. Sokol envisioned the project as a way to keep urban residents connected with the Russian traditions of gardening and working the land and to raise awareness about health and the environment as well. The secret to the success of the project, according to Sokol, was its ability to address needs unrelated to the environment, such as growing food for residents' own use. Sokol believed that the gardens provide a kind of relief to those suffering from the effects of economic uncertainty and other maladies, while also providing them some economic support. By 2004 there were approximately fifteen rooftop gardens and one hundred participants in St. Petersburg (Equator Initiative 2004).

An environmental issue of particular concern to local residents is the health effects of pollution. The Radimichi organization of Bryansk Oblast has focused on the link between health and the environment in the Chernobyl zone. The leader of Radimichi, Pavel Vdovichenko, said that his group became interested in the environment because members realized that it is an essential part of their ongoing work on public welfare and economic development. Vdovichenko remarked, "We understand that ecology is part of where we live—this is unavoidable—but we like to think about it broadly as the ecology of the individual."[17]

In contrast to grassroots groups, professionalized organizations have developed vibrant transnational ties, and their connection to local communities often languishes. From their founding, professionalized organizations

---

15. Gizhitskaia interview.

16. Alla Sokol, author interview, St. Petersburg Club of Urban Gardeners/EkoDom, St. Petersburg, April 22, 1999.

17. Vdovichenko interview.

tended to be more distant from the general public than grassroots groups owing to their leaders' professional positions, often as scholars or researchers. Professionalized leaders also have emphasized the importance of expert opinion in policymaking and are less likely to advocate for the input of average citizens. Evgenii Sobolevskii of Ekolog spoke perhaps for many professionalized leaders when he extolled the virtues of having a "team of experts" leading his environmental organization.[18]

The value placed on expertise, combined with the academic backgrounds of many professionalized activists, reinforces the elite nature of professionalized environmental organizations in Russia. These environmental leaders tend to be uncertain about how they, as activists, should interact with the public. In the mid-1990s, Maria Tysiachniouk and Alexander Karpov asked predominantly professionalized environmentalists in St. Petersburg about their contact with citizens and received responses such as: "We do not know what to say to people and what to call them for"; "We do not know where to find interested people, nor do we know what to suggest to them"; "We do not know how to mobilize people for constructive action and are afraid of misunderstandings;" and "We do not have experience talking to people" (Tysiachniouk and Karpov 1998). Other activists attribute their reluctance to reach out to the public to the sense that average citizens, understandably, have been preoccupied by economic concerns. Yulia Fomenko of WWF-Far East commented, "The conditions here are such that people can't feed their families or heat their houses, so it is not always correct to talk to people about the environment. People often have no choice; it is a question of survival."[19] Oleg Bodrov also recognized that the reason many citizens are reluctant to protest against the Leningrad Atomic Energy Station, even though they fear for their health and safety, is because they know "atomic energy is what feeds us; it is the opportunity to earn a wage, to have a job."[20]

Members of the public rarely approach professionalized organizations. Aleksei Chizhevskii, a leader of Erika, commented, "It is hard to get adults to gather for anything because they are preoccupied with economic problems.... We need a generation for many ideas to change. Right

---

18. Sobolevskii interview.
19. Fomenko interview.
20. Bodrov interview.

now many people don't feel personal responsibility or they feel ineffective or inadequate."[21] Natalia Litvinenko of the Amuro-Ussuriskii Center for Bird Diversity noted that in the seven years her organization had been operating, only three prospective members from among the general citizenry of Vladivostok approached the group, although a great number of foreign bird-watchers contacted them. She contrasted their situation with one of their foreign partners, the Wild Bird Society of Japan, which has forty thousand members. To highlight their difficulty, Litvinenko recounted that their three prospective members felt themselves to be oddballs (*chudaki*) because of their love for birds, with one saying, "All my life, friends and relatives have mocked me, saying that I am some kind of fool because I like to look at birds with binoculars." When questioned further, however, Litvinenko admitted that the center did not develop relations with these individuals as they were not sure how to integrate them into the group's largely research-based activities.[22]

Over time, Russia's professionalized environmental activists have become increasingly aware that if their projects are carried out independently of the interest or even knowledge of local communities, this lack of support might hinder the movement's sustainability and future success. Valentina Kubanina, for example, traced the difficulties of her organization Ekologos to the fact that its founding mission—providing information and technological support for environmental groups—was in part prompted by the availability of funds from foreign donors for that mission, and not the result of the public's interest. Kubanina recognized that "this is not an idea that springs out of the demands of society in general."[23] When donor priorities shifted to other issue areas, there was no local interest in the organization's survival. This lack of funding, combined with the death of the group's leader, imperiled Ekologos's ability to continue as an organization.

Kubanina noted that many Russian citizens are reluctant to participate in social organizations even once they learn about their activities. She remarked, "There are two attitudes toward the third sector. One, people look back at socialism, at the *subbotniki* and collectivism and remember having

---

21. Chizhevskii interview.
22. Litvinenko interview.
23. Kubanina interview.

to pay membership fees. Two, there is another attitude that the third sector has been introduced by foreign organizations."[24] Natalia Proskurina of ISAR-FE argued that many social groups have failed to publicize themselves and to demonstrate their ability to solve social problems.[25]

Public skepticism about environmental groups is at least partly attributable to organizations' weak roots in local communities. Olga Pitsunova, a leader of the Center of Ecological Initiatives Assistance in Saratov, a longstanding environmental organization, believed that funding from foreign donors was the key factor behind the disconnect between the public and environmental groups in the 1990s:

> In the past years, riding on a wave of grants, very many social organizations became specialized nonprofit organizations...[and] formed what they call the "third sector," working without or almost without connections with the population. But if we are to have a movement, not just nonprofit organizations, then we should have many mass social organizations and groups of citizens' initiatives, groups for which environmentalism is not a profession (Luneva 1998, 24).

Ultimately, external funding can lead to a bifurcation between an organization's "constituency in principle" and a "constituency in practice." The constituency in principle is the Russian population, and environmentalists' projects certainly are designed to improve the environmental situation in Russia. In practice, however, many organizations need to justify their projects to external supports in order to survive. Thus, their constituency in practice has become the critical funders themselves.

Research by Greenpeace Russia indicates that popular mobilization is possible if environmental organizations pay attention to citizens' concerns. In the late 1990s, Greenpeace reported that interviewees in seven Russian cities said that they would prefer to support actions to protect the environment near their home or neighborhood; the actions that they were least likely to support were "pressuring the authorities and business for the

---

24. Kubanina interview. Kubanina also laughed as she recounted how, after asking her what her profession is, people sometimes say that she can't possibly work in a social organization because social organizations do not exist.

25. Proskurina interview. Whitefield (2003) and Tynkkynen (2006) have come to similar conclusions.

goal of resolving environmental problems" and "the battle against global climate change" (Greenpeace Russia 1999). In focus groups, respondents again indicated that they would rather give money to resolve environmental problems in their neighborhood or city than give money for global projects. One interviewee said, "I would not give money to Greenpeace, but I would give money to a local environmental organization to protect nature" (Greenpeace Russia 2000, 9). Another remarked, "If I knew that the money would go to resolve concrete problems, then ten or twenty rubles wouldn't be too big a sum for me—I would give that money for the environment because it ultimately affects the health of my children" (ibid.). Respondents also stated, however, that they did not know of any organizations that met their requirements for donation.

A few professionalized organizations have made efforts to tailor international environmental projects to local circumstances. For example, the TACIS-funded Environmental Awareness Program in St. Petersburg spent significant time and energy reworking the international Global Action Plan, designed to cultivate environmental practices in the home, in order to fit the realities of post-Communist life. Many of these adjustments were as simple as recognizing that urban Russians are likely to live in apartment buildings and that the plan's prescriptions for energy savings and waste disposal in freestanding homes needed to be altered to fit Russian conditions. This effort to redesign a program from the bottom up is exceptional, however.

Finally, leaders of government affiliates frequently expressed confidence in their leading role in the environmental movement, although they offered few specific examples of public mobilization. Galina Esiakova of the Vladimir branch of VOOP attributed state officials' willingness to work with her group (and not with other green organizations) to the fact that "no other society is so big and stable."[26] A few government affiliates do have long-standing educational programs that bring them into contact with the public. There is anecdotal evidence that these groups are better able to work in relatively more conservative educational environments. Although there are many small green parties and a number of branches of the Green Party of Russia throughout the country, Vladimir Shemetov

---

26. Esiakova interview.

of the St. Petersburg branch of KEDR repeatedly insisted that his group is the "real Green Party—the others just call themselves green parties."[27]

There are some positive trends for public mobilization. By 2005–2006, the majority of environmentalists I interviewed agreed that public interest in the environment was increasing.[28] Activists attributed this interest to growing concern about the relationship between the environment and health, visible problems with garbage and other waste in Russian cities, and a small increase in the amount of information available to the public about environmental risks. The minority who stated that the public was less interested in green issues attributed that fact to their lack of faith in the government's accountability and to what they feel is general cynicism and social apathy. A St. Petersburg activist argued, "People are tired of this topic [the environment] where nothing is being done—strange 'greens' protest, but nothing changes from the point of view of the man in the street."[29] A Siberian activist who believed that public interest in the environment is growing as citizens' lives are personally affected, still offered the following pessimistic assessment of the public mind-set toward social activism:

> Citizen participation, social consultation, and control over administrative agencies so far are still rare in our lives. [Why?] Inertia, a lack of faith in their own power, combined with infantilism, the conviction that the authorities shouldn't be troubled by the population, and so forth. In many minds there is still the ideal of a paternalistic model of government—the government as the father.[30]

The emergence of upper and middle classes was noted by several activists as potentially significant for environmental activism, but they did not necessarily agree on what the impact of the change would be. An activist from Novosibirsk said, "Naturally, the middle class are actively interested—they are property owners—but the rest of the population, at the lower level, just survives."[31] A St. Petersburg environmentalist found

---

27. Shemetov interview.
28. Of those responding directly to the question, fifteen agreed that public interest had increased, while five felt that public interest was the same or lower.
29. Environmental activist T, March 2, 2006.
30. Environmental activist U, July 18, 2005.
31. Environmental activist H, July 12, 2005.

that wealthy residents in her area have started to care more about the environment, but they are mostly interested in problems located in their immediate neighborhoods.[32] A St. Petersburg group representative offered an example of this, noting that although their group had permission from the city authorities to use a local island as a base of operations, wealthy residents had prevented the organization from carrying out activities there "with threats and criminal acts."[33] A Siberian activist expressed concern that the public has become "infected with consumer aspirations."[34] Another environmentalist offered this analysis, "According to statistics, the charitable activities of the rich are increasing, but that is not perceptible in the regions far from Moscow and places without oil."[35] Several activists asserted that the public would be more likely to offer donations to social organizations if there were laws to support charitable giving.

Overall, environmentalists' failure to mobilize citizens who are generally concerned about environmental quality is a failure of communication and framing. A 2008 Public Opinion Foundation poll found that 78 percent of Russian respondents are personally concerned about the environmental situation, yet 57 percent do not feel that they are able to participate in resolving environmental problems (Fond Obshchestvennoe Mnenie 2008). On the whole, Russia's environmentalists have not demonstrated the link between environmental quality and standards of living or health. Or perhaps it is more accurate to say that environmentalists have not convinced citizens that social organizations will help them achieve these goals of improved health and well-being. Russian citizens feel aggrieved, but they do not feel optimistic or efficacious nor do they believe that social organizations are trustworthy. This failure to mobilize local support allows environmentalists' opponents, in particular government officials, to question greens' legitimacy and take punitive action against them without fear of public outcry

Acting as Intermediaries: Relations with the State

While they have built strong ties with relatively small groups in society, grassroots activists are not inclined to engage government officials.

32. Environmental activist T, March 2, 2006.
33. Environmental activist R, November 7, 2005.
34. Environmental activist U, July 18, 2005.
35. Environmental activist AA, July 14, 2005.

Although not advocating a return to Communist rule, grassroots leaders are more likely than professionalized environmentalists to offer a mixed assessment of the post-Soviet period, lamenting the loss of services for children and the orderliness of Soviet society.[36] Their cautious attitude toward political issues in general contributes to grassroots activists' desire to maintain a neutral or accommodating relationship with local authorities, sometimes preferring to go unnoticed altogether.

The majority of grassroots groups relate to the government only indirectly, through community institutions. Grassroots environmental activists draw a clear distinction between bureaucrats responsible for education and culture and elected officials. As one leader remarked, "We work through the education administration. We don't go to the authorities."[37] To sympathetic officials who work on education and social services, grassroots organizations can justify their projects in terms of child development and public health. Other grassroots groups, including Green Attitude of Bryansk, also are adamantly apolitical. Natalia Knizhnikova emphasized, "I decided that Green Attitude will never be involved in politics, never." Asked for the reasons behind this decision, she said that politics is not an effective route to meeting the public's needs: "The government still has the attitude that they know what is good for people and that they don't need to ask them what they want."[38] Other environmentalists worry that state support implies that "they [state officials] will impose their full control, including their ideology" (Solovyova 1995). Groups tackling issues perceived as

---

36. The ideological orientations of grassroots leaders appear to be more diverse than those of professionalized and government-affiliate leaders. Two examples illustrate this. Boris Kulakov, leader of the Society for the Protection of Krestovskii Island, recalled an idealized past, "Earlier, that is during the Soviet period, the Soviet authorities were different.... One of the differences was that the authorities acted in the interest of the majority. So that if we would have announced to the governor that we were going to protest, then—without any conversation—there would have been no construction [on the island]. As soon as it was said that we were going to protest, that they were cutting down trees, then immediately the authorities would have accepted it because they acted in interest of the majority. That is what Communist power is—the interest of the majority" (Kulakov interview). Galina Kuchina, of Save the Ob!, remembered a more negative political environment: "We lived in a epoch of totalitarian education. They dictated everything to us: what was possible, what was impossible, that man was the owner of nature, that it was possible to subjugate nature. These ideas took root, and still are what guide us right now. For that reason we work with adolescents, with schoolchildren, the next generation" (Kuchina interview).

37. Gizhitskaia interview.

38. Knizhnikova interview.

politically sensitive have a more difficult time. The leader of the Bryansk group Bell of Chernobyl said, "The government's attitude is that there never was and is not a Chernobyl."[39]

Grassroots organizations occasionally come into conflict with the authorities, even when they believe that they are pursuing nonideological goals that focus on upholding existing laws not expanding political rights. One example of this is the St. Petersburg Society for the Protection of Krestovskii Island. The society was created in 1995 to combat the rapid increase in the construction of single-family homes, or *kottedzhi,* in one of the city's green zones. Krestovskii Island has been a "zone of culture and recreation" for the city of St. Petersburg since the mid-1800s, and its status was confirmed in the city's 1985 general plan. In the mid-1990s, island residents and park users discovered a private construction firm's plan to tear down old apartment buildings and put up new private homes. The leader of the group, Boris Kulakov, voiced their fears, "They want to destroy the area...to cut down the trees, to build cottages for the rich, but when those cottages are built they will fence off the area for themselves. For that reason we needed to create this organization to collectively defend the interests of the city."[40] The group claimed fifteen active members and thousands of supporters by the late 1990s. To recruit supporters and circulate petitions, the society looked not only to other green groups, but also to "councils of veterans, blockade survivors, women's groups, and so forth." The society's tactics included publicizing the jeopardized status of the island among city residents and finding allies among the representatives of St. Petersburg's local self-government (*mestnoe samoupravlenie*), the lowest rung of the city administration. They also found a lawyer willing to work pro bono to file a claim for them in the local courts. Most important, however, the group "depend[ed] upon the general plan" of the city, the existing body of law and regulation, as a resource for their activism. The reason for their group, Kulakov stated vehemently "is not just an idea—it's the general plan!" While Kulakov believed that government officials were being paid off by the construction companies, he was confident of the group's eventual victory because "the law is on our side." As of 2008, this protracted battle continues in the courts, as does building on the island (Kovalev 2004; Gazeta.SPB 2008).

---

39. Bell of Chernobyl representative interview.
40. Kulakov interview.

When government officials do interact with grassroots groups, it often is because these organizations represent real constituencies for candidates who would like their support, although candidates are generally reluctant to make any concrete commitments. Natalia Proskurina, the director of ISAR-FE, noted that social organizations more and more frequently are used to strengthen candidates' images.[41] She points out that in the 1998 elections in Primorskii Krai, even Governor Nazdratenko met with youth groups and pensioners' organizations—something he had never done in the past. Her assessment was that "the motives of the governor are very obvious and transparent," even to the groups involved, and do not indicate that the governor "is doing something real to help people." Elected officials' willingness to meet with these groups, even if they do not respond directly to groups' demands, does acknowledge implicitly that grassroots organizations represent real constituencies.

Environmentalists from professionalized organizations tend to have an ambivalent attitude toward the state. They frequently oppose state policies and often are critical of the government's environmental-protection strategies, but their skepticism coexists with a strong desire to work with and through the state, arguably the only institution that can achieve comprehensive nature protection and other environmental goals. What these environmentalists seek is a fundamental reform of state agencies and practices. When questioned about the relationship between their organization and the local and regional authorities, professionalized activists frequently responded that the relationship is "complicated" (*slozhnoe*). It remains difficult for environmental organizations to arrange meetings with government officials, access government information, or cultivate a productive dialogue. Liliia Kondrashova, a Vladivostok activist, chalks these difficulties up to the fact that "social movements are very active and change very easily, while government organizations are more conservative."[42]

State officials largely remain uninterested in projects designed to facilitate their cooperation with social organizations. Elena Kobets, a member of the Transboundary Environmental Information Agency (TEIA) of St. Petersburg, recounted the response of local government officials to the NGO directory that her group published with foreign support: "This

---

41. Proskurina interview.
42. Kondrashova interview.

directory that we published didn't provoke their interest. People call me, for example, from many different funders, and they ask for the directory. There is a mass of foreign organizations that is interested. But not one [local] official called me.... Here no one demonstrated any interest."[43] Officials' impression of environmentalists is often linked to the mass demonstrations of the perestroika period. They feel that activists who "go around with megaphones and flags, who make noise and gather crowds" do not need to be taken seriously, according to Yuri Shirokov of ISAR-Siberia.[44] Professionalized activists also are often quite pessimistic about the government's ability to reform itself. A Vladivostok environmentalist said, "They don't want to listen. They don't listen to anything that we explain to them."[45] Ogorodnikov of EkoDom offered the opinion, "The relationship between environmentalists and politicians will never be genuine. They [politicians] are after their own financial goals. Politicians are not people who are motivated by a great ideal."[46]

Even when the opportunity arises, professionalized environmental activists recognize risks in cooperating with the government. Their cooperation might appear to be acceptance of the institutions and procedures as legitimate when they in fact are critical of these entities as only nominally democratic and superficially interested in environmental protection. In the 1990s, environmentalists who were asked about their reluctance to work with the government commented that "laws exist only in theory" and "the President himself violates the laws" (Tysiachniouk and McCarthy 1999, 8, 14). Another risk is that social organizations will be drawn into criminal patronage networks. One Vladivostok activist said that criminal influence and money permeate the local government where her organization operates. She said her organization has found it difficult to find partners within the government, noting, "There are lots of different interests within the government, and you can't always guess someone's interests based on their [official] position."[47] The fact that formal laws are superseded by informal

43. Elena Kobets, author interview, Transboundary Environmental Information Agency, St. Petersburg, April 7, 1999.

44. Shirokov interview.

45. Nataliia Litvinenko, author interview, Amuro-Ussuriskii Center for Bird Diversity, Vladivostok, October 20, 1999.

46. Ogorodnikov interview.

47. Anonymous.

interests in the administration leads professionalized organizations to be cautious.

Environmentalists in St. Petersburg have acted most directly of all the regions studied to develop a model of critical engagement with the state. The city's Agenda 21 Working Group, a coalition of environmental organizations and a few other social groups, have worked at the level of the federal city since 1997.[48] These activists initiated a program called Dialogue 21 designed to raise the issue of sustainable development with local government officials and business people. One of their efforts included a March 1999 seminar entitled "Principles and Mechanisms of Taking Public Opinion into Account in Policymaking at the City Level" for social organizations and representatives of the St. Petersburg city legislature. At the seminar, organizers suggested that the participation of social organizations should be formally structured into each phase of policymaking.[49] Participants tried to persuade legislators that if the public knew more about their work, they would have a more positive attitude toward their representatives.

When formal institutions prove difficult to work with, environmentalists search for sympathetic individuals inside the state bureaucracy. Vladimir Gushchin, leader of several St. Petersburg organizations, said that he has found willing partners in the local administration and emphasized that "the administration is not a single whole" (Fedorov and Kobets 1999c). Vdovichenko of Radimichi commented: "It is easy to say we are good and the government is bad, but on every floor of every government building there is at least one good, normal person, and if you tell them what you are doing and don't ask for something right away, they may offer to help later."[50] Environmentalists sometimes devise creative ways of getting

---

48. Evgeniia Makhonina of Green World led the Agenda 21 effort in the late 1990s. She recognized that some aspects will need to be changed to fit local conditions, "Agenda 21 is an innovation from the West, from outside, but fell on soil that has its own features.... We work closely with other Baltic states but can't just transfer a blueprint from them. We need to analyze our own situation" (Evgeniia Makhonina, author interview, Green World/Local Agenda 21, St. Petersburg, May 14, 1999).

49. Representatives even provided a list of the "normative bases" for public participation in policymaking, including thirteen federal-level laws, seven regional laws, and five city laws.

50. Vdovichenko interview. Operating in Bryansk, Radimichi has come into conflict with the local authorities on several occasions. In the mid-1990s the local government agreed to allow Radimichi to accept humanitarian aid from Germany for victims of the Chernobyl disaster. When

around the hostility of state officials. When the Friends of Bryansk Forest faced the possibility of opposition from then Governor Yuri Lodkin, they headed off the problem by making him an honorary board member of their organization.

In contrast, leaders of government-affiliate organizations suggested that their groups offer the most promising route to creating more effective environmental protection practices from within the government, not from below as other social organizations envision. This strategy has worked to a certain degree. When asked which environmental organizations they cooperate with, Russian regional government officials most frequently mentioned government affiliates. For example, Anatolii Baev, director of the Department of Nature Protection for St. Petersburg, recounted that his department works with government affiliates, including Association Clean City, KEDR, and VOOP (Fedorov and Kobets 1999a, 5). Yet in spite of this support, the government-affiliate niche encompasses the fewest organizations, indicating the authorities' lack of interest in cultivating ties to social organizations and in environmental protection. Even given their restricted agendas, government affiliates occasionally come into conflict with other social actors and need to appeal for government support. Conflicts such as these may force government officials to make choices between economic interests and environmental concerns, perhaps gradually reinforcing the state's commitment to environmental protection. Yet the survival of government affiliates depends on the sufferance of an essentially indifferent government, and environmentalists recognize that officials could withdraw their support at any time.

Given their heavy reliance on the state, one could question whether government-affiliate organizations are really self-organized groups within civil society. Their official status as independently registered organizations and their persistent advocacy of environmental issues within a largely

---

officials later proved uncooperative, Vdovichenko used the government's earlier agreement letter to shame them for not doing more to help. The group has not been able entirely to avoid problems with the local authorities, however. Radimichi needs to show that it is "cleaner than anyone else," according to Vdovichenko (author interview). He recalled that tax inspectors audited the group when their volunteer accountant was absent; they were given a hefty fine for paying some taxes late and making minor mistakes on the complex forms. To get them to revoke what he saw as unfair charges, Vdovichenko threatened to take the problem to the regional authorities and then to Moscow. More optimistically, Vdovichenko said, "We have noticed the following: where they start to know us, they accept us." (Luneva 1999).

indifferent government may enable these government affiliates to serve as sites of association and debate in the public sphere. Aleksei Gurnev acknowledged that "society has no influence on decision making." In fact, he believes that it was easier to cooperate with the Communist Party–dominated government in the Soviet period. But Gurnev also thinks that government-affiliate organizations like his, which bring industrial and state officials together, can create "a new field of social action" that is more appropriate for Russia and is more likely to succeed than the strategies of other environmental groups.[51] Critics argue that government affiliates lend state institutions the appearance of consultation and responsiveness without actually altering practices that exclude public participation.

In a later survey, five years after my initial interviews, environmentalists' perceptions about state interest in environmental issues continued to vary by organization type. Professionalized activists, with only one exception, responded that the authorities' level of interest in the environment was the same as in the past—in other words, quite low. Grassroots activists were split, with half arguing that the authorities' interest had increased and half saying that it was the same or lower. Several grassroots activists commented that the local authorities had been forced to respond to growing public concern about the environment, health, and safety in cities because of public outcry. A Vladivostok activist argued that poor living conditions can lead to cooperation among greens, commercial firms, and the government. She suggested that these kind of pragmatic coalitions are more likely to happen in smaller towns and cities where there is more contact and trust among these groups.[52]

Three grassroots activists who responded to the survey said that they have taken steps to engage more directly in the public sphere, one by becoming a deputy on the raion-level education commission, another by joining the United Russia Party, and the third by joining the reformulated KEDR Party, now known as the Russian Ecological Party. In the case of the environmentalist who joined United Russia, the pro-Kremlin dominant party in Russia, a representative of the organization reported that the leader "felt that this was the only way to struggle against the new rich and other illegal powers" and, indeed, "the party has helped us in several

51. Gurnev interview.
52. Environmental activist J, January 17, 2006.

cases."[53] The activist who joined the reformulated KEDR Party after his smaller green party failed to survive moved from a grassroots organization to a government affiliate, based on the designations in this study. He acknowledged that his current party is based wholly on the state's sanitary-epidemiological bureaucracy and a circle of industrialists, and he contrasted its state affiliation with "informal" greens that he worked with in the past. He recounted, "The earlier party 'Greens' was founded by these [informal] green activists, but it died step by step because the majority of them did not want to gather in one party and to act in the framework of a political party." He also offered this analysis of the political situation that led him to make the switch:

> There is almost no opposition to the authorities, or maybe there is but they do not have access to television. That means that an opposition can only exist in Moscow because on the rest of the Russian territory the people don't read newspapers and the Internet, and they worry above all about material problems. The word "democracy" has become an expletive and, most important, the numerous bureaucracies do not respond to our critiques in any way.... That is why our party of Greens is now trying in every possible way to become closer to the president, hoping for compassion for its activities.[54]

This activist went on to say that his new party has been able to attract funding from businessmen in the region and to achieve modest electoral returns of just over 1 percent.

Relations within Russia's Green Movement

The growing number of social organizations populating the Russian political landscape does not automatically signify the development of civil society, particularly if these organizations are not linked in broader networks. Environmentalists across organizational types have struggled to knit together their ties to state and society actors and establish constructive dialogue with one another. Environmental activists face significant barriers to intramovement cooperation, including Russia's vast distances,

---

53. Environmental activist R, November 7, 2005.
54. Environmental activist X, July 29, 2006.

encompassing eleven time zones, and poor transportation and communications infrastructure. More important barriers are related to different visions of the appropriate relationship between the state and society. Thus far, environmental organizations have few incentives to cooperate with each other. Instead, environmentalists have tried to differentiate themselves from other organizations in order to attract attention. However, focusing on their differences has left many greens feeling that Russia no longer has an environmental "movement."[55]

Activists had different theories to explain their own apparent weakness as political and social actors. Professionalized organizations attributed their lack of influence in the political system to the lack of an open policy-making process and an impartial rule of law in Russia. Grassroots organizations cited the public's preoccupation with economic concerns and lack of leisure time. Representatives from government affiliates in turn argued that social organizations are weak because the state is functioning well—in other words, the government is responsive to demands from society, assimilates them, and takes necessary action in the environmental sphere, making social organizations less important.

Activists' opinions of how environmental organizations relate within the movement also varied. Some environmentalists argued that green organizations are generally cooperative since they are more developed and more active than other Russian social organizations. They also noted the broad spectrum of environmental problems in Russia, suggesting that

---

55. The environmental movement in St. Petersburg stands out as exceptional because environmental organizations of all stripes gather together relatively often, yet they have quite conflicted relations with each other. In contrast, environmentalists in other regions, particularly Vladivostok, bemoan the long distances and lack of e-mail access in the Far East as obstacles to creating a broader green movement. St. Petersburg greens span the ideological spectrum, from anarchists to hippies to nationalists to those nostalgic for the Soviet years. Notably, St. Petersburg greens are involved in a self-conscious debate about what the environmental movement is and how it should behave. For example, I attended a Green Party conference that tried to unite St. Petersburg's numerous green parties in 1999. At the conference, Yuri Shevchuk, the leader of Green Cross, and Antonina Kuliasova debated which organizations can be called "environmental." Shevchuk declared that eco-spirituality should not be considered part of the movement. Their conversation then broadened to include other greens attending the conference, segueing into a somewhat acrimonious discussion of which groups were included and which were left out of a directory of environmental NGOs. Even though groups in St. Petersburg do not always agree, the interaction and dialogues have given the region a much greater sense of having a "movement" than in other cities.

there is room for many different groups. However, most environmentalists seemed to think that green organizations interact "negatively," are too critical of each other, and do not cooperate enough. Valentina Kubanina argued that the groups don't cooperate with each other because most of them are weak and uncertain about the future: "Only when a group is successful itself can it afford to be generous."[56] Sergei Pashchenko saw an opposite problem: "I have noticed the following: when organizations are founded, they love each other like small children. Only as they grow do they start to quarrel because they don't have any money to share, because they are trying to develop their own unique image."[57] Meanwhile, Oleg Bodrov attributed the lack of cooperation among environmental groups to a more deeply rooted problem: "We don't have a democratic tradition or culture of democratic abilities to communicate among different nongovernmental organizations."[58]

The environmental movement is highly decentralized, but many regional activists agree that the Socio-Ecological Union (SEU) plays a leading role in coordinating activism. The SEU, based in Moscow, is an umbrella organization that attempts to combine the strengths of professionalized environmental groups while taking into account their leaders' preferences for autonomy (Sotsial'no-Ekologicheskii Soyuz 1992). The organization started as a way to continue ties among Druzhina groups from the Soviet period, and now maintains cooperative relations with more than two hundred environmental organizations throughout the former Soviet Union. Yet although these affiliated groups are technically members, the SEU's leader, Sviatoslav Zabelin, prefers to think of the SEU's affiliates as a community rather than an organization. After environmentalists' experience with state-sponsored mass organizations in the Soviet period, Zabelin maintains that a sense of organizational freedom is essential to the development of the movement overall.[59] Thus Zabelin runs the most successful environmental umbrella group in Russia through his ability to "lead without leading."[60]

---

56. Kubanina interview.
57. Pashchenko interview.
58. Bodrov interview.
59. Sviatoslav Zabelin, author interview, Socio-Ecological Union, Moscow, April 20, 2000.
60. Zabelin noted that the umbrella-organization strategy is also a way to discourage government interference while still uniting the energies of many environmentalists. Since the SEU

Aside from a few sponsoring relationships, grassroots and professional-ized groups do not meet very often and engage in few cooperative projects. Vladimir Aramilev from Vladivostok's Institute for Sustainable Natural Resource Use noted that he and his colleagues "do not have much in com-mon with teachers' organizations.... Teachers' organizations don't need the kind of advanced information we provide."[61] Pashchenko of Sibe-rian Scholars for Global Responsibility does not approve of environmental groups that are not "professional."[62] In return, grassroots activists charge that professionalized groups are "closed" to them. Grassroots environmen-talists occasionally suggested that professionalized groups were founded merely to receive grant money, not because of their leaders' conviction about environmental issues.

What activists from grassroots and professionalized organizations share is a suspicion of any organization that cooperates too closely with the gov-ernment. As one activist suggested, "Local governments fund their own organizations in order to fulfill [foreign] donors' requests that society and the government cooperate.... This type of cooperation is based on per-sonal relationships and is bad because it excludes many different groups."[63] Many environmental groups refused to work with the green party KEDR because they think the party is not a "real" environmental organization but a vehicle for the political ambitions of the state officials who founded the party. Some professionalized activists also have a negative impression of another government affiliate, the All-Russian Society for Nature Pro-tection, which is seen as bound by its Soviet past. A professionalized envi-ronmentalist commented, "It was a very bureaucratic organization during the time of the Soviet Union and it was very ineffective. It had a central-ized administration, and the opportunities to influence decision making within the organizations were very limited. It was a bureaucratic orga-nization—a manifestation of the totalitarian system."[64] Government af-filiates respond by disassociating themselves from the activities of other green groups. Galina Esiakova of VOOP-Vladimir said that she is not con-cerned about the sustainability of environmental groups that do not receive

---

has no real leader or hierarchical structure, there is no particular person that the government can target or try to co-opt (author interview).

61. Aramilev interview.
62. Pashchenko interview.
63. Anonymous environmental activist, author interview.
64. Anonymous environmental activist, author interview.

government funding, noting that "it may be good if there are fewer social organizations because it will be easier to coordinate them."[65]

The lack of networking among environmental groups has meant that they have not been able to compensate for each others' weaknesses as civil society actors. For example, grassroots groups have not provided professionalized organizations the legitimacy of a real constituency, and professionalized organizations have not represented the issues and needs of greens at the grassroots to the government. This may be changing, partly because of the Russian government's increasing neglect of the environment and hostility towards environmentalists.

The Russian Government Reframes Green Activism

Russia's political system does not simply set the stage for environmental organizations' development and activities. Political officials and agencies also react to environmentalists' activities and engage in their own framing of green mobilization. The result is a relationship of give-and-take and constant readjustment in language and tactics by environmentalists and state actors alike. State officials learned the lesson of the perestroika period that popular mobilization even on a seemingly benign issue can be destabilizing and they attempt to manage these risks. Within the state apparatus, officials see the environmental movement as a threat for two reasons. First, environmental mobilization could interfere with the government's plans to develop the economy, particularly its plans for economic development through exploitation of natural resources such as timber and petroleum. The president's former economic adviser Andrei Illarionov expressed this opinion about certain types of green activism.[66] Second, environmentalists could pose a threat to political stability, a particular concern for the powerful law-and-order coalitions based in the security services who enjoyed increasing influence during Putin's tenure as president.

The state's response to green activism has taken several forms. First, laws related to social organization are often applied in a politicized way. State officials have charged that Russian environmental groups operate

---

65. Esiakova interview.
66. For example, Andrei Illarionov was a vocal critic of the Kyoto Protocol, calling the Kyoto Treaty an "economic Auschwitz" for Russia (Osborn 2004).

under foreign control and spy on the Russian military and industry. Government officials have used tax audits and other inspections punitively against environmentalists, in particular charging that groups that receive foreign funding are security threats for their "anti-Russian" behavior. Officials also have increasingly clamped down on the free flow of information in Russia; the arrest of and treason charges against Aleksandr Nikitin and Grigorii Pasko for publicizing pollution by the military are examples of this trend.

The state's successful reframing of environmental activism threatens to widen the gulf between citizens and the movement, increasing the population's suspicion of environmentalists. It has legitimized political officials' hostility to greens at the regional and local levels. However, the Russian officals' harsh reaction to environmental mobilization also indicates that a green critique of Russia's current political and economic system is potentially powerful.

Environmentalists Labeled Anti-Russian

In general, the Russian state has not looked favorably upon environmentalists' efforts to act as watchdogs chronicling the state's failure to enforce its own environmental laws. Russian government officials make a number of charges against environmentalists: that they are too "emotional," are inclined to exaggerate, and are opposed to economic growth.[67] The government's most damaging accusation, however, is that environmentalists do not work to improve conditions for Russian citizens. President Putin and other political officials have painted environmental activism as threatening to the state and the economy, accusing environmentalists of representing the interests of the West. In July 1999, just prior to becoming president, Putin was quoted in *Komsomolskaia Pravda* as saying, "Sadly, foreign secret service organizations use not only diplomatic cover but very actively

---

67. In just one example, when Greenpeace sent the St. Petersburg administration a proposal for a waste-sorting facility, where recyclable materials such as plastic, paper, glass, and fabrics would be sorted, Andrei Vassiliev, the head of project development at the Committee for Power Supply and Engineering for the city, responded by saying, "Greenpeace officials are far too emotional in their approach to the problem of waste.... Their figures are also exaggerated and hardly reflect reality" (Bigg 2002).

use all sorts of ecological and public organizations."[68] For many Russian observers, the charge that greens are anti-Russian is lent credibility by their reliance on foreign funding, which undermines their legitimacy as social actors and generates suspicion among the public and local and regional officials.

This rhetoric has been adopted by officials in the regions. For example, Aleksei Frolov, a representative of the Committee for Nature Protection of St. Petersburg, responded to the question of how he would evaluate the green movement of St. Petersburg by saying:

> Let's say I have a sufficiently negative relationship with the St. Petersburg green movements. First of all, when discussing questions of nature protection, social organizations often lack professionalism. Second, I am disturbed by the abundance of foreign grants which these parties and movements receive. I understand that each movement needs to survive somehow. But it seems to me that very often representatives of these green organizations are not based on the Russian side. (Fedorov and Kobets 1999b, 4)

Environmentalists particularly have faced problems in more conservative areas. As a Russian activist in Siberia recounted, "Especially in the villages they scold us: 'You are an American spy. You are from an American organization and you want to find out something. What is with you? You could be sitting in America, but you are active here—that is incomprehensible.'"[69] Journalists also have picked up on the suspicion that greens are anti-Russian. For example, the St. Petersburg paper *Petrovskii Kur'er* printed an article wrongly implying that the groups Green World and *Deti Baltiki* (Children of the Baltic) were taking money from Western sources for their opposition to the construction of a port on the southern bank of the Gulf of Finland.[70]

The government's implicit campaign against environmentalists is not simply rhetorical. Environmental organizations, particularly those receiving foreign grants, have been subjected to an unusually high number of audits by the Federal Security Service (FSB) and the tax police, and some

---

68. As cited in *RFE/RL Newsline,* July 20, 1999.
69. Novosibirsk environmental activist.
70. Bodrov interview.

environmental groups have been evicted from their state-owned premises owing to unsubstantiated suspicion about their activities (Cox 2000). In St. Petersburg, Green World was subjected to a tax audit that they believe was politically motivated.[71] Later Oleg Bodrov, the organization's leader, was physically attacked outside the group's office and hospitalized for ten days; the location of the attack and the fact that none of his valuables were taken led Bodrov's colleagues to link the attack to his environmental activities (Digges 2002). Marina Rikhanova, of Baikal Environmental Wave, has said that her group was audited twice by authorities in 2007 on the basis of their annual report. She suspects the audits have to do with the group's opposition to plans for a uranium-processing facility near Baikal. Rikhanova remarked, "The registration service has oversight over 3,000 NGOs in the Baikal region and our organization gets searched twice in a year?" (Eckel 2008). Liudmila Komogortseva of the Bryansk group For Chemical Safety, recalls that at one point "if we decided to participate in a certain demonstration, the authorities threatened to liquidate the organization" (as quoted in Khalii 1998, 12). Dmitrii Lisitsyn, whose organization Sakhalin Environment Watch was audited in early 2000, thinks that the government's actions are an effort to show "who is the master of the house" (*kto v dome khoziain*).[72] The Socio-Ecological Union has taken the position that there is no basis for these inspections of environmental groups, but that they occur because "social environmental organizations have become 'bones in the throats' of the authorities."[73] They note that the SEU has been called a terrorist group by government officials. Many greens believe that harassment from inspections and audits is so widespread that they must have been ordered by the president himself. Activists also express concern that the 2006 law on NGOs represents a tightening of state control on social organizations and gives officials the power to deny some groups their legal registration and to harass others (Von Twickel 2007).[74]

---

71. *Baltic News,* no. 53, February 22, 2000.

72. Speech given at the World Affairs Council, San Francisco, January 24, 2002.

73. *Vesti SoES,* March 2000, http://www.seu.ru/vesti/2000-03/index.htm.

74. The 2006 NGO law officially has the uninformative title "On Introducing Amendments into Certain Legislative Acts of the Russian Federation." During previous instances requiring re-registration, environmentalists said they did not feel personally threatened by the process but were frustrated by the time and energy required, not to mention the uncertainty generated by their interactions with the bureaucracy. For example, when the Bryansk organization Viola attempted to register a branch office of their group in the town of Novozybkov, they were informed by the

When environmentalists have held firm against government harassment, officials have turned their attention to state employees who cooperate with greens. For example, in November 2002 the FSB opened criminal investigations into the work of Baikal Environmental Wave and that of two geologists, employees of the Sosnovgeos State Geological Institute, who cooperated with the environmental organization to produce maps of radioactive pollution around the city of Angarsk near Lake Baikal (Meyer 2002). Both parties denied that the maps were secret, pointing out they had sent copies of the maps to various state bodies earlier that year, along with their report. FSB officers confiscated the organization's computers and a list of foreign volunteers. Finally, in December 2003, the charges were dropped, but the message to the employees of state research institutes and universities was clear.[75]

The government's punitive measures toward certain environmental organizations are a powerful disincentive even for groups that have not yet been targeted. The government's negative depiction of green organizations also discourages potential political allies from lending their support because the perceived cost of challenging the government is simply too high. In addition, the authorities' reframing of environmental activism as anti-Russian almost certainly reduces support for these groups among the public, especially given the lack of other available information about environmental organizations.[76] A WWF-Vladivostok survey from the late 1990s found that 11.7 percent of the public in the Far East thought that

---

authorities that the group Radimichi was already working on similar issues in the area and that one social organization was enough for that town (Grishina and Dzhibladze 2000, 9).

75. Aleksei Yablokov sees this as a very worrisome trend: "If we don't manage to protect these people, no one will cooperate with us in the future, and it will be very difficult for us to work. We absolutely must save our sources" (Borisova 2002).

76. If a group is confident of the service it is providing to society, however, it may be able to respond to these charges. Pashchenko and the Siberian Scholars for Global Responsibility hosted a group of U.S. environmentalists during the summer of 2000 in order to conduct joint monitoring at four nuclear facilities in Siberia. While taking measurements outside the Novosibirsk Uranium Chemical Complex, the scientists were arrested by the local police and FSB officers who accused them of being in a restricted area. They were released after several hours, but then a Novosibirsk paper ran an article saying that spies had been found outside of the complex. Pashchenko and his U.S. colleagues then did something unprecedented: they went to the newspaper office to meet with reporters to tell their side of the story. In response, the reporters wrote a more detailed and balanced follow-up article identifying them as environmentalists, not spies (Pashchenko, e-mail message to author August 21, 2000; Carpenter 2001).

international environmental groups were working for their own profit, spying or exploiting raw materials (WWF-Far East 1998, 24). One clear drawback of greens' reliance on transnational resources is that it has provided the Russian government with a foundation for challenging the goals and legitimacy of the movement as a whole, offering some credence to the government's charges in the eyes of the general public.

This kind of harassment of environmental organizations makes it even more challenging for groups to critically and usefully engage with the state. For example, environmentalists are divided over the intentions and effects of the Public Chamber, established in 2005 to institutionalize regular communication between representatives of social organizations and the state. Some have vowed not to work with the chamber, claiming that is an attempt to manage social organizations and discourage opposition. Vladimir Zakharov of the Center for Russian Environmental Policy in Moscow takes another view, however. He accepted a nomination to the body and heads the Commission on Environmental Policies and Nature Protection.[77] Zakharov said that he prefers to keep an open mind, participating in the chamber as long as it appears to be an opportunity for constructive engagement with the state, while maintaining the option to leave at any time.[78]

Environmental Information and Charges of Treason

Under the Putin administration, the state increasingly tightened its control over access to information. Alexei Simonov, a leading human-rights campaigner with the Moscow-based Glasnost Defense Foundation, compares the government's information policy to that of the Soviet era: "The habit of special services people is to keep as many secrets as possible for as long as possible.... The problem of Putin, as was the problem of his predecessors, is that they believe sources of information for the public should not be the press but the special services" (Crosbie 2002). Simonov cites numerous cases of arrest and even murder of journalists in Russia in order to support his opinion.

---

77. Information on the commission can be found at http://www.oprf.ru/structure/comissions2008/114.

78. Vladimir Zakharov, author interview, Center for Russian Environmental Policy, Moscow, June 28, 2005.

Environmentalists feel the effects of the government's attitude toward public information, complaining that it has been difficult to gain access to information about current government and industrial projects in order to do environmental-impact assessments because it is often declared confidential (Cherp 2000; Ostergren and Jacques 2002). Problems of secrecy are particularly acute in Russia's former closed cities, generally sites of military importance or scientific research (Garb and Komarova 1999; Kutepova and Tsepilova 2007; Mironova, Tysiachniouk, and Reisman 2007). Sergei Pashchenko commented that in order to address environmental problems effectively, "we need to get out from under this vulture of secrecy—we must insist on that."[79] He called the environmental information that is available "a joke," noting that you need to "add two zeros" to the statistics in order to understand the magnitude of Russia's problems.

Two prominent environmental activists were charged with treason for publicizing information about environmental damage caused by the military. In both cases, the environmentalists insisted that the information was freely available and that they had merely put together a summary report. Aleksandr Nikitin, a former Russian naval officer, was arrested in 1996 while working on a report for the Norwegian environmental organization Bellona on the risks of radioactive pollution from Russia's Northern Fleet. In his report, he called the leaking of the military submarines' nuclear reactors "a Chernobyl in slow motion" (Bellona 1998). Nikitin was charged with espionage and the disclosure of state secrets. He defended himself against the espionage charges by asserting that all of the information in his reports had come from public sources. The Russian Minister of Atomic Energy argued that Nikitin's report "inflicts colossal damage to national interests—even if it [the information] may have been published before."[80] Nikitin became the first "prisoner of conscience" in Russia designated by Amnesty International since the Soviet era. In August 2000, after a long series of legal battles, Nikitin finally was acquitted when the court ruled that the laws he had been charged under were applied retroactively.[81] Grigorii Pasko was charged in a similar legal suit after giving

---

79. Pashchenko interview.
80. Interfax, November 5, 1998, in Johnson's Russia List 2467.
81. Nikitin's case was investigated for five years and entailed thirteen court decisions. The Russian prosecutor's office then filed an appeal to overturn the acquittal while Nikitin was in the

information to a Japanese television crew about nuclear-waste dumping by Russia's Pacific Fleet. Although acquitted of nine out of ten charges, Pasko was convicted of espionage in December 2001 and sentenced to four years' imprisonment.[82] Pasko served more than half of his sentence before being released on parole in 2003. A St. Petersburg activist, who supports Nikitin and Pasko, commented that the two environmentalists' direct employment by Western organizations and reliance on Western funding opened them up to the charge of espionage. He traced the lack of popular support for Nikitin and Pasko to the public's impression that environmental organizations act on behalf of Western interests. Nikitin and Pasko remain prominent figures in Russia's environmental movement. Nikitin is the head of the St. Petersburg branch of the Bellona environmental organization and Pasko continues to work as an environmental journalist.

In my follow-up study in 2005–2006, most environmentalists surveyed believed that state and public hostility toward environmental activism persisted. A Siberian activist asserted that the general perception was that "all environmental undertakings are the machinations of foreign intelligence services, and [the public's] convictions are formed under the influence of politicians, especially from the power ministries."[83] Others agreed that the image of NGOs in Russia is not positive. The organization in the survey that has employed the most confrontational tactics—including petitions, protests, and a lawsuit—has also faced the greatest harassment by the authorities, including several tax inspections, document seizures, and a physical attack against the group's leader that members believe is linked

United States accepting the Goldman Prize for Environmental Activism (known as the environmental Nobel Prize). The grounds for the appeal were the numerous violations of Nikitin's rights during the course of his trial and imprisonment. Yuri Schmidt, Nikitin's lawyer, was outraged by this strategy given that he had filed many complaints about violations of his client's rights over the five-year period, all of them rejected by the prosecutor's office. "In forty years of legal practice, I've never seen worse cynicism, worse abuse of the constitution and human rights—for the prosecution to justify overturning an acquittal with the very violations it committed" (as quoted in Lambroschini 2000).

82. In an earlier court hearing, in 1999, Pasko gave the following defense: "The agents of the federal security service [FSB] placed me under all types of psychological and physical pressure during the preliminary investigation and wanted to hear from me an unconditional recognition of my guilt.... Yes I am guilty...of striving to win foreign investment for my country in order to solve its environmental problems, of not noticing how glasnost had ended in our country and how the seed of democracy had dried out" (as reported in *Transitions Online* 1999).

83. Environmental activist U, July 18, 2005.

to local officials.[84] Interestingly, the former leader of a government-affiliate organization, who has since started a new organization that also works closely with the city administration and industry, cited the high levels of corruption in the administrative apparatus as one of the biggest obstacles to his work.[85]

Greens Cooperate: Campaigning against Nuclear Waste

The Russian government's negative response to environmental activism appears to significantly constrain environmentalists' ability to act as state-society intermediaries in the near future. Yet the ferocity of the government's response to green activism may be a sign of environmentalists' power—or at least their potential power—as political actors. The government's repression of the environmental movement indicates its awareness of greens' potential to upset the political and economic status quo. The government's hostility may also serve to radicalize the movement. When environmentalists can find a way to navigate the internal and external obstacles to cooperative action, they stand at the forefront of efforts to transform the current political system.

The 2000–2001 campaign against importing nuclear waste into Russia demonstrated that it is possible for environmentalists to cooperate across organizational types. The battle over importing and storing nuclear waste in Russia underscored environmentalists' inability to change state policy on substantive issues but had implications for the role they could potentially play in transforming Russia's political system. The fight against importing nuclear waste also prompted greens to adopt a deeper, more nuanced assessment of the type of transnational cooperation that Russian environmentalists need in order to be successful.

Immediately following the dissolution of State Committee on Ecology in 2000, the Ministry of Atomic Energy proposed that Russia begin importing nuclear waste from other countries in exchange for valuable hard currency (Felgenhauer 2001). In May 2000, the ministry proposed legislation allowing Russia to import twenty-one thousand tons of radioactive

---

84. Environmental activist C, July 17, 2005.
85. Environmental activist I, December 28, 2005.

waste for reprocessing and storage, allowing the country to earn approximately $20 billion over ten years. According to government officials, importing foreign nuclear waste could be the key to resolving Russia's own nuclear-waste problems since the proceeds would pay for an environmental-cleanup program and the development of more-efficient nuclear reactors.[86]

Russian greens vociferously protested the proposed law. They argued that the measure posed a danger to public health and a threat to future generations; that Russia is incapable of storing its own waste safely; and that importing waste would increase the threat of terrorists gaining control of nuclear material.[87] In June 2000, more than 170 environmental activists met in Moscow to form an initiative group for organizing a referendum on importing nuclear waste, one of the few legal avenues available to the public to affect policymaking.[88] Green activists publicized the environmental and health risks of the plan, including writing open letters to President Putin, dumping contaminated soil from the Urals on the steps of the Duma, and organizing numerous small protests across the country (*Moscow Times* 2001). Public opinion in Russia was clearly on the environmentalists' side: a ROMIR poll found that 93 percent of Russians were opposed to the proposal (Reuters News Service 2000).

In response to the referendum initiative, the government created its own forum of environmental groups to oppose the referendum (Yablokov 2001).[89] Prime Minister Mikhail Kasyanov derided the idea of citizen input by means of a referendum, arguing, "Such a vote could only be an emotional decision" (Stolyarova 2000). NGOs' efforts were met with allegations of espionage as well. Duma deputy Anatolii Lukianov charged that anyone opposing the nuclear-waste bill must be an "American agent" (Felgenhauer

---

86. Throughout the debate the Minister of Atomic Energy, Ryumantsev, argued, "We are not going to make mega-profits. Everything will go to the environment" (Zyatkov 2002).

87. Russia already has an estimated fourteen thousand tons of its own nuclear waste.

88. Russian law then allowed for a citizen-initiated referendum if a registered group of more than one thousand citizens collects at least two million signatures within two months.

89. According to the 1995 federal law On the Use of Nuclear Energy, the Ministry of Atomic Energy is required to consult with the public on issues of nuclear safety and to allow for public participation in policymaking. According to Aleksei Yablokov, the ministry created the Ecological Forum, an organization made up of nuclear scientists and led by the general director of the Union of Regional Nuclear Power Companies, to fulfill this requirement. It was this forum that opposed the referendum.

2001). And Piotr Romanov, a Duma deputy chairman said, "It isn't hard to understand that the current 'environmental campaign' against the Nuclear Energy Ministry...[is] organized in the West and directed from the West. The West does not want Russia in this particular market; it wants high-tech development in Russia to end" (Kucherenko 2001). The Ministry of Atomic Energy also produced a damning brochure against the greens entitled "The Socio-Ecological Union's Antinuclear Campaign for Nuclear Safety: Methods and Resources for Disinformation." The brochure stated:

A number of these NGOs receive significant financial support from overseas, and in several cases could not exist without such support. The situation can only be seen as paradoxical: the attempt to liquidate one of the most important, life-saving branches of the Russian economy has become a mercenary activity, entered into openly, even with a certain pride and bravado in referring to their foreign bosses....Most conversation about saving the Russian environment is an attempt to misinform the Russian public, and is based on lies and garbled facts, often bordering on anti-scientific raving....For a decade the "green" figures of the ecological movement have worked carefully and purposefully to discredit the Russian atomic complex....The theme of nuclear waste importation for them is just a new reason to show themselves off. (Ministry of Atomic Energy 2001)

In spite of the government's vigorous campaign against the referendum, a coalition of grassroots and professionalized environmental organizations successfully gathered almost 2.5 million signatures in support of a referendum—an unprecedented level of public support for an environmental issue in the post-Soviet period.[90] However, the Central Election Commission ruled that only 1,873,000 signatures were authentic, causing the campaign to fall short of the two million signatures required. Many inside and outside the movement suspected the commission of bowing to official pressure in order to derail the referendum.

Although the referendum was not held, the petition drive was tremendously successful at demonstrating public opposition to the plan. Given the social apathy throughout post-Soviet Russia, the vast distances involved, and the need to coordinate thousands of activists, environmentalists' ability

---

90. This number is even more impressive than might first appear since signing a petition for referendum required each individual to give his or her passport information, including address.

to collect 2.5 million signatures was nothing less than remarkable. Why was this effort more successful at mobilizing society than earlier green activities? There are three reasons. Most important, professionalized and grassroots groups were able to bridge the divide between them and worked together to unite the capacity and political knowledge of the former with the local contacts and legitimacy of the latter. Second, environmentalists were able to cooperate in this way because they focused their activism on an issue that genuinely concerned the public. Russians were understandably anxious about the long-term and irreversible nature of the plan to import waste, and in particular the link between radioactive contamination and public health. And third, the concerns of Russian and transnational environmentalists aligned as well. Groups were able to share information and resources in a joint campaign, rather than Western organizations attempting to achieve their goals through the activities of Russian groups.[91]

Achieving Transformational Goals?

Environmentalists build their relationships with the state and society in different ways that in turn have differing implications for their ability to demand change in the political arena. They may be weak, but the character of their weakness varies. Government-affiliate organizations are the most inscrutable in this regard. These organizations are populated by individuals who appear to be genuinely dedicated to addressing environmental issues, yet they could be seen as an extension of the state bureaucracy and as an effort by the state to construct civil society according to its preferences. Activists in government-affiliate organizations have kept alive many of the Soviet-era nature-protection organizations and may slowly restructure them in response to new incentives and pressures. For now, however, these groups demonstrate that the current regime is most willing

---

91. Environmentalists were unable to activate U.S. government pressure on Russia, however. Through licensing agreements related to nonproliferation treaties, the United States controls up to 90 percent of spent nuclear fuel worldwide. Far from supporting the environmentalists, the Clinton administration encouraged the Russian government to develop the storage project, and the idea has been supported strongly by the U.S.-based Nonproliferation Trust. Documents leaked from the U.S. Energy Department during the George W. Bush administration also seemed to indicate support for the project (Brown 2001).

to cooperate with social organizations that operate under narrow, state-circumscribed conditions. Government-affiliate leaders' activism encompasses incremental efforts to change government practices from within. They have little incentive to interact closely with social groups when government decision making is generally autonomous of public opinion. The question remains, however, of what government affiliates can achieve within an administration that places such a low priority on environmental issues. Are they merely a manifestation of the state's continuing instinct to control society? Or are government affiliates a kind of Trojan horse of environmental activism inside the walls of the state?

For grassroots groups, environmentalism generally has a broader meaning than for other green organizations, encompassing varieties of both spirituality and day-to-day life that are not usually associated with environmentalism in the West. Grassroots environmental organizations tend to operate on a very small scale and reflect and accept the general public's aversion to politics. Grassroots leaders enter into activism already endowed with community ties and resources and build on existing networks and institutions in their communities—in effect recycling and reusing them—to transform their meaning and impact. While reliance on narrow personal networks has been seen as a sign of weakness in civil society (Howard 2003, 27–28), for grassroots environmentalists these networks, however limited, provide one of the few resources available for generating community change.[92] As individuals who work at some of the few community-wide institutions, teachers are well positioned to draw together otherwise unacquainted citizens into environmental activities. At the same time, they influence the next generation's ideas about the environment and the responsibilities of citizenship. However, as long as grassroots organizations avoid the political arena, they will serve simply to build social capital in society—certainly an important contribution—but will not act as real intermediaries between the state and society.

Professionalized environmental organizations have received the most attention as agents of civil society development because they have been

---

92. In the case of post-Soviet Russia, Gibson finds that Russian social networks exhibit the type of weak ties that are likely to facilitate the development of civil society. Gibson argues that in Russia, "In general, social networks appear to be an important source of learning—from others and from experience—about the meaning of democratic institutions and processes" (2001, 64).

singled out by donors and scholars as generators of social change. Professionalized organizations' access to foreign support has allowed them to tackle more complex issues, to marshal the talents and energies of a professional staff, and to use their independence from domestic sources of financing in order to challenge the government's policies and practices. However, in the early post-Soviet period, professionalized organizations have appeared to be inattentive to the need to frame their activities for average citizens. This is due in part to their relatively elite status in their previous professions as scientists or researchers and in part to the advantages of foreign funding, which provide professionalized activists with little incentive to engage the Russian public.[93] Connecting with local communities may be even harder once professionalized groups have adopted transnational goals and rhetoric.[94] As Russian environmentalists succeed in the arena of grant competitions, they begin adopting a new transnational language of "projects" and "fundraising" that mimics the donors' rhetoric but has been unfamiliar and even alienating to potential local partners.[95] In the case of professionalized organizations, the question arises: What happens when a social organization is transnational before it is local? Transnational partners' and donors' promotion of a transnational culture of social activism is one of the greatest advantages for professionalized groups, but it also estranges them from the rest of Russian society.

This state of affairs has been recognized by Russian activists and Western donors alike. Some professionalized activists have begun to doubt the efficacy of Western funding. The leader of Siberian Scholars for Global Responsibility noted the drawbacks of foreign support: "Several years ago when we drew in Western sources [of funding], it helped a lot. Now I'm

93. Bruno (1998, 184) went so far as to argue that foreign assistance has created a new socioeconomic group in the former Soviet Union.

94. Donor training has undoubtedly raised the professional qualifications of many environmental leaders. The risk, however, is that the number of people trained and the amount of information disseminated, as an easily quantifiable measure of civil society development, becomes the primary activity and objective of an organization. Many donor reports emphasize the importance of training and use training statistics to measure progress. See, for example, World Learning 1998, 20–25. For a discussion of the difficulty of evaluating foreign assistance, see Carothers (1999, 281–302).

95. As one grassroots leader noted, "Many organizations now work on 'projects.' This is new. In the past we all worked toward a goal [*po napravleniiu*], not on a project. This is a purely Western innovation" (Knizhnikova interview).

afraid that a reverse wave is occurring.... Now they say, 'Oh! Pashchenko receives money from America in order to close the factories because America wants to control all the atomic energy, so that when the gas runs out it will have everything.'"[96] Donors are also increasingly aware of the pitfalls of foreign support and have begun to demand more interaction with the public in environmental groups' projects. As the representative of the Moscow office of a U.S.-based private foundation remarked, "NGO leaders often say, 'The public doesn't understand us,' but they need to ask themselves what they are doing to involve the public—what are they doing to serve the public."[97]

In recent years, environmentalists have responded to donors' new incentives and their own desire to be more effective and are beginning to make an effort to expand the movement. For example, representatives from Green World have attempted to recruit other social groups, such as veterans and pensioners, to their campaign against the construction of a new port in the Finnish gulf. They also started a project that focuses on what is positive about the Baltic regional environment rather than only on problematic issues, inviting residents of the south bank of the Finnish gulf to contribute their thoughts on the environment, including the area's natural history, culture, and recreational opportunities. WWF-Vladivostok also began to think more broadly about tiger protection, taking political and social questions into account as well as biodiversity protection. Scientists have recognized that although poachers kill the tigers in order to sell their fur, they are paid relatively little for each skin. Small-business opportunities and ecotourism might make poaching less tempting to economically-disadvantaged local residents.

Russian environmentalists have experienced mixed outcomes in their roles as intermediaries between state and society and contributors to the development of civil society. Each organization type fulfills only part of the idealized role of intermediary, exhibiting strengths and weaknesses. What the experience of Russian environmentalists demonstrates is that it is difficult to be politically engaged in a community exhausted by seventy years of politicization, and it is difficult to be autonomous when the state still

---

96. Pashchenko interview.
97. Lawder interview.

dominates public discourse and controls most resources. Thus far, greens have had to choose which of these difficulties they will try to overcome.

In the context of what theories of civil society outline as the role of civic organizations, Russia's environmental groups thus far appear as ineffective intermediaries between state and society. While surveys demonstrate that Russian citizens are extremely dissatisfied with the quality of the country's environment, the environmental movement has been unable to tap into those grievances to gain public support for their organizations and encourage participation. State officials also remain unreceptive to Russian activism, and activists are left to publicize environmental degradation rather than prevent it. Greens have had difficulty broadening public participation, demanding consultation on public policies, and protecting themselves from arbitrary action by state agents. Even the most modest sign of success in terms of civil society development—the regime's acceptance of the organizations' right to exist—has not been fully achieved in Russia.

Still environmentalists have developed different aspects of their intermediary role, exhibiting varied strengths and weaknesses. Government affiliates push for the application of existing laws on nature protection. While the existence of government affiliates indicates that the Russian state has not made a profound break with the past in its relations with social organizations, their presence demonstrates government officials' growing awareness of the need to incorporate public participation in policymaking, if only for the sake of appearances. These environmentalists within the walls of the state may be able to bolster the government's sense of responsibility for environmental protection and prevent further erosion in state nature-protection agencies. Government affiliates are not engaged in transformation as much as they are in maintaining the status quo. They could turn out to be sites of environmental activism in the future or early examples of a new style of state co-optation of social organizations.

Grassroots organizations, on the other hand, reuse and recycle Russia's community institutions, giving them greener (and more democratic) content. As most Russian citizens are too overwhelmed by the effects of rapid economic and social change in the post-Soviet period to think about bears, tigers, or toxic waste, grassroots environmentalists focus on issues that will improve citizens' daily lives. The type of participation encouraged by grassroots groups may not be overtly political, yet the issues they tackle reaffirm the mutual rights and responsibilities of local government and citizens. Grassroots organizations face the challenge of keeping people active who aren't activists at heart. In doing so, they have encouraged more people to opt into society and to expand their affiliations beyond a small circle of family and friends. At the same time, however, grassroots groups' reliance on scarce local resources has limited the scope of their activism and left them organizationally weak and reluctant to challenge the authorities.

Professionalized organizations are a new type of organization in Russian society. They have attracted many talented individuals to the green movement, trained new leaders, increased the technological capacity of activists, and expanded the potential for international cooperation. Professionalized groups have also monitored and critiqued the state's environmental-protection record, offering an independent voice to counterbalance the government's rhetoric about the environment. At the same time, it is undeniable that these organizations have developed in a way which has left them disconnected from the primary beneficiaries of their activism—local communities—and opened them up to the government's "environmentalism-as-treason" rhetoric. Of course, social movements do not simply reflect public opinion; they are generally at the forefront of social change. Yet thus far professionalized organizations have spent little time framing their activities in ways that will resonate with local communities or mobilize public opinion in their favor. Their societal disconnection also can limit the impact of their research findings and policy proposals; professionalized environmentalists have generated an impressive amount of information about the environment but have not stimulated a corresponding demand for it. Thus, professionalized environmental organizations occupy a space somewhere between state and society, but for the most part they do not yet play a linking or mediating role. They remain, in effect, "schools for democracy" that educate only a few elite members of society.

Even as environmental organizations seem to fall short of an ideal role in civil society, they are laying the framework for the potential transformation of Russia's political system and social practices in the future. Government affiliates symbolize the state's grudging acceptance of social organizations. Grassroots activists are building social capital and drawing Russians out of the private sphere, and professionalized groups are calling the state to account. The latter two groups represent participation without advocacy and advocacy without participation respectively. The question is, Will these groups be able to cooperate in the future to minimize their weaknesses and strengthen their impact?

The events of the past decade demonstrate the difficulty of creating civil society "from outside" using external funding. While the persistence and growth of environmental organizations in Russia is a major achievement given the country's political and economic instability, foreign funding for civil society development has not lived up to donors' hopes. Grant programs have supported many professionalized organizations, but the same programs also make it possible for professionalized groups to maintain their elite orientation and weak ties with society. As one foreign donor noted, Russian organizations modeled on Western NGOs have developed an ivory tower of activism.[98] A Siberian NGO-resource-center administrator concluded, "We have been building strong organizations, but they work in a vacuum."[99] Many social movements begin within a social elite. But they are less effective when they remain elite, failing to make themselves relevant to the general population.

The primary obstacle to the development of the environmental movement is not found outside Russia, however. The Russian authorities' uncompromising response to green activism has narrowed the public space in which environmentalists operate. Yet the very intensity of the state's reaction may be promoting the idea that environmental protection and democracy are intimately intertwined.[100] The government's increasing efforts to repress the movement by manipulating the law and violating activists' civil liberties have led many environmentalists to argue publicly that they are struggling not only on behalf of the environment but for democracy as well. Consequently some greens have begun to cooperate more closely with activists in the human-rights movement to share ideas, tactics, and even resources. Vladimir Slivyak, leader of the national group Ekozashchita (Ecodefense), responded to the Central Electoral Commission's

---

98. Ibid.

99. Anatolii Zabolotnyi, author interview, Siberian Civic Initiative Support Center, Novosibirsk, December 3, 1999.

100. In a study of European antinuclear movements, Herbert Kitschelt noted, "The less innovative and more immobile a political regime, the greater the risk that this inflexibility itself will trigger demands that go beyond the immediate policy issue to ones threatening to legitimacy of the regime" (Kitschelt 1986, 82).

ruling against the greens' referendum petition on nuclear waste with strong language: "The government doesn't want a real democracy to be developed in our country. But there is one thing which is not taken into account so far—millions of people supported an initiative by environmental activists. Those people may start to protest...in more radical forms" (*Reuters News Service* 2000). The Russian government has not yet taken the people into account. If environmental activists do, then their organizations will present a formidable challenge to the current political regime.

A Greener Future?

Civil society and social mobilization are believed to be the keys to democracy and sustainable economic development. Optimism about the power of social groups, however, is based on a limited understanding of the causes and consequences of activism—particularly in postauthoritarian societies, the very settings where political change is most eagerly sought. To amend this gap in our knowledge we need to study how social organizations survive under challenging political and economic conditions and how this struggle shapes their activities and effectiveness. The impact of political liberalization on civil society and of civil society on liberalization is portrayed in its ideal form as a virtuous circle: the incremental expansion of political rights generates demand for greater political openness and government accountability, leading to further growth in citizen participation. In practice, however, the relationship between political liberalization and civil society is complex and unpredictable. For example, the Russian regime's hybrid of authoritarian and democratic features has not generated an upwelling of citizen activism, nor have citizens' groups thus far successfully demanded that the Russian state engage in further political liberalization.

In analyzing how activists have managed to continue their environmental advocacy in adverse circumstances, this book illuminates tensions and trajectories of change within civil society in order to increase the explanatory power of civil society as a concept. Examining the organizational diversity that exists within civil society—its sources and consequences—improves our understanding of the sustainability of social mobilization and its ability to bring about policy change and alter the political system. This approach moves beyond simplistic characterizations of strength or weakness to a multifaceted depiction of social mobilization that enhances our powers of analysis and prediction.

An Organizational Approach Revisited

An organizational approach knits together insights from various scholarly literatures through the concept of "organizational niches," which serves as a synthesizing mechanism to explain why certain varieties of activism are more or less likely to emerge in a given political context. Factors such as grievance, resource flows, and political opportunities interact in a society's mobilizational field, creating a limited number of niches for organizational development. Thus, an organizational approach demonstrates that there is not one strategy, nor are there many strategies, for managing limited political opportunities and resource scarcity. Instead, organizations locate themselves within a restricted number of niches in the mobilizational field in which they can sustain and expand their organizations.

An organizational approach demonstrates the crucial role that social organizations play in a social movement by institutionalizing activists' response to the broader political and economic incentive structure. Organizations, once created, then shape varieties of activism. Examining the role of organizations in structuring mobilization also highlights the importance of leaders' preferences and perceptions. Political and economic opportunities must be recognized to be exploited. Organization leaders will be more inclined and more able to exploit some opportunities than others depending on the norms, networks, and institutions with which they are affiliated. Competing, and at times mutually exclusive, logics of appropriate political action exist in any society but are particularly stark in conditions of political and economic dislocation found in postauthoritarians societies. Leaders envision the appropriate behavior of social organizations in the political system and direct their organization's search for funding and allies accordingly.

In a context of scarce resources, organizations are likely to seek funders with a similar view of the problem they address and to develop dependencies on critical funders. Grievances matter for social mobilization because they stimulate different constituencies, activating the ideas, tactics, and resources of certain groups and not others. Therefore, it is the source, not just the level, of critical resources that shape social organizations' development. Dependent organizations will try to manage these relationships in order to achieve beneficial terms, but they cannot avoid being profoundly shaped by the organizational field. Ultimately, resource dependence does not necessarily pose a problem for organizations—in fact, it is inevitable—but an erratic or unreliable stream of resources from key actors can threaten organizational survival.

Social Activism and the Soviet Legacy

In addition to contributing to broader debates about social mobilization, this book also offers insight into the development of social organizations in Russia. First, even as I adopt an organizational approach to the study of social mobilization, I recognize that the effort to construct formal organizations has generated benefits and constraints for Russian environmentalists. While the number of environmental groups now active across Russia is a sign of the movement's growing capacity, maintaining an organization requires a significant expenditure of time, energy, and resources, and is a task that may draw activists away from their substantive work. In addition, formal organizations, once developed, may be difficult to change and may constrain future opportunities for activism.

Most important, this study of social activism in Russia suggests that we could fruitfully rethink the effects of the Soviet legacy within post-Soviet Russian society. Many aspects of the Soviet legacy are indeed obstacles to the development of civil society in Russia, as has long been recognized, but the reality of how Soviet norms, networks, and institutions continue to influence mobilization is more complicated in practice than earlier studies would lead us to expect. The Soviet legacy's effects vary across social groups—groups that had different experiences under the Soviet regime and interpret the current political context differently. Activists engage in social action based on what they perceive and believe about state-society relations. Thus, each of the three organizational types positions itself in relation to the state and society in part because of the leaders' orientation toward the Soviet past, a perspective that is shaped by each leader's professional background. Decisions about whether to oppose, cooperate with, or avoid the state and how to interact with members of the public depend on how each leader envisions the goals and strategies of environmental activism and are in part a reaction to the Soviet era. This dynamic process of social mobilization under the strong influence of the previous regime is broadly applicable to other movements in the postcommunist region of more than twenty-five states, and arguably to other postauthoritarian societies as well.

These findings also suggest that some features of post-Soviet society, such as the persistence of friendship and personal-survival networks, do not necessarily have a deleterious effect on social activism, as has been previously thought. While post-Soviet Russia may not be the most fertile soil for building social organizations, it does offer some resources to social activists. Out of necessity, these activists have learned to make effective use of Soviet-era institutions, activities, and networks. Each organization finds elements of a usable past within the Soviet legacy on which to base their activism. Organizations that combine elements of Soviet-era mobilization with new practices may be the most in tune with their potential constituents, as Russian citizens are also learning to blend new and old survival strategies.

Russia's Post-Soviet Environmental Movement

What effect has the juxtaposition of the Soviet legacy with new opportunities and incentives had on the mediating role played by Russian environmental organizations between state and society? Since most grassroots environmental organizations generally avoid engaging the authorities, they are limited in their role as intermediaries. Yet they still make a contribution to civil society development in Russia. The issues prompting grassroots activism are linked to the concerns of the local population and are therefore more likely to encourage participation. Consequently grassroots organizations are more accountable to beneficiaries of activism and more likely to attract the passive support of the local bureaucrats, even if they do not generate dramatic political change. Small grassroots groups also provide both solidarity and material benefits for participants. While many of these groups do not make demands on the government directly, they do tend to pull Russians out of the private sphere into interaction with their fellow citizens, possibly building social capital to provide a basis for future cooperation.

Government affiliates address a restricted range of environmental issues and generally do not consult the public. Yet some of these long-standing organizations have names that are familiar to the public from the Soviet era, and citizens who are skeptical about new Western-style organizations may be more likely to consider supporting a government-affiliate organization. Their close relationship to the state prompts the question of whether government affiliates are truly self-organized groups in civil society. None of the government affiliates studied had been created purely to fulfill the state's requirement for political participation and each harbors dedicated activists whose views of how environmental goals should be pursued differs from that of grassroots and professionalized activists. Although they are not state-created, the political passivity of these organizations represents continuity with the state-society relations of the Soviet era and seems to offer little likelihood of greater public participation or state accountability.

Professionalized organizations have persistently demanded access to government information, have advocated for transparent and accountable policymaking, and have networked with their transnational counterparts to exert pressure on Russian state officials. After almost two decades of activism, however, these groups have yet to become accepted as regular actors in Russian politics. Many Russian government officials do not see a role for societal participation in policymaking or, when the desirability of participation is accepted in theory, officials often have not accepted the environmentalists' claim to speak on behalf of the public. As a general strategy, the movement's disengagement from local communities jeopardizes the development of a robust civil society. Without the support of Russian

citizens for environmental issues and projects, these professionalized organizations' demands lack legitimacy and open them to charges that they are
not working in the interests of the Russian people.

Professionalized leaders are aware that their difficulty generating public support is a problem. But they have not yet identified effective strategies
for changing the public's mind-set around green issues and drawing them
in as supporters. By waiting for Russian citizens to become financially secure before trying to recruit them as supporters, these groups may have
missed a window of opportunity during the immediate post-Soviet period
when new practices and attitudes were taking shape. While the conditions
for developing a mass environmental movement may not have been pro-
pitious during the post-Soviet period, professionalized activists may have
unwittingly given up the benefits of (even low) levels of public support,
such as greater legitimacy in the political arena.

One social group that environmentalists from professionalized organizations do worry about a great deal is the next generation of scientists,
those who will carry on their work in the future. "The scientific institutions are vanishing," noted Dale Miquelle of the Hornocker Institute, a
group that employs a number of Russian scientists. "There are empty halls
and few people entering the fields. This is the real problem."[1] Vladimir
Aramilev of the Institute of Sustainable Development also feared "there is
no next generation of people who will be able to do this work."[2] Aramilev
has recruited local university students to his organization and has applied
for grants (so far without success) to support young scientists by operating an inexpensive dormitory for them. When I spoke to him, however,
he acknowledged that "we can't offer them a future." The St. Petersburg
Society of Naturalists tries to support scientific education by sponsoring
competitions for the best scientific dissertations, offering the winners small
stipends to carry on their research, attend conferences, or publish their
findings. Professionalized environmentalists hope that this next generation will populate the state bureaucracies and universities in the future,
generating a change in how the government views the environment.[3]

---

1. Miquelle interview.
2. Aramilev interview.
3. The two representatives I interviewed from the Amuro-Ussuriskii Center for Bird Diversity engaged in a humorous debate on this issue: "They will be good bureaucrats, these children."

Two-Way Transnationalism

My work with environmentalists in Russia confirms the increasing significance of transnational factors in domestic social activism but highlights the fact that transnational factors affect movements unevenly, influencing some issues and organizations to a great extent, but others very little. It also suggests that transnational support is not always an asset for social organizations. The development of social organizations in Russia shows that transnational factors are sometimes empowering and other times constraining for domestic social activism. To be sure, without transnational support many Russian environmental organizations would not exist, and many worthwhile environmental projects would not have been undertaken. Transnational support for social organizations has proven to be a mixed blessing, however. It has enabled professionalized organizations to develop their organizational capacity beyond their grassroots and government-affiliate counterparts and permitted these groups to maintain a great degree of autonomy from the state, giving them the independence to critique state policies. Yet this funding raises other dilemmas, including constituency confusion in which activists have little incentive to frame their activities for the domestic audience, resulting in weak roots in local communities. This weakness has given Russian government officials the opportunity to portray these groups as anti-Russian. While this predicament is most obvious in the case of professionalized organizations, the development of all environmental groups exhibits a kind of path dependency in which the construction of early relationships and dependencies constrain future options.

The problems of environmental protection in Russia are increasingly transnational. Russia is becoming a supplier of raw materials to the world economy and a consumer of global goods and services, with all of the attendant environmental consequences of those roles. During the past fifteen years, the flow of transnational ideas and support for environmentalism has been largely one way—toward Russian activists. The poorly developed feedback loop between Russian activists and their transnational

---

When they are bureaucrats, they won't be such idiots." "But [the government] won't accept bureaucrats from our side!" "Of course, that's right, they won't take them. 'What? You like birds? Get out of here!'"

counterparts has led the Russians to borrow more from transnational environmental rhetoric than they have been able to contribute. Transnational actors, both those interested in promoting democracy internationally and those pursuing environmental protection, have found a comparative advantage in working in Russia where—it was thought—even minimal amounts of funding could achieve big improvements in the quality of governance and the state of the environment. In fact, it is easier for many Western activists to focus on the glaring violations of democratic principle and environmental protection in Russia than it is to push for more difficult incremental political and economic reforms in their own society. As Natalia Proskurina of ISAR-FE argues, "Those who give money to Russian organizations do not get less than those who receive it!"[4] To increase their effectiveness in the future, however, Russian activists need to have a greater role in agenda setting and more flexibility in how they use transnational funds. Otherwise they simply have traded a relationship with an overbearing state for one with a hegemonic community of funders promoting a new orthodoxy. In addition, transnational environmental activists could support Russians by spending time and resources monitoring the actions and investments of Western companies that operate in Russia and the international economic institutions that guide Russia's economic development.

Domestic Politics and Civil Society Development

Ultimately, the long-term success of the Russian environmental movement depends on domestic factors—opportunities to work within Russia's political system and the support of the Russian public. Even if Russian environmental organizations are able to sustain themselves in the future, the Russian government and its policies will remain the primary obstacle to and enabler of environmental protection in Russia. As a Vladivostok environmentalist noted, "The future of our organization depends to a great degree on the policies of our government. Will it support the activities of society?"[5] The actions of the Putin and Medvedev administrations

4. Proskurina interview.
5. Sobolevskii interview.

indicate that the authorities' default preference is still for state control—control of both natural resources and social activism. Pluralism in terms of economic structures, political opposition, and civil society is viewed with suspicion. State actors have been quick to take repressive action against environmentalists. In this way, the authorities have magnified the public's perception of the risk involved in participating in or cooperating with social organizations, yet another hurdle that environmental activists must overcome.

The combination of varied funding opportunities and political constraints does leave space for social mobilization, but social organizations must make difficult choices that ultimately compromise their role as agents of civil society development. Green organizations can oppose the government, publicizing the government's failure to provide environmental protection, for example, as professionalized organizations do; they can focus on apolitical issues of community improvement, as grassroots organizations do; or they can work within the limitations of the government's interest in environmental protection, as government affiliates do. If they choose to oppose the state, however, they open themselves up to harassment by the state security services and occasionally even arrest. If they choose to cooperate with the state, they severely circumscribe the scope of their activism. The choice to work only on apolitical social issues limits their impact on Russian politics, making the transformation that many supporters of civil society development hope for that much less likely.

This book also raises the question of whether social organizations are able to move society toward a transformational goal such as deepening democracy by working within existing political institutions in a closed political system. Is a certain level of political pluralism a necessary precursor to successful environmentalism? Under Russia's political conditions, is transformation a question of simply building on existing government institutions? Or is it a matter of fundamentally changing political practices and culture? Do social organizations have more to gain from cooperating with or opposing the government? What is the most effective mix of the two tactics? This is a debate that continues among Russian environmentalists themselves. Although there seems to be a growing sense that the cause of democratization is unlikely to be furthered when social organizations work within the rules of a procedural democracy that lacks substantive opportunities for real participation, a number of environmental groups are searching for opportunities to pragmatically cooperate with the state in order to do what they can to protect the environment.

Ironically, in their limitations as civil society actors these environmental organizations may resemble nothing so much as our own nongovernmental organizations in the West. While our expectations for these groups are often based on an idealized vision of civil society drawn from the "golden era" of associations in the West (Skocpol 2003), social organizations in Russia have many of the same positive and negative features as our own interest groups.[6] For the last thirty years, scholars of American nongovernmental organizations in particular have bemoaned diverse trends including advocacy organizations' disconnect from the public and their reliance on funding from foundations; the increasing number of GONGOs, or government-organized NGOs; and the unwillingness of citizens in local communities to abandon their television screens for civic-engagement opportunities in bowling leagues and soccer teams. These tendencies in the West raise the question of what it means to come of age as a social organization at the turn of the twenty-first century in an increasingly transnational environment enabled by the rapid flow of ideas, activists, and resources.

Conclusion

Environmentalists in Russia can be assured of a long and tumultuous battle for environmental protection and political change. The country's tremendous wealth in terms of natural resources and untouched wilderness areas that can still be preserved promises to draw the attention of political, economic, and social actors for years to come. Greens have struggled in adverse conditions. But the organizations they have constructed are some of the few sites of potential political change in a system that is increasingly focused on managed democracy and economic growth regardless of the environmental cost. The collapse of the Soviet system opened a window for new ideas and practices in Russia, but this window is rapidly closing

---

6. For example, in a study of U.S. interest groups in the early 1980s, Walker found that they increasingly survived "not by inducing large numbers of new members to join their groups…but by locating important new sources of funds outside the immediate membership" (Walker 1983, 397).

as post-Soviet practices stabilize and become entrenched as a new nor-malcy or equilibrium. In Russia's current political context, environmen-talists have had only limited success in promoting nature protection and political change. The Russian green movement's long-term success is in-extricably bound up in the attitudes and support of the Russian popula-tion, support that greens have spent little time cultivating. Yet given the very real grievances surrounding environmental degradation, the exis-tence of these green organizations does hold out the possibility of a broader role for public participation in the future. The question now is, How can the movement grow beyond its activist base? Russian environmentalists face the challenges of transforming the population's concern about green issues into action; of organizing around issues of local concern that will at-tract participants; and of making people feel politically effective so that they have an incentive to join in.

Environmentalists recognize the link between an open polity and envi-ronmental protection. As Greenpeace Russia spokesman Evgenii Usov re-marked, "It is impossible to build up a democratic society in Russia while ignoring ecological problems."[7] Greens also know that it is impossible to resolve environmental issues without a more participatory political system. If they can continue to work from the political margins, they can show Russian citizens that, time and time again, government actions diverge from public preferences. By pointing to the gap between the what the gov-ernment says about environmental protection and what the reality is—air quality that endangers public health, dangerous waste disposal practices, unregulated construction, and the arrest of peaceful protesters—environ-mental organizations may be able to facilitate public mobilization in the future.

The most important question about the social organizations operating in Russia in the early post-Soviet period is, Will they be able to adapt to changing political and economic conditions? Identifying organizational types allows us to anticipate how the movement might change as new re-sources become available and others decline, as the political arena opens further or continues to contract. In general, the diversity of orientations, activities, and organizational types bodes well for the sustainability of the

7. "Russian Greenpeace Branch Publicizes Its Agenda for 2002," *RFE/RL Security Report,* January 10, 2002.

environmental movement in some form even as Russia's political and economic fortunes continue to shift in unpredictable ways. There are several reasons to be optimistic. Environmentalists have proven to be ingenious at recycling Soviet institutions and networks. They have done a remarkable job of navigating the clash of political incentives, resource streams, and cultural imperatives that have left them on uncertain ground, between the Soviet system on the one hand, and the evolution of the new post-Soviet values and behaviors on the other. Compared to the early 1990s, environmental groups today also have unprecedented access to technology. Greens have a new self-confidence and, having escaped the isolation of the Soviet years, they will not easily be isolated again.

Appendix A

ORGANIZATIONS STUDIED IN
EACH REGIONAL CAPITAL

Novosibirsk

All-Russian Society for Nature
    Protection (VOOP)
AVES
Center for Ecological Initiatives
EkoDom
Ekoklub NGU
ENSI
ISAR-Siberia

League for the Defense of Wolves
League to Save the Steppe
Novomir
Save the Ob!
Siberian Ecological Fund
Siberian Scholars for Global
    Responsibility
Social Ecology

Vladimir

All-Russian Green Party
All-Russian Society for Nature
    Protection (VOOP)
Center of Ecological Education
Club of the Green Movement
Druzhina

Fund for Ecological
    Technology
Kukushkin Pond
Society of Hunters and Fishers
Socio-Ecological Union,
    Vladimir branch

Vladivostok

Amuro-Ussuriskii Center for Bird
   Diversity
Association Krug
Bluebirds
Ekolog
GSN-Phoenix
Hornocker Institute
In Defense of the Sea
Initiative Group Nadezhda
Institute for Sustainable Natural
   Resource Use

ISAR-FE
Laboratory of Ecological Education
Primorskii Krai Social Fund
   Ekologos
Resource Information Center for
   Ecological Education (RITs)
Russian Scouts
Society for Promotion of Sustainable
   Development
WWF-Vladivostok
Zov Taigi

Bryansk

Bell of Chernobyl
Bryansk Ecological Union
Center of Ecology and People-Detskii
   Sad "Ladushka"
Egida
Erika
For Chemical Safety

Friends of the Bryansk Forest
Green Attitude
Radimichi
Russian Society of Ginseng
   Growers
Viola
Youth Agency of Chemical Safety

St. Petersburg

Agenda 21 Working Group
Association Clean City
Baltic Fund for Nature
Center for the Development of
   Perception
Children of the Baltic
Children's Ecolology Center of
   Admiralty District
Coalition Clean Baltic
Committee of Spiritual Revival
Constructive Ecological Movement
   KEDR
Cultural-Enlightenment Youth
   Organization "Mir"
Ecol-Analytic Information Center
   "Soyuz"

Ecological Party of Russia KEDR
Ecological program of Sosnovii Bor
   School No. 7
Federation for Environmental
   Education
Gatchina-St. Petersburg
Green Cross
Green Party of the Northwest
Green World
Healthy Family
Holy Nature
Libra
Neva Clear Water
Non-Government Ecological
   Coordination Council
Russian Green Party

Sailors-Veterans for Ecology

Society for Protection of Animals

Society for Protection of Krestovskii Island

St. Petersburg Society of Greenpeace Supporters

St. Petersburg Society of Naturalists

St. Petersburg Urban Gardening Club

TACIS Environmental Awareness Program

Transboundary Environmental Information Agency

Appendix B

REGIONAL INDICATORS

TABLE B1. Economic Performance Indicators

	GDP per capita by PPP (in U.S. dollars)[a]	Average per capita monetary income (in U.S. dollars)[b]	Private firms per 1,000[c]	Average
Primorskii Krai	6,104 (0.94)	850 (0.80)	12 (0.43)	0.72
Novosibirsk	5,117 (0.79)	778 (0.73)	18 (0.64)	0.72
Vladimir	5,482 (0.85)	589 (0.56)	9 (0.32)	0.57
Bryansk	4,860 (0.75)	554 (0.52)	7 (0.25)	0.51
St. Petersburg	6,476 (1.00)	1,060 (1.00)	28 (1.00)	1.00

Note: In order to compare economic indicators, each value is calculated as a percentage of the highest regional indicator (in this case, as a percentage of St. Petersburg) in parentheses following each value.

[a] United Nations 2001.
[b] Goskomstat Rossii 1999, 106–7.
[c] Ibid., 316–17.

TABLE B2. Development Indicators

	UNDP Human Development Index[a]	Students per 10,000[b]	Small businesses per 1,000[c]	Doctors per 1,000[d]	Research organizations per 1,000,000[e]	Newspaper output per 1,000[f]	Average
Primorskii Krai	0.683 (0.87)	227 (0.42)	4.6 (0.19)	5.1 (0.70)	19 (0.19)	637 (0.24)	0.44
Novosibirsk	0.723 (0.92)	331 (0.61)	7.4 (0.31)	5.2 (0.71)	45 (0.46)	575 (0.22)	0.54
Vladimir	0.703 (0.90)	120 (0.22)	4.1 (0.17)	3.6 (0.49)	25 (0.26)	263 (0.10)	0.36
Bryansk	0.717 (0.92)	129 (0.24)	2.5 (0.10)	3.6 (0.49)	20 (0.20)	289 (0.11)	0.34
St. Petersburg	0.783 (1.00)	546 (1.00)	24 (1.00)	7.3 (1.00)	98 (1.00)	2,646 (1.00)	1.00

Note: Development indicators are calculated as a percentage of the region with the highest value (in this case, as a percentage of St. Petersburg) in parentheses following each value.

[a] United Nations 1999, 102–3. The method of computing the Human Development Index in the Russian Federation was changed in 1997. This table uses the old method.
[b] Goskomstat Rossii 1999, vol. 2, 210–12.
[c] Ibid., 318–319.
[d] Ibid., 213–15.
[e] Ibid., 706–7.
[f] Ibid., 252–53.

TABLE B3. Political Indicators

	Electoral Data			McMann and Petrov democracy ranking[c]	Regional executive-legislative relations during interview period[d]
	Yeltsin vote less Zyuganov, 1996	Classification of regions, 1991–95 elections[a]	Vote for Yabloko in 1999[b]		
Primorskii Krai	12.9	Region with unstable preferences	6.78	−75	Split: governor dominates
Novosibirsk	−5.2	Region with unstable preferences	9.82	19	Split: balanced
Vladimir	9.7	Moderate reformist region	5.85	0	United: governor dominates
Bryansk	−22.9	Conservative region	2.53	−31	United: governor dominates
St. Petersburg	52.8	Firmly reformist region	11.18	88	Split: balanced

[a] McFaul and Petrov 1998, vol. 1, 288–93.
[b] EastWest Institute, *Handbook of Russian Regions*, http://www.iews.org/rrabout.nsf.
[c] McMann and Petrov 2000.
[d] Characterization based on author's survey of regional press and political information available about region.

References

Agency WPS. 2003. "It Is Getting Increasingly Fashionable among Russian Oil Companies to Take Care of Environmental Protection," December 19. *Russian Environmental Digest* 5, 51 (December 15–21, 2003). http://teia.pu.ru/publications/.

Aksenova, Olga, Liubov Luneva, and Irina Khalii. 1998. *Mesto pod solntsem: posobie dlia ekologicheskikh obshchestvennykh organizatsii. Instrumentarii deiatel'nosti.* Moscow: Arc Consulting.

Alexseev, Mikhail. 2003. "Centre-Periphery Conflict as a Security Dilemma: Moscow v. Vladivostok." In *Russian Regions and Regionalism: Strength through Weakness,* Edited by Graeme P. Herd and Anne Aldis, 164–84. London: Routledge Curzon.

Alimov, Rashid. 2005. "Russian Nuke Whistleblower Files for Asylum in Finland." *Bellona.* http://www.bellona.no/bellona.org/english_import_area/international/russia/envirorights/info_access/40553.

Babcock, Glenys A. 1997. "The Role of Public Interest Groups in Democratization: Soviet Environmental Groups and Energy Policy-Making, 1985–1991." PhD diss., Rand Graduate School.

Badkhen, Anna. 1999a. "Nuclear Plant Whistleblower 'Silenced.'" *St. Petersburg Times,* September 7.

———. 1999b. "Officials Play Down Toxic Threat to Ladoga." *St. Petersburg Times,* February 16.

——. 1999c. "Slimy Toxic Sludge, a Silent Spring Surprise." *St. Petersburg Times,* March 26.

Bellona. 1998. "The Most Important Trial in Russian Legal History." October 3. http://www.bellona.no/bellona.org/english_import_area/international/russia/envirorights/nikitin/c-court1999/8207.

Berman, Sheri. 1997. "Civil Society and the Collapse of the Weimar Republic." *World Politics* 49, 3:401–29.

Bermeo, Nancy. 2003. *Ordinary People in Extraordinary Times: The Citizenry and the Breakdown of Democracy.* Princeton, NJ: Princeton University Press.

Bigg, Claire. 2002. "Activists Propose Waste Solution." *St. Petersburg Times,* June 21.

——. 2005. "Russia: Environmentalists Go Political." *RFE/RL Newsline,* June 5. http://www.rferl.org/featuresarticle/2005/06/c8768834–3a35–456a-bad2-c836241f8546.html.

——. 2006. "Russia: Scrutiny of Foreign Funds Hurts Democracy Programs." *RFE/RL Newsline,* February 15. http://www.rferl.org/featuresarticle/2006/02/29a5798f-70ec-4093–8947-c6b25c73db53.html.

Blacksmith Institute. 2006. *Annual Report 2006.* New York: Blacksmith Institute. http://www.blacksmithinstitute.org/docs/2006ar.pdf.

Borisova, Yevgeniia. 2002. "Maps Put Geologists on FSB's Hit List." *Moscow Times,* November 27.

Bourdieu, Pierre. 1984. *Distinction: A Social Critique of the Judgment of Taste.* Translated by Richard Nice. Cambridge, MA: Harvard University Press.

——. 1993. *The Field of Cultural Production: Essays on Art and Literature.* Edited by Randal Johnson. New York: Columbia University Press.

Bradshaw, Michael J. 2006. "Observations on the Geographical Dimensions of Russia's Resource Abundance." *Eurasian Geography and Economics* 47, 6:724–46.

Bransten, Jeremy. 2002. "Russia: In Windfall for Polluters, Supreme Court Orders Refund of Environmental Fines." *RFE/RL Weekday Magazine,* June 11. http://www.rferl.org/features/2002/06/11062002161859.asp.

Breslauer, George W. 1999. "Boris Yeltsin as Patriarch." *Post-Soviet Affairs* 15, 2: 186–200.

Bridger, Sue, and Frances Pine, eds. 1998. *Surviving Post-Socialism: Local Strategies and Regional Responses in Eastern Europe and the Former Soviet Union.* London: Routledge.

Brown, Paul. 2001. "U.S. Backs Plan for Russia to Import Nuclear Waste." *Guardian,* February 19.

Bruno, Marta. 1998. "Playing the Cooperation Game: Strategies around International Aid in Post-Socialist Russia." In *Surviving Post-Socialism: Local Strategies and Regional Responses in Eastern Europe and the Former Soviet Union,* edited by Sue Bridger and Frances Pine, 170–87. London: Routledge.

Brysk, Alison. 2000. *From Tribal Village to Global Village: Indian Rights and International Relations in Latin America.* Palo Alto, CA: Stanford University Press.

Bunce, Valerie. 1999. *Subversive Institutions: The Design and Destruction of Socialism and the State.* Cambridge: Cambridge University Press.

Burstein, Paul. 1998. "Interest Organizations, Political Parties, and the Study of Democratic Politics." In *Social Movement and American Political Institutions,* edited by

Anne N. Costain and Andrew S. McFarland, 39–56. Lanham, MD: Rowman and Littlefield.

Burstein, Paul, Rachel L. Einwohner, and Jocelyn A. Hollander. 1995. "The Success of Political Movements: A Bargaining Perspective." In *The Politics of Social Protest: Comparative Perspectives on States and Social Movements,* edited by J. Craig Jenkins and Bert Klandermans, 275–95. Minneapolis: University of Minnesota Press.

Carothers, Thomas. 1999. *Aiding Democracy Abroad: The Learning Curve.* Washington, DC: Carnegie Endowment for International Peace.

Carpenter, Tom. 2001. "Blowing the Whistle on Russia's Nuclear Roulette." *Give and Take* 4, 1 and 2 (Spring/Summer): 45.

Center for Russian Environmental Policy. 1999. "Resolution of the Second All-Russia Congress on Environmental Protection." *Towards a Sustainable Russia,* 12, 1 (September): 9–12.

Chambers, Simone, and Jeffrey Kopstein. 2001. "Bad Civil Society." *Political Theory* 29, 6:837–65.

Charities Aid Foundation. 1998/99. "Russia Annual Review," Moscow.

Chernyakova, Nonna. 1999. "The Wild World of Russia's Far East." *Transitions Online,* July 1999. archive.tol.cz/jul99/specr05005.html.

Cherp, Oleg. 2000. "Environmental Impact Assessment in the Russian Federation." In *Environmental Assessment in Countries in Transition,* edited by Ed Bellinger, Norman Lee, Clive George, and Anca Paduret, 114–25. Budapest: Central European University Press.

Chizhevskii, Aleksei. 1998. "Put' 'Eriki.'" In *Sila dvizhenie,* edited by Iu. V. Saiapina, 163–67. Moscow: ISAR-Moscow.

Civicus. 1999. *Civil Society at the Millennium.* West Hartford, CT: Civicus and the Kumarian Press.

Cockburn, Patrick. 2000. "Putin Puts Future of Siberian Tiger at Risk." *Independent,* July 5.

Cohen, Jean L., and Andrew Arato. 1992. *Civil Society and Political Theory.* Cambridge, MA: MIT Press.

Cole, Luke W., and Sheila R. Foster. 2001. *From the Ground Up: Environmental Racism and the Rise of the Environmental Justice Movement.* New York: New York University Press.

Collier, Ruth Berins, and James Mahoney. 1999. "Adding Collective Actors to Collective Outcomes: Labor and Recent Democratization in South America and Southern Europe." In *Transitions to Democracy,* edited by Lisa Anderson, 97–119. New York: Columbia University Press.

Cox, Rory. 2000. "Putin Sets Back Ecological Clock." *Pacific Environments* 2, 2 (Summer): 1, 4–5.

Crosbie, Judith. 2002. "Russia Is Still a Secret Society." *Irish Times,* November 8.

Crotty, Jo. 2003. "The Reorganization of Russia's Environmental Bureaucracy: Regional Response to Federal Changes." *Eurasian Geography and Economics* 44, 6:462–75.

———. 2006. "Reshaping the Hourglass? The Environmental Movement and Civil Society Development in the Russian Federation." *Organisation Studies* 27, 9:1319–38.

Dalton, Russell J. 1995. "Strategies of Partisan Influence: Western European Environmental Groups." In *The Politics of Social Protest: Comparative Perspectives on States and Social Movements,* edited by J. Craig Jenkins and Bert Klandermans, 296–323. Minneapolis: University of Minnesota Press.

———. 2005. "The Greening of the Globe? Cross-national Levels of Environmental Group Membership." *Environmental Politics* 14, 4:441–59.

Darst, Robert G. 2001. *Smokestack Diplomacy: Cooperation and Conflict in East-West Environmental Politics.* Cambridge, MA: MIT Press.

Davies, James C. 1962. "Toward a Theory of Revolution." *American Sociological Review* 27: 5–19.

Davis, Gerald F., Doug McAdam, W. Richard Scott, and Mayer N. Zald. 2005. *Social Movements and Organization Theory.* Cambridge: Cambridge University Press.

Dawson, Jane. 1996. *Eco-Nationalism: Anti-Nuclear Activism and National Identity in Russia, Lithuania, and Ukraine.* Durham, NC: Duke University Press

DeBardeleben, Joan. 1985. *The Environment and Marxism-Leninism: The Soviet and East German Experience.* Boulder, CO: Westview Press.

DeBardeleben, Joan, and Kimberly Heuckroth. 2001. "Public Attitudes and Ecological Modernization in Russia." In *The Struggle for Russian Environmental Policy,* edited by Ilmo Mass and Veli-Pekka Tynkkynen, 49–76. Helsinki: Kikimora.

Della Porta, Donatella. 2004. *Transnational Protest and Global Activism.* Lanham, MD: Rowman and Littlefield.

Della Porta, Donatella, Hanspeter Kriesi, and Dieter Rucht, eds. 1999. *Social Movements in a Globalizing World.* New York: St. Martin's Press.

Diamond, Larry. 1999. "Toward Democratic Consolidation." In *The Global Resurgence of Democracy,* 2nd ed., edited by Larry Diamond and Marc F. Plattner, 227–40. Baltimore: Johns Hopkins University Press.

———. 2001. *Developing Democracy: Toward Consolidation.* Baltimore: Johns Hopkins University Press.

Diani, Mario. 1995. *Green Networks: A Structural Analysis of the Italian Environmental Movement.* Edinburgh: Edinburgh University Press.

Digges, Charles. 2002. "Green World Activist Attacked." *Bellona,* March 15. http://www.bellona.org/english_import_area/international/russia/npps/leningrad/23348.

DiMaggio, Paul J., and Walter W. Powell. 1983. "The Iron Cage Revisited: Institutional Isomorphism and Collective Rationality in Organizational Fields." *American Sociological Review* 48:147–60.

Dubinin, Aleksandr. 1998. "Gde gnezditsia chernyi aist?" In *Sila dvizhenie,* edited by Iu. V. Saiapina, 33–36. Moscow: ISAR-Moscow.

Dunlap, Riley E., George H. Gallup, and Alec M. Gallup. 1993. "Of Global Concern: Results of the Health of the Planet Survey." *Environment* 35:7–15, 33–39.

Dzhibladze, Yuri. 1999a. "My ne trebuem l'got!" *Zapiski c Dal'nego Vostoka* (May–June): 15–16.

———. 1999b. "Russian NGOs Fight for Fair Taxation." *Give and Take* 2, 1 (Winter 1999): 4–5.

EastWest Institute. "Handbook of Russian Regions." http://www.iews.org/rrabout.nsf (accessed October 15, 2001; site now discontinued).

Eckel, Mike. 2008. "Rights Groups: Thousands of Russian NGOs Face Closure for Not Meeting Onerous Rules." *Associated Press,* April 16. http://www.usatoday.com/news/world/2008-04-16-2075579040_x.htm.

Edwards, Bob, Michael W. Foley, and Mario Diani. 2001. *Beyond Tocqueville: Civil Society and Social Capital Debate in Comparative Perspective.* Hanover, NH: University Press of New England.

Edwards, Michael, and David Hulme. 1992. *Making a Difference: NGOs and Development in a Changing World.* London: Earthscan.

Ehrenberg, John. 1999. *Civil Society: The Critical History of an Idea.* New York: New York University Press.

Elliot, Karin V. 1998. "The Evolution of an NGO: 'Phoenix' Rises out of Government Effort to Stop Poaching." *Give and Take* 1, 1 (Summer): 11.

Equator Initiative. 2004. "Rooftop Revolution—Russia," January. http://www.tve.org/ho/doc.cfm?aid=1400.

Erastova, Anastasia. 1999. "Tsentr Popova: ekologicheskogo prosveshcheniia na ostrove." *DV uchenyi,* September 14.

Esman, Milton J., and Norman T. Uphoff. 1984. *Local Organizations: Intermediaries in Rural Development.* Ithaca, NY: Cornell University Press.

Evans, Alfred B. 2008. "The First Steps of Russia's Public Chamber: Representation or Coordination?" *Demokratizatsiya* 16, 4:345–62.

Fedorov, Aleksandr, and Elena Kobets. 1999a. "Administratsiia-obshchestvennost': neprostie otnosheniia." *Most-Silta,* 1:5.

———. 1999b. "Rossiia-Finliandia: spad sotrudnichestva v okhrane prirody?" *Most-Silta,* 1:4.

———. 1999c. "Zelenoe dvizhenie: tri vzgliada iznutri." *Most-Silta,* 1:9.

Felgenhauer, Pavel. 2001. "Why Russia Wants Waste." *Moscow Times,* January 4.

Feshbach, Murray, and Alfred Friendly, Jr. 1992. *Ecocide in the USSR: Health and Nature under Siege.* New York: Basic Books.

Field, Mark G. 2000. "The Health and Demographic Crisis in Post-Soviet Russia: A Two-Phase Development." In *Russia's Torn Safety Nets,* edited by Mark G. Field and Judyth L. Twigg, 11–42. New York: St. Martin's Press.

Finnemore, Martha. 1996. *National Interests in International Society.* Ithaca, NY: Cornell University Press.

Fish, M. Steven. 1995. *Democracy from Scratch: Opposition and Regime in the New Russian Revolution.* Princeton, NJ: Princeton University Press.

———. 2000. "The Executive Deception: Superpresidentialism and the Degradation of Russian Politics." In *Building the Russian State: Institutional Crisis and the Quest for Democratic Governance,* edited by Valerie Sperling, 177–92. Boulder, CO: Westview.

———. 2001. "Authoritarianism despite Elections: Russia in Light of Democratic Theory and Practice." Paper presented at the annual meeting of the American Political Science Association, San Francisco, August 30–September 2.

Fomichev, Sergei. 1997. *Raznotsvetnye zelenye.* Moscow and Nizhnii-Novgorod: TsoDP SoES/Tretii Put'.

Fond Obshchestvennoe Mnenie. 2001a. "Obshchestvennye organizatsii v Rossii," June 28. http://www.fom.ru/virtual/body.

———. 2001b. "Problemy Ekologii," November 22. http://www.fom.ru/reports/frames/short/d014406.html.

———. 2005. "Deistviia po zashchite okruzhaiushchei sredi," July 7. http://bd.fom.ru/report/map/tb052711.

———. 2007. "Ekologiia v Rossii: otsenka situatsii." http://bd.fom.ru/report/map/d073222.

258   *References*

———. 2008. "Ekologicheskaia situatsiia v Rossiiskom massovom soznanii." December 23. http://bd.fom.ru/report/map/ekologija_otchet08.

Foweraker, Joe, and Todd Landman. 1997. *Citizenship Rights and Social Movements: A Comparative and Statistical Analysis.* Oxford: Oxford University Press.

Fowler, Alan. 1997. *Striking a Balance: A Guide to Enhancing the Effectiveness of Non-Governmental Organisations in International Development.* London: Earthscan.

Freedom House. 2008. "Russia (2008)." http://www.freedomhouse.org/template.cfm?page=22&year=2008&country=7475.

Fremin, Yulii. 1997. "Federalnoye agentstvo s delami." *Itogi.* In *Ekokhronkia,* 3/4 (33/34): 18.

Friedgut, Theodore H. 1979. *Political Participation in the USSR.* Princeton, NJ: Princeton University Press.

Gambrell, Jamey. 2004. "Philanthropy in Russia: New Money under Pressure." *Carnegie Reporter* 3, 1. http://www.carnegie.org/reporter/09/philanthropy/index.html

Gamson, William. 1975/1990. *The Strategy of Social Protest.* Belmont, CA: Wadsworth.

Garb, Paula, and Galina Komarova. 1999. "A History of Environmental Activism in Chelyabinsk." In *Critical Masses: Citizens, Nuclear Weapons Production, and Environmental Destruction in the United States and Russia,* edited by Russell J. Dalton, Paula Garb, Nicholas P. Lovrich, and John M. Whiteley, 165–92. Cambridge, MA: MIT Press.

Gazeta.SPB. 2008. "Krestovskii ostrov zakryt dlia obychnykh grazhdan." March 17. http://www.gazeta.spb.ru/30671-0/.

Gellner, Ernest. 1994. *Conditions of Liberty: Civil Society and Its Rivals.* New York: Allen Lane, Penguin Press.

Gel'man, Vladimir. 1999a. "New Law on Regional Institutions Preserves Status Quo." *Russian Regional Report,* 4, 41, November 5.

———. 1999b. "Regime Transition, Uncertainty and Prospects for Democratisation: The Politics of Russia's Regions in a Comparative Perspective." *Europe-Asia Studies* 51, 6:939–56.

Gel'man, Vladimir, Sergei Ryzhenkov, and Michael Brie. 2003. *Making and Breaking of Democratic Transitions: The Comparative Politics of Russia's Regions.* Lanham, MD: Rowman and Littlefield.

Gibson, James L. 2001. "Social Networks, Civil Society, and the Prospects for Consolidating Russia's Democratic Transition." *American Journal of Political Science* 45, 1:51–68.

Giugni, Marco G., Doug McAdam, and Charles Tilly, eds. 1998. *From Contention to Democracy.* Lanham, MD: Rowman and Littlefield.

———. 1999. *How Social Movements Matter.* Minneapolis: University of Minnesota Press.

Glushenkova, Helena I. 1999. "Environmental Administrative Change in Russia in the 1990s." *Environmental Politics* 8, 2:157–64

Goffman, Erving. 1974. *Frame Analysis: An Essay on the Organization of Experience.* New York: Harper Colophon.

Golosov, Grigorii. 2004. *Political Parties in the Regions of Russia: Democracy Unclaimed.* Boulder, CO: Lynne Rienner Publishers.

Gorbachev, Mikhail. 1995. *Memoirs.* New York: Doubleday.

Gorelov, Nikolai. 1999a. "Bryansk governor presses to consolidate hold over media." *Russian Regional Report,* 4, 8, March 4.

———. 1999b. "Bryansk mayor resigns over conflict with deputies." *Russian Regional Report,* 4, 6, February 18.

Goskomstat Rossii. 1999. *Regiony Rossii: Staticheskii Sbornik.* Moscow: Gosudarstvennyi Komitet Rossiiskoi Federatsii po statistiki.

Gosudarstvennaia Duma, Komitet po delam obshchestvennykh ob"edinenii i religioznykh organizatsii. 2000. "Statisticheskie dannye po nekommercheskim organizatsiiam razlichnykh organizatsionno-pravovykh form," March 3. Moscow.

Granovetter, Mark. 1973. "The Strength of Weak Ties." *American Journal of Sociology* 78, 6:1360–1380.

Greenpeace Russia. 1999. "Blagotvoritel'nost' v Rossii i Greenpeace: Resultaty kolichestvennogo issledovaniia," July. Moscow.

———. 2000. "Razvitie blagotvoritel'nosti v Rossii: Formy i metody privlecheniia chastnykh pozhertvovanii v Rossii," April 14–15. Moscow.

Grishina, Elena, and Iurii Dzhibladze. 2000. "Report: On the Violations Committed in the Course of Registration and Re-Registration on Public Associations in the Russian Federation in 1999." Moscow: Information Center of the Human Rights Movement and Center for the Development of Democracy and Human Rights, February 15.

Gurr, Ted. 1970. *Why Men Rebel.* Princeton, NJ: Princeton University Press.

Hahn, Gordon M. 2004. "Managed Democracy? Building Stealth Authoritarianism in St. Petersburg." *Demokratizatsiya* 12, 2:195–231.

Hahn, Jeffrey W. 2002. "The Development of Political Institutions in Three Regions of the Russian Far East." In *Regional Politics in Russia,* edited by Cameron Ross, 95–119. Manchester: Manchester University Press.

Hale, Henry E. 2002. "Civil Society from Above? Statist and Liberal Models of State-Building in Russia." *Demokratizatsiya* 10, 3: 313–17.

———. 2005. *Why Not Parties in Russia?: Democracy, Federalism, and the State.* Cambridge: Cambridge University Press.

Hann, Chris. 1996. "Introduction: Political Society and Civil Anthropology." In *Civil Society: Challenging Western Models,* edited by Chris Hann and Elizabeth Dunn, 1–24. London: Routledge.

Hannan, Michael T., and John Freeman. 1989. *Organizational Ecology.* Cambridge, MA: Harvard University Press.

Hanson, Stephen E. 2007. "The Uncertain Future of Russia's Weak State Authoritarianism." *East European Politics and Society* 21, 1:67–81.

Hawley, Amos. 1968. "Human Ecology." In *International Encyclopedia of the Social Sciences,* edited by David Phillips, 328–37. New York: MacMillan.

Hemment, Julie. 2007. *Empowering Women in Russia: Activism, Aid and NGOs.* Bloomington: Indiana University Press.

Henderson, Sarah L. 2003. *Building Democracy in Contemporary Russia: Western Support for Grassroots Organizations.* Ithaca, NY: Cornell University Press.

Henry, Laura A. 2009. "Thinking Globally, Limited Locally: The Russian Environmental Movement and Sustainable Development." In *Environmental Justice and Sustainability in the Former Soviet Union,* edited by Julian Agyeman and Yelena Ogneva-Himmelberger, 47–69. Cambridge, MA: MIT Press.

Henry, Laura A., and Lisa McIntosh Sundstrom. 2007. "Russia and the Kyoto Protocol: Seeking an Alignment of Interests and Image." *Global Environmental Politics* 7, 4 (November): 47–69.

Hipsher, Patricia L. 1998. "Democratic Transitions and Social Movement Outcomes: The Chilean Shantytown Dweller's Movement in Comparative Perspective." In *From Contention to Democracy,* edited by Marco G. Giugni, Doug McAdam, and Charles Tilly, 275–90. Lanham, MD: Rowman and Littlefield.

Hirschman, Albert O. 1970. *Exit, Voice, and Loyalty.* Cambridge, MA: Harvard University Press.

Hoffman, David E. 2000. *The Oligarchs: Wealth and Power in the New Russia.* New York: PublicAffairs.

Howard, Marc Morje. 2003. *The Weakness of Civil Society in Post-Communist Europe.* Cambridge: Cambridge University Press.

Human Rights Watch. 2008. "Choking on Bureaucracy: State Curbs on Independent Civil Society Activism" 20, 1 (February).

Huntington, Samuel P. 1993. *The Third Wave: Democratization in the Late Twentieth Century.* Norman: University of Oklahoma Press.

Institute of Natural Resources Management. 1997. "Draft Evaluation of the Impact Made by the USAID/Moscow Assistance Program on Environmental Activism and Non-Government Organizations (NGOs)." Working paper, USAID, Moscow.

Interfax. 2002a. "Environmentalists Forbidden from Protesting Plans to Build New Factory in Oryol." *Russian Environmental Digest* 4, 30 (July 22–28). http://teia.pu.ru/publications/.

——. 2002b. "200,000 Russians Receive Letters with an Appeal to Make Donations for Nature Conservation," May 16. *Russian Environmental Digest* 4, 20 (May 13–19). http://teia.pu.ru/publications/.

ISAR-Dal'nii Vostok and USAID. 1998. *Obshchestvennye ob"edineniia Dal'nego Vostoka: informatsionyi spravochnik.* Vladivostok.

ITAR-TASS. 2002. "Two Million Russians Live in Radiocontaminated Regions," April 26. *Russian Environmental Digest* 4, 17 (April 22–28). http://teia.pu.ru/publications/.

Iur'ev, Sergei. 1999. *Pravovoe regulirovanie deiatel'nosti nekommercheskikh organizatsii v Rossiiskoi Federatsii.* Moscow: ZAO "BINOM."

Jakobson, Lev, Boris Rudnik, and Sergei Shishkin. 1997. "Russia." In *The New Civic Atlas: Profiles of Civil Society in 60 Countries,* Liza W. Poinier, 115–17. Washington, DC: Civicus.

Jancar, Barbara. 1987. *Environmental Management in the Soviet Union and Yugoslavia: Structure and Regulation in Federal Communist States.* Durham, NC: Duke University Press.

Janos, Andrew C. 2000. *East Central Europe in the Modern World: The Politics of the Borderlands from Pre- to Postcommunism.* Palo Alto, CA: Stanford University Press.

Jenkins, J. Craig, and Bert Klandermans, eds. 1995. *The Politics of Social Protest.* Minneapolis: University of Minnesota.

Jenkins, J. Craig, and Charles Perrow. 1977. "Insurgency of the Powerless: Farm Workers Movements." *American Sociological Review* 42:249–68.

Johnson, Avery. 2002. "Urban Group Dreams of Eco-Friendly Settlement." *Moscow Times,* November 12.

Johnson, Janet E. 2009. *Gender Violence in Russia: The Politics of Feminist Intervention.* Bloomington: Indiana University Press.

Jowitt, Kenneth. 1992. *The New World Disorder: The Leninist Extinction.* Berkeley: University of California Press.

Kaiumov, Askhat. 2001. "Regional'nye aspekty stanovleniia konstruktivnogo vlasti i obshchestva." *Vesti SoES* 4, 19. http://www.seu.ru/vesti/2001–04/04.htm.

Kaliuzhnova, E. M. 1998. "Fond 'Kukushkin Prud': nasha istoriia." *Zelenaia Politika,* 2 (November): 1.

Karatnycky, Adrian, Alexander Motyl, and Amanda Schnetzer, eds. 2001. *Nations in Transit 2001.* New York: Freedom House.

Karl, Terry. 1990. "Dilemmas of Democratization in Latin America." *Comparative Politics* 23, 1 (October): 1–21.

Karl, Terry, and Philippe C. Schmitter. 1991. "Modes of Transition in Latin America, Southern and Eastern Europe." *International Social Science Journal* 43, 2 (May): 269–84.

Keane, John. 1998. *Civil Society: Old Images, New Visions.* Palo Alto, CA: Stanford University Press.

Keck, Margaret E. 1995. "Social Equity and Environmental Politics in Brazil: Lessons from the Rubber Tappers of Acre." *Comparative Politics* 27, 4 (July): 409–24.

Keck, Margaret E., and Kathryn Sikkink. 1998. *Activists beyond Borders: Advocacy Networks in International Politics.* Ithaca, NY: Cornell University Press.

Khalii, Irina. 1998. "Chelovecheskie resursy." Copy of article given to author by Rosa Khatskelevich, Tsentr RNO, St. Petersburg, April 1999.

Kirkow, Peter. 1997. "Local Self-Government in Russia: Awakening from Slumber?" *Europe-Asia Studies* 49, 1 (January): 43–58.

Kitschelt, Herbert P. 1986. "Political Opportunity Structures and Political Protest: Anti-Nuclear Movements in Four Democracies." *British Journal of Political Science* 51:57–85.

Kjeldsen, Stig. 2000. "Financing of Environmental Protection in Russia: The Role of Charges." *Post-Soviet Geography and Economics* 41, 1:48–62.

Kommersant. 2007. "75 Successors Too Many," June 12. http://www.kommersant.com/p773140/Russian_presidential_elections_successor_/.

Konovalova, Evgeniya. 2007. "Russia: Reactionary Revolutionaries." *Transitions Online,* May 15.

Kotilainen, Juha, Maria Tysiachniouk, Antonina Kuliasova, Ivan Kuliasov, and Svetlana Pchelkina. 2008. "The Potential for Ecological Modernisation in Russia: Scenarios from the Forest Industry." *Environmental Politics* 17, 1:58–77.

Kotov, Vladimir, and Elena Nikitina. 2002. "Reorganisation of Environmental Policy in Russia: The Decade of Success and Failures in Implementation and Perspective Quests." Working paper, Fondazione Eni Enrico Mattei (July). http://www.feem.it/Feem/Pub/Publications/WPapers/WP2002–057.htm.

Kouzmina, Anna, and Oleg Yanitsky. 1999. "Interpersonal Networks of Russian Greens." In *Towards a Sustainable Future: Environmental Activism in Russia and the United States; Selected Readings,* edited by Maria Tysiachniouk and George W. Mc-Carthy, 173–90. St. Petersburg: Institute of Chemistry of St. Petersburg University.

Kovalev, Vladimir. 2004. "Bill to Save Green Areas Suspended at City Hall." *St. Petersburg Times,* January 9.

Krestnikova, Irina, and Ekaterina Levshina. 2002. "Korporativnaia filantropia: mify i realnost.'" Moscow: Charities Aid Foundation. http://www.cafrussia.ru/researches.shtml.

Kriesi, Hanspeter. 1996. "The Organizational Structure of New Social Movements in a Political Context." In *Comparative Perspectives on Social Movements: Political Opportunities, Mobilizing Structures, and Cultural Framings,* edited by Doug McAdam, John D. McCarthy, and Mayer N. Zald, 152–84. Cambridge: Cambridge University Press.

Kriesi, Hanspeter, Ruud Koopmans, Jan Willen Duyvendak, and Marco G. Giugni. 1995. *New Social Movements in Western Europe: A Comparative Analysis.* Minneapolis: University of Minnesota Press.

Kucherenko, Vladimir. 2001. "A Nuclear Portfolio for the New Minister." *Rossiiskaia gazeta,* April 5. In *Russian Environmental Digest* 3, 14 (April 2–8). http://teia.pu.ru/publications/.

Kutepova, Nadezhda L. 2001. "Public Opinion Surveys Help Counter Pro-Nuclear Misinformation." *Give and Take* 4, 1 and 2 (Spring/Summer): 14–15.

Kutepova, Nadezhda L., and Olga Tsepilova. 2007. "Closed City, Open Disaster." In *Cultures of Contamination: Legacies of Pollution in Russia and the U.S.,* edited by Michael R. Edelstein, Maria Tysiachniouk, Lyudmila V. Smirnova, 147–64. Amsterdam: Elsevier.

Kyodo News Service—Japan Economic Newswire. 2004. "Russian NGO Fights Poachers to Protect Endangered Siberian Tigers," February 21. *Russian Environmental Digest* 6, 8 (February 16–22). http://teia.pu.ru/publications/.

Lambroschini, Sophie. 2000. "Russia: Acquitted Environmentalist May Face Retrial." *RFE/RL Newsline,* August 1.

———. 2001. "Russia: Environmental Woes Grow One Year After Watchdog Group Dissolved." *RFE/RL Newsline,* June 6.

Lapidus, Gail W. 1999. "Asymmetrical Federalism and State Breakdown in Russia." *Post-Soviet Affairs,* 15, 1 (January-March): 74–82.

Ledeneva, Alena V. 1998. *Russia's Economy of Favors: Blat, Networking, and Informal Exchange.* Cambridge: Cambridge University Press.

Lee, Yok-Shui F., and Alvin Y. So, eds. 1999. *Asia's Environmental Movements: Comparative Perspective.* Armonk, NY: M. E. Sharpe.

Levinsky, Alex. 1998. "Bryansk Opposition Unites against Communist Governor." *Russian Regional Report,* 3, 14 (April 9). http://www.res.ethz.ch/kb/search/details.cfm?id=14468&lng=en.

Levitsky, Steven, and Lucan Way. 2002. "The Rise of Competitive Authoritarianism." *Journal of Democracy* 13, 2 (April): 51–65.

Lindemann-Komarova, Sarah. 2008. "The Parallel Universes of NGOs in Russia," April 18. In Johnson's Russia List 2008-79. http://www.cdi.org/russia/johnson/2008-79-25.cfm.

Linz, Juan J., and Alfred Stepan. 1996. *Problems of Democratic Transition and Consolidation: Southern Europe, South America, and Post-Communist Europe.* Baltimore and London: Johns Hopkins University Press.

Lipset, Seymour Martin. 1959. "Some Social Requisites of Democracy: Economic Development and Political Legitimacy." *American Political Science Review* 53 (March): 69–105.

Luneva, Liubov'. 1998. "Obshchestvennoe dvizhenie ili tretii sektor?" *Biulleten' Moskovskogo ISAR* 7 (Fall/Winter): 24–25.

Luneva, Liubov'. 1999. "Otsenka deiatel'nosti." Photocopy given to author by Rosa Khatskalevich, RNO Center, St. Petersburg, April 1999.

Maleshin, Nikolai. 2003–2004. "The Farcical Third All-Russian Congress of Nature Conservation." *Russian Conservation News* 34 (Fall/Winter): 2–3.

March, James G., and Johan P. Olsen. 1989. *Rediscovering Institutions: The Organizational Basis of Politics.* New York: Free Press.

Maslennikova, Irina. 2000a. "Internet Booming in Novosibirsk." *Russian Regional Report* 5, 11 (March 22). http://www.res.ethz.ch/kb/search/details.cfm?id=14221&lng=en.

———. 2000b. "NGO Fairs an Instrument for Social Partnership," *Russian Regional Report* 5, 26 (July 6). http://www.res.ethz.ch/kb/search/details.cfm?id=14197&lng=en.

McAdam, Doug. 1982/1999. *Political Process and the Development of Black Insurgency, 1930–1970.* Chicago: University of Chicago Press.

———. 1998a. "Conclusion: The Future of Social Movements." In *From Contention to Democracy,* edited by Marco G. Giugni, Doug McAdam, and Charles Tilly, 229–45. Lanham, MD: Rowman and Littlefield.

———. 1998b. "On the International Origins of Domestic Political Opportunities." In *Social Movements and American Political Institutions,* edited by Anne N. Costain and Andrew S. McFarland, 251–67. Lanham, MD, and Boulder, CO: Rowman and Littlefield.

McAdam, Doug, John D. McCarthy, and Mayer N. Zald, eds. 1996. *Comparative Perspectives on Social Movements: Political Opportunities, Mobilizing Structures, and Cultural Framings.* Cambridge: Cambridge University Press.

McAdam, Doug, Sidney Tarrow, and Charles Tilly. 1997. "Toward an Integrated Perspective on Social Movements in Revolutions." In *Comparative Politics: Rationality, Culture, and Structure,* edited by Mark Irving Lichbach and Alan S. Zuckerman, 142–73. Cambridge: Cambridge University Press.

———. 2001. *Dynamics of Contention.* Cambridge: Cambridge University Press.

McCarthy, John D., and Mayer N. Zald. 1977. "Resource Mobilization and Social Movements: A Partial Theory." *American Journal of Sociology* 82, 6:1212–41.

McFaul, Michael. 2001. *Russia's Unfinished Revolution: Political Change from Gorbachev to Putin.* Ithaca, NY: Cornell University Press.

McFaul, Michael, and Nikolai Petrov, eds. 1998. *Politicheskii al'manakh Rossii 1989–1997.* 2nd ed. Moscow: Moscow Carnegie Center.

McMann, Kelly M., and Nikolai V. Petrov. 2000. "A Survey of Democracy in Russia's Regions." *Post-Soviet Geography and Economics* 41, 3:155–82.

Melucci, Alberto. 1989. *Nomads of the Present: Social Movements and Individual Needs in Contemporary Society.* Edited by John Keane and Paul Mier. Philadelphia: Temple University Press.

Mendelson, Sarah, and John K. Glenn. 2002. *The Power and Limits of NGOs: A Critical Look at Building Democracy in Eastern Europe and Eurasia.* New York: Columbia University Press.

Meyer, Henry. 2002. "Ecologists in Russia Feel the Heat Again from State Probe," Agence France Presse, November 27. *Russian Environmental Digest* 4, 48 (November 25–December 1).

Michels, Robert. 1962. *Political Parties: A Sociological Study of the Oligarchical Tendencies of Modern Democracy.* New York: Free Press.

Ministry of Atomic Energy, Press Service, Department of Safety and Emergency Situations. 2001. "The Socio-Ecological Union's Antinuclear Campaign for Nuclear Safety: Methods and Resources for Disinformation," translated by Eliza Klose. Reprinted in *Give and Take* 4, 1 and 2 (Spring/Summer): 7.

Mironova, Natalia, Maria Tysiachniouk, and Jonathan Reisman. 2007. "The Most Contaminated Place on Earth: Community Response to Long-Term Radiological Disaster in Russia's Southern Urals." In *Cultures of Contamination: Legacies of Pollution in Russia and the U.S.,* edited by Michael R. Edelstein, Maria Tysiachniouk, and Lyudmila V. Smirnova, 165–83. Amsterdam: Elsevier.

Mirovitskaya, Natalia. 1998. "The Environmental Movement in the Former Soviet Union." In *Environment and Society in Eastern Europe,* edited by Andrew Tickle and Ian Welsh, 33–66. Harlow, UK: Longman.

Mischenko, Vera. 1998. "Ecojuris Institute Wins Forest Protection Case," February 17. http://forests.org/archive/europe/russforv.htm.

Mishina, Anastasia. 2000. "Siberian NGOs Grow and Become More Professional." *Russian Regional Report* 5, 26 (July 6).

Morris, Aldon, and Suzanne Staggenborg. 2004. "Leadership in Social Movements." In *The Blackwell Companion to Social Movements,* edited by David A. Snow, Sarah A. Soule, and Hanspeter Kriesi, 171–96. Malden, MA: Blackwell.

Moscow Times. 2001. "Protestors Slam Nuclear Waste Bill," February 20.

Moshkin, Mikhail. 2008. "Grants: The Public Chamber; State Support of Non-Governmental Organization Is Rapidly Increasing." *Vremya Novostei,* April 24. Available through Johnson's Russia List 2008–80.

Munck, Gerardo L., and Carol Skalnik Leff. 1999. "Modes of Transition and Democratization: South America and Eastern Europe and Comparative Perspective." In *Transitions to Democracy,* edited by Lisa Anderson, 193–216. New York: Columbia University Press.

Newell, Josh. 2004. *The Russian Far East.* McKinleyville, CA: Daniel and Daniel.

Oates, Sarah. 2007. "The Neo-Soviet Model of the Media." *Europe-Asia Studies* 59, 8:1279–97.

Oberschall, Anthony. 1973. *Social Conflict and Social Movements.* Englewood Cliffs, NJ: Prentice-Hall.

Obshchestvennaia Palata Rossiiskoi Federatsii [Public Chamber of the Russian Federation]. 2008. *Doklad sostoianii grazhdanskogo obshchestva v Rossiiskoi Federatsii.* Moscow. http://www.oprf.ru/files/Doklad-OPRF-2008.pdf.

O'Donnell, Guillermo, and Philippe C. Schmitter. 1986. *Transitions from Authoritarian Rule: Tentative Conclusions about Uncertain Democracies.* Baltimore: Johns Hopkins University Press.

Offe, Claus. 1985. "New Social Movements: Challenging the Boundaries of Institutional Politics." *Social Research* 52, 4 (Winter): 817–68.

Oldfield, Jonathan, D. 2005. *Russian Nature: The Environmental Consequences of Societal Change.* Burlington, VT: Ashgate.

Organisation for Economic Cooperation and Development. 1999. *Environmental Performance Reviews: The Russian Federation.* Paris: OECD.

———. 2007. *Policies for a Better Environment: Progress in Eastern Europe, Caucasus and Central Asia.* Paris: OECD. http://www.oecd.org/document/17/0,3343,fr_2649_3429 1_39305233_1_1_1_1,00.html.

Osborn, Andrew. 2004. "Kyoto Treaty Is an Auschwitz for Russia, Says Putin's Adviser," *Independent,* April 15.

Ostergren, David M., and Peter Jacques. 2002. "A Political Economy of Russian Nature Conservation Policy: Why Scientists Have Taken a Back Seat." *Global Environmental Politics* 2, 4:102–24.

Ottaway, Marina, and Thomas Carothers, eds. 2000. *Funding Virtue: Civil Society Aid and Democracy Promotion.* Washington, DC: Carnegie Endowment for International Peace.

Pasko, Grigory. 2008. "Interview with Russian Environmental Activist Alexey Yablokov," October 8. http://www.robertamsterdam.com/2008/10/grigory_pasko_interview_with_r.htm.

Pchela. 1997. "Zelenyi Peterburg v voprosakh i otvetakh," 11:78–88.

Pellow, David Naguib. 2007. *Resisting Global Toxics: Transnational Movements for Environmental Justice.* Cambridge, MA: MIT.

Peluso, Nancy Lee, and Michael Watts, eds. 2001. *Violent Environments.* Ithaca, NY: Cornell University Press.

Peterson, D. J. 1993. *Troubled Lands: The Legacy of Soviet Environmental Destruction.* Boulder, CO: Westview Press.

———. 2000. "Putin Regime Pressures Russian Environmental Activists." *Give and Take* 3, 3 (Fall): 6.

Peterson, D. J., and Eric K. Bielke. 2001. "The Reorganization of Russia's Environmental Bureaucracy: Implications and Prospects." *Post-Soviet Geography and Economics* 42, 1:65–67.

Petrov, Mikhail. 2002. "60 Percent of Russians Live in Bad Environment." ITAR-TASS, November 25.

Petrova, A. 1999. "Only One-Third of Russians Are Satisfied with the Environment." Fond Obshchestvennye Mnenie, June 5. http://english.fom.ru/reports/frames/eof992405.html.

Pfeffer, Jeffrey. 1982. *Organizations and Organization Theory.* Boston: Pitman.

Pfeffer, Jeffrey, and Gerald R. Salancik. 1978. *The External Control of Organizations: A Resource Dependence Perspective.* New York: Harper and Row.

Piven, Frances Fox, and Richard A. Cloward. 1977. *Poor People's Movements: Why They Succeed, How They Fail.* New York: Pantheon Books.

Powell, Leslie. 2002. "Western and Russian Environmental NGOs: A Greener Russia?" In *The Power and Limits of NGOs: A Critical Look at Building Democracy in Eastern Europe and Eurasia,* edited by Sarah E. Mendelson and John K. Glenn, 126–51. New York: Columbia University Press.

Pryde, Philip. 1991. *Environmental Management in the Soviet Union.* Cambridge: Cambridge University Press.

Pustintsev, Boris. 2001. "The Kremlin and Civil Society." *Moscow Times,* October 22.

Putnam, Robert D. 1993. *Making Democracy Work: Civic Traditions in Modern Italy.* With Robert Leonardi and Raffaella Y. Nanetti. Princeton, NJ: Princeton University Press.

Quigley, Kevin F. F. 1997. *For Democracy's Sake: Foundations and Democracy Assistance in Central Europe.* Washington, DC: Woodrow Wilson Center Press.

Rau, Zbigniew, ed. 1991. *The Reemergence of Civil Society in Eastern Europe and the Soviet Union.* Boulder, CO: Westview Press.

Ray, Raka. 1999. *Fields of Protest: Women's Movement in India.* Minneapolis: University of Minnesota Press.

Reporters sans Frontieres. "Worldwide Press Freedom Index 2007." http://www.rsf.org/article.php3?id_article=24025.

Reuters News Service. 2000. "Russia Denies Referendum on Nuclear Waste Import," November 29. http://www.forest.ru/eng/problems/control/publication15.html.

RFE/RL Newsline. 2001. "Putin Inaugurates Two Export Terminals," December 28. http://www.rferl.org/newsline/2001/12/281201.asp.

——. 2008. "Public Chamber Criticizes Application of NGO Registration Law," April 10. http://www.rferl.org/newsline/2008/04/1-rus/rus-100408.asp.

RIA Novosti. 2006. "Putin Restates Opposition to Overseas Financing for NGOs." July 4. Available through Johnson's Russia List, 2006–151.

RIA OREANDA. 2004. "WWF of Russia, Greenpeace of Russia Accuse Ministry of Natural Resources of Falsifying 3d Congress Resolution," January 23. *Russian Environmental Digest* 6, 4, (January 19–25).

Richter, James. 2009. "Putin and the Public Chamber." *Post-Soviet Affairs* 25, 1 (January–March 2009): 39–65.

Rose, Richard, William Mishler, and Christian Haerpfer. 1998. *Democracy and Its Alternatives: Understanding Post-Communist Societies.* Baltimore: Johns Hopkins University Press.

Rose, Richard, William Mishler, and Neil Munro. 2006. *Russia Transformed: Developing Popular Support for a New Regime.* Cambridge: Cambridge University Press.

Ross, Cameron, ed. 2002. *Regional Politics in Russia.* Manchester: Manchester University Press.

Rucht, Dieter. 1997. "Limits to Mobilization: Environmental Policy for the European Union." In *Transnational Social Movements and Global Politics,* edited by Jackie Smith, Charles Chatfield, and Ron Pagnucco, 195–213. Syracuse, NY: Syracuse University Press.

——. 1999. "The Impact of Environmental Movements in Western Societies." In *How Social Movements Matter,* edited by Marco Giugni, Doug McAdam, and Charles Tilly, 204–24. Minneapolis: University of Minnesota Press.

Salamon, Lester M., and Helmut K. Anheier. 1996. *The Emerging Nonprofit Sector: An Overview.* Manchester: Manchester University Press.

——. 1997. *Defining the Nonprofit Sector: A Cross-National Analysis.* Manchester: Manchester University Press.

Salmenniemi, Suvi. 2008. *Democratization and Gender in Contemporary Russia.* New York: Routledge.

Sampson, Steve. 1996. "The Social Life of Projects: Importing Civil Society to Albania." In *Civil Society: Challenging Western Models,* edited by Chris Hann and Elizabeth Dunn, 121–42. London: Routledge.

Schmitter, Philippe C. 1997. "Civil Society East and West." In *Consolidating the Third Wave Democracies: Themes and Perspectives,* edited by Larry Diamond, Marc F. Plattner, Yun-han Chu, and Hung-mao Tien, 239–62. Baltimore: Johns Hopkins University Press.

Scott, W. Richard, Martin Ruef, Peter J. Mendel, and Carol A. Caronna. 2000. *Institutional Change and Healthcare Organization: From Professional Dominance to Managed Care.* Chicago: Chicago University Press.

Seligman, Adam B. 1992. *The Idea of Civil Society.* New York: Free Press.

Shevchuk, Yuri. 1995. "Deiatel'nost', struktura, i kharakternye osobennosti ekologicheskikh organizatsii Sankt-Peterburga." *Spravochnik proektov i programm obshchestvennykh organizatsii Sankt-Peterburga.* St. Petersburg: BINKO/euroCom.

Shuvalova, Natalia, ed. 2006. "Otnoshenie k blagotvoritel'nosti v Rossii: Obzor materialov issledovaniia." Moscow: Forum Donorov. http://donorsforum.ru/_files/156_54.doc.

Sibirskii Tsentr Podderzhki Obshchestvennykh Initsiativ. 1998. *Obshchestvennye ob"edineniia Sibirskogo Regiona: Novosibirskaia Oblast'.* Novosibirsk.

Skocpol, Theda. 2003. *Diminished Democracy: From Membership to Management in American Civic Life.* Norman: University of Oklahoma Press.

Smelser, Neil. 1968. *Essays in Sociological Explanation.* Englewood Cliffs, NJ: Prentice Hall.

Smillie, Ian, and Henny Hemlich, eds. 1999. *Government-NGO Partnerships for International Development.* London: Earthscan.

Smith, Jackie, Charles Chatfield, and Ron Pagnucco, eds. 1997. *Transnational Social Movements and Global Politics.* Syracuse, NY: Syracuse University Press.

Smith, Kathleen. 1996. *Remembering Stalin's Victims: Popular Memory and the End of the USSR.* Ithaca, NY: Cornell University Press.

Smyth, Regina. 2006. *Candidate Strategies and Electoral Competition in the Russian Federation: Democracy without Foundation.* Cambridge: Cambridge University Press.

Snow, David A., and Robert D. Benford. 1992. "Master Frames and Cycles of Protest." In *Frontiers in Social Movement Theory,* edited by Aldon D. Morris and Carol McClurg Mueller, 133–55. New Haven, CT: Yale University Press.

Snow, David A., E. Burke Rochford, Jr., Steven K. Worden, and Robert D. Benford. 1986. "Frame Alignment Processes, Micromobilization, and Movement Participation." *American Sociological Review* 51:464–81.

Solovyova, Alla V. 1995. "Some Thoughts on Charity and Funding Sources and Donors' Motives." In *Handbook of Projects and Programs of Social Organizations of St. Petersburg,* 31–36. St. Petersburg: TACIS.

Sotsial'no-Ekologicheskii Soyuz. 1992. *30 let dvizheniia: neformal'noe prirodokhrannoe molodozhnoe dvizhenie v SSSR. Fakty i dokumenty 1960–1992.* Kazan': SoES.

Sperling, Valerie. 1999. *Organizing Women in Contemporary Russia: Engendering Transition.* Cambridge: Cambridge University Press.

Staggenborg, Suzanne. 1988. "The Consequences of Professionalization and Formalization in the Pro-Choice Movement." *American Sociological Review* 53 (August): 585–606.

Starr, S. Frederick. 1988. "Soviet Union: A Civil Society." *Foreign Policy* 70 (Spring): 26–41.

State Environmental Protection Committee of the Russian Federation. 1997. "Russian Federation Country Profile: Implementation of Agenda 21," April. http//:www.un.org/esa/earthsummit/rusia-cp.htm.

Stenning, Alison. 1999. "Marketisation and Democratisation in the Russian Federation: The Case of Novosibirsk." *Political Geography* 18, 5 (June): 591–617.

Stolyarova, Galina. 2000. "Nuclear Waste Referendum Progresses." *St. Petersburg Times,* October 24.

Stoner-Weiss, Kathryn. 1997. *Local Heroes: The Political Economy of Russian Regional Governance.* Princeton, NJ: Princeton University Press.

Sundstrom, Lisa McIntosh. 2006. *Funding Civil Society: Foreign Assistance and NGO Development in Russia.* Palo Alto, CA: Stanford University Press.

Swidler, Ann. 1986. "Culture in Action: Symbols and Strategies." *American Sociological Review* 51, 2:273–86.

TACIS. 1995. *Spravochnik proektov i program obshchestvennykh organizatsii Sankt-Peterburga.* St. Petersburg: BIKNO and EuroCom.

Tarrow, Sidney. 1994. *Power in Movement: Collective Action, Social Movements, and Politics.* Cambridge: Cambridge University Press.

——. 1996. "States and Opportunities." In *Comparative Perspectives on Social Movements: Political Opportunities, Mobilizing Structures, and Cultural Framings,* edited by Doug McAdam, John D. McCarthy, and Mayer N. Zald, 41–61. Cambridge: Cambridge University Press.

——. 2005. *The New Transnational Activism.* Cambridge: Cambridge University Press.

Taylor, Bron, ed. 1995. *Ecological Resistance Movements: The Global Emergence of Radical and Popular Environmentalism.* Albany: State University of New York Press.

Taylor, Verta. 1989. "Social Movement Continuity: The Women's Movement in Abeyance." *American Sociological Review* 54:761–75.

Tilly, Charles. 1999. "Conclusion: Why Worry about Citizenship?" In *Extending Citizenship, Reconfiguring States,* edited by Michael Hanagan and Charles Tilly, 247–59. Lanham, MD: Rowman and Littlefield.

Tkachenko, Stanislav L. 2003. "Regionalisation of Russian Foreign and Security Policy." In *Russian Regions and Regionalism: Strength through Weakness,* edited by Graeme P. Herd and Anne Aldis, 204–23. London: Routledge Curzon.

Tocqueville, Alexis de. 1835/1990. *Democracy in America.* New York: Vintage Classics, Random House.

Touraine, Alain. 1981. *The Voice and the Eye: An Analysis of Social Movements.* Translated by Alan Duff. Cambridge: Cambridge University Press.

Transitions Online. 1999. "Russia: The Green Menace." August 2. http://www.archive.tol.cz/itowa/aug99rus.html.

Treisman, Daniel. 1999. *After the Deluge: Regional Crises and Political Consolidation in Russia.* Ann Arbor: University of Michigan.

Trotsky, Leon. 1925. *Literature and Revolution.* Translated by Rose Strunsky. London: George Allen and Unwin.

Tsepilova, Olga. 1999. "Emerging Public Participation in Decision Making (Kirishi Case)." In *Towards a Sustainable Future: Environmental Activism in Russia and the United States; Selected Readings,* edited by Maria S. Tysiachniouk and George W. McCarthy, 61–83. St. Petersburg: Institute of Chemistry of St. Petersburg University.

Tynkkynen, Nina. 2006. "Action Frames of Environmental Organisations in Post-Soviet St. Petersburg." *Environmental Politics* 15, 4:639–49.

Tysiachniouk, Maria. 2006. "Forest Certification in Russia." In *Confronting Sustainability: Forest Certification in Developing and Transitioning Countries,* Report No. 8, edited by B. Cashore, F. Gale, E. Meidinger, and D. Newsom, 261–95. New Haven, CT: Yale School of Forestry and Environmental Studies.

Tysiachniouk, Maria, and Alla Bolotova. 1999. "Environmental Activism in the St. Petersburg Region." In *Towards a Sustainable Future: Environmental Activism in Russia and the United States; Selected Readings,* edited by Maria S. Tysiachniouk and George W. McCarthy, 191–209. St. Petersburg: Institute of Chemistry of St. Petersburg University.

Tysiachniouk, Maria, and Alexander Karpov. 1998. "Development of Environmental Nongovernmental Organizations in Russia." Paper presented at the Third International Conference of the International Society for Third Sector Research, Geneva, Switzerland, July 8–11.

Tysiachniouk, Maria, and George McCarthy. 1999. "A Comparison of Attitudes of Russian and U.S. Environmentalists and Suggested Policies to Promote Sustainable Development." In *Towards a Sustainable Future: Environmental Activism in Russia and the United States; Selected Readings,* edited by Maria S. Tysiachniouk and George W. McCarthy, 1–18. St. Petersburg: Institute of Chemistry of St. Petersburg University.

Tysiachniouk, Maria, and Jonathan Reisman. 2004. "Co-Managing the Taiga: Russian Forests and the Challenge of International Environmentalism." In *Politics of Forests: Northern Forest-Industrial Regimes in the Age of Globalization,* edited by Ari Auku-sti Lehtinen, Jakob Donner-Amnell, and Bjornar Saether, 157–75. Aldershot, UK: Ashgate.

United Nations. 1999. *Human Development Report 1999: Russian Federation.* Moscow: UNDP.

———. 2001. *Human Development Report 2001: Russian Federation.* Moscow: UNDP.

———. 2002. *Johannesburg Summit 2002: Russian Federation Country Profile.* http://www.un.org/esa/agenda21/natlinfo/wssd/russianfed.pdf.

———. 2003. *Human Development Report: Russian Federation, 2002/2003.* Moscow: UNDP.

United States Agency for International Development (USAID). 1999. "NGO Sustainability Index." http://www.usaid.gov/locations/europe_eurasia/dem_gov/ngo index/1999/.

———. 2002. "USAID/Russia Strategy Amendment 1999–2005," February. http://www.usaid.ru/en/more_info/publications/strategy-public_version.doc.

United States Agency for International Development (USAID), Center for Democracy and Governance. 1998a. "Democracy and Governance: A Conceptual Framework," November. http://www.usaid.gov/democracy/pubsindex.html.

———. 1998b. "Handbook of Democracy and Governance Program Indicators," August. http://www.usaid.gov/democracy/pubsindex.html.

United States Agency for International Development (USAID), Office of the Inspector General. 2005. "Audit of USAID/Russia's Democracy Program," Report No. B-118-05-002-P. Budapest: USAID, March 31. http://www.usaid.gov/oig/public/fy05rpts/b-118-05-002-p.pdf.

Urban, Michael. 1997. *The Rebirth of Russian Politics*. With Vyacheslav Igrunov and Sergei Mitrokhin. Cambridge: Cambridge University Press.

Vakil, Anna C. 1997. "Confronting a Classification Problem: Toward a Taxonomy of NGOs." *World Development* 25, 12:2057–70.

Varshavskaya, Anna. 2002. "Russians Keen to Join Battle to Preserve Wildlife and Environment." *BBC Monitoring International Reports,* May 16. *Russian Environmental Digest* 4, 20 (May 13–19).

Von Twickel, Nikolaus. 2007. "NGOs Buried by Mountain of Paper." *Moscow Times,* August 24.

Walker, Edward W. 1996. "The Dog That Didn't Bark: Tatarstan and Asymmetrical Federalism in Russia." *The Harriman Review* 9, 4 (Winter): 1–35.

———. 2003. *Dissolution: Sovereignty and the Breakup of the Soviet Union*. Lanham, MD: Rowman and Littlefield.

Walker, Jack. 1983. "The Origins and Maintenance of Interest Groups in America." *American Political Science Review* 77 (June): 390–406.

Warren, Mark E. 2001. *Democracy and Association*. Princeton, NJ: Princeton University Press.

Wedel, Janine R. 1992. *The Unplanned Society: Poland during and after Communism*. New York: Columbia University Press.

Weidel, Henry. 2004. "The Sad State of Vladivostok." *Eurasia Daily Monitor* 1, 69 (August 9). http://www.jamestown.org/publications_details.php?volume_id=401&issue_id=3042&article_id=2368380.

Weigle, Marcia A. 2000. *Russia's Liberal Project: State-Society Relations in the Transition from Communism*. University Park: Pennsylvania State University Press.

Weiler, Jonathan. 2004. *Human Rights in Russia: A Darker Side of Reform*. Boulder, CO: Lynne Rienner.

Weiner, Douglas R. 1988. *Models of Nature: Ecology, Conservation, and Cultural Revolution in Soviet Russia*. Bloomington: University of Indiana Press.

———. 1999. *A Little Corner of Freedom: Russian Nature Protection from Stalin to Gorbachev*. Berkeley: University of California Press.

White, Anne. 1999. *Democratization in Russia under Gorbachev, 1985–91*. New York: St. Martin's Press.

Whitefield, Stephen. 2003. "Russian Mass Attitudes toward the Environment, 1993–2001." *Post-Soviet Affairs* 19, 2 (April): 95–113.

World Bank. 2004. "Russian Economic Report." February. http://www.worldbank.org.ru/ECA/Russia.nsf/ECADocByUnid/0CF40EF2E501A275C3256CD1002B7D90/$FILE/RER7_eng.pdf.

World Learning. 1998. "Partnership across Borders." Copy given to author by World Learning representative, Moscow, 2000.

WWF-Far East. 1998. "Opros naseleniia." *Zov Taigi,* 5–6 (40–41):24.

WWF-Russia. 2007. *WWF Annual Report 2006,* Moscow.

Yablokov, Alexei. 2001. "Minatom's NGO—Friend or Foe?" *Give and Take* 4, 1 and 2 (Spring/Summer): 17.

Yanitsky, Oleg. 1993. *Russian Environmentalism: Leading Figures, Facts, Opinions.* Moscow: Mezhdunarodnoye Otnoshenie.

——. 1995. "Ekologicheskaia politika i ekologicheskoe dvizhenie v Rossii." Unpublished speech, presented at the Working Group of Eco-sociologists and Leaders of Ecological Organizations, Moscow, May 19–21, as quoted in Weiner 1999, 437.

——. 1996. *Ekologicheskoe dvizhenie Rossii: kriticheskii analiz.* Moscow: Russian Academy of Sciences, Institute of Sociology.

Zakharov, Vladimir M., ed. 1999. *Priorities for Russia's National Environmental Policy.* Moscow: Center for Russian Environmental Policy.

Zald, Mayer N., and John D. McCarthy, eds. 1987. *Social Movements in an Organizational Society.* New Brunswick, NJ: Transaction Books.

Zapiski c Dal'nego Vostoka. 1999. "Analis uslug i potrebnostei NKO Dal'nego Vostoka," (May–June): 28–35.

Ziegler, Charles E. 1987. *Environmental Policy in the USSR.* Amherst: University of Massachusetts Press.

Zolotov, Andrei Jr. 2001. "Civic Activists Storm the Kremlin." *Moscow Times,* November 22.

Zubarevich, Natalya. 2003. "Russia Case Study on Human Development Progress toward the MDGs at the Sub-National Level." Occasional Paper, Human Development Report Office, United Nations Development Program.

ZumBrunnen, Craig, and Nathaniel Trumbull. 2003. "Environmental Policy Challenges." In *Russia's Policy Challenges: Security, Stability, and Development,* edited by Stephen K. Wegren, 250–75. Armonk, NY: M. E. Sharpe.

Zyatkov, Nikolai. 2002. "Will Russia Become a Nuclear Waste Dump?" *Argumenty i Fakty,* April 24, as cited by Agency WPS, April 25, 2002. *Russian Environmental Digest* 4, 17 (April 22–28).

INDEX

Page numbers in *italics* indicate figures; those with a t indicate tables.

demonstrations by, 153; forest campaign of, 174; *Goskomekolgiia* and, 53n20; members of, 91, 198–99; St. Petersburg supporters of, 104, 165–66, 193–94; visibility of, 188

green political parties, 81, 147n13; fragmentation of, 105n21, 194n14, 209; KEDR and, 199–200; in St. Petersburg, 191–92

Green World, 89, 113, 165, 166, 227; Agenda 21 and, 206n48; legal issues of, 110, 173; strategies of, 148–49; tax audit of, 216; transnational networks and, 190–91, 215

gross domestic product (GDP), 249t; Putin's policies and, 46–47

Gulbina, Anna, 140–41, 192

Gurnev, Aleksei, 156, 191–92, 208

Gushchin, Vladimir, 154n25, 206

health hazards, 35, 49, 65, 138, 171–72

Hirschman, Albert O., 187

Hornocker Institute, 80, 166, 178, 237

Houses of Children's Creativity, 103, 144, 170n59

Howard, Marc Morje, 22, 23, 75

Human Development Index, 35, 63, 250t

human rights, 41, 47, 218; groups for, 72n8, 149–50; monitoring of, 58

Illarionov, Andrei, 213

In Defense of the Sea group, 100, 140–41, 192

infant mortality, 35

Institute for Sustainable Natural Resource Use, 113, 162–63, 177, 212, 237

Institute of Marine Biology, 80

Institute of Soil Science, 80

interest groups, 9, 11, 17, 111, 241

ISAR, 80, 148, 150–51, 169

ISAR-FE, 103–7, 116, 152, 169, 198, 204, 239

ISAR-Siberia, 128, 191, 205

Japan, 197, 220

Jenkins, J. Craig, 42

W. Alton Jones Foundation, 109

Joselyn, Bernadine, 58n32, 117n45, 127, 169n57

Jowitt, Kenneth, 22–23

judiciary system, 44, 59, 203, 214–18

Kaiumov, Askhat, 48n12, 51

Karpov, Alexander, 111, 196

Kasyanov, Mikhail, 34, 222

Kazakova, Marina, 144n7, 169n58

Keck, Margaret E., 21–22

KEDR Party, 123, 156, 199–200, 207–9, 212

KGB, 42. *See also* Federal Security Service

Kharitonov, Sergei, 148–49

Khasan, Lake, 178

Khodorkovsky, Mikhail, 120

Khrushchev, Nikita, 37

Kitschelt, Herbert, 28, 230n100

Klandermans, Bert, 42

Knizhnikova, Natalia, 106, 131, 202, 226n95

Kobets, Elena, 204–5

Kolomyts, Lev, 166, 171n60

Komogortseva, Liudmila, 89, 132, 175–76, 216

Komsomol, 36, 37, 146–47

Kondrashova, Liliia, 107–8, 114, 170n59, 204

Kouzmina, Anna, 190

Krestovskii Island, 132, 192, 202n36, 203

Kriesi, Hanspeter, 28

Krug organization, 107, 144–45

Krylova, Tatiana, 106

Kubanina, Valentina, 118n49, 126, 192, 197–98, 211

Kuchina, Galina, 106, 177n76, 202n36

Kukushkin Pond group, 141–43, 192

Kulakov, Boris, 132, 202n36, 203

Kuliasov, Ivan, 147, 162, 172–73

Kuliasova, Antonina, 53, 102, 106, 210n55

Kulikov, Aleksandr, 129n70

Kutsenko, Viktor, 172

Kyoto Protocol, 159, 213n66. *See also* climate change